W9-BRN-586

The Communists and Peace

with
A Reply to Claude Lefort

Jean-Paul Sartre

The Communists and Peace

with A Reply to Claude Lefort

GEORGE BRAZILLER / *New York*

The Communists and Peace has been translated from the French by Martha H. Fletcher, with the assistance of John R. Kleinschmidt.

A Reply to Claude Lefort has been translated from the French by Philip R. Berk.

Les Communistes et la Paix originally appeared in *Les Temps Modernes,* nos. 81, July 1952; 84-85, October-November 1952; 101, April 1954. *Réponse à Claude Lefort* originally appeared in *Les Temps Modernes,* no. 89, April 1953.

Les Communistes et la Paix was originally published in book form in Jean-Paul Sartre, *Situations,* VI, copyright © 1964, Editions Gallimard. *Réponse à Claude Lefort* was originally published in book form in Jean-Paul Sartre, *Situations,* VII, copyright © 1965, Editions Gallimard.

For information, address the publisher:
George Braziller, Inc.
One Park Avenue
New York, New York 10016

Library of Congress Catalog Card Number: 68-17390
Designed by Jennie R. Bush
Printed in the United States of America

Contents

The Communists and Peace

The Communists and Peace has been translated from the French by Martha H. Fletcher, with the assistance of John R. Kleinschmidt.

In preparing the translation of *The Communists and Peace* for publication, the editors alone have been responsible for establishing certain stylistic conventions, among them the style of verb-tense usage throughout the translation.—Editor's Note

When the police (C.R.S.) were charging the miners, the right-wing press published victory bulletins: that's what had made me think that *Le Figaro* doesn't like the workers. But I was wrong. I apologize to everyone and particularly to Mr. Robinet. For he simply adores the workers. He didn't want to admit it—too bashful, I suppose. But after the free-for-all at the Renault factory, he has finally declared his pretty sentiments. It surprised me at first, I must admit, to read his huge headline: "Workers' victory." For, after all, I thought, over whom did the working class win this victory, if not the employers and the police, in other words, over the readers of *Le Figaro*? But I wasn't with it at all: no, the proletariat didn't conquer the cops. Or the bourgeoisie. It triumphed over the Communist Party—the only political organization that represents it in the National Assembly—over the *Force Ouvrière*—the largest and oldest of its trade union federations. In short, the proletariat has stripped itself of its weapons, it has thrown down its arms; a last effort is expected of it: if it dissolves its unions, votes for the Independents in the by-elections, then it will know the finest victory of all: victory over itself. Yes, that's how the workers are liked: without weapons, bare-handed, open-armed. How fine were the masses at Fourmies, on May 1, 1891: no shock troops then, nor para-military organizations: people in the streets, lots of people, in disorder. Children, lilies of the valley; a girl holding a sprig of mistletoe. Major Chapuis' soldiers could take aim deliberately, without haste, and fire point-blank.

Perhaps convenient opportunities of this sort will come back. I can understand people's being pleased: The Fourmies massacre undoubtedly belongs to that category of spectacles which Mr. Mauriac calls "scandalous but sensible." But what is beyond my understanding is the imbecilic contentment evinced by certain left-wing men and newspapers. Poor fellows, once again the C.P. has pulled it off: they loved it, they left it regretfully; it crapped on them, they hate it. A love affair. I run into these outcasts from time to time; they have kept their tender smiles but the expression in their eyes is a bit haggard: the contradiction of our age has installed itself in them. How can you believe *at the same time* in *both* the historic mission of the proletariat and the betrayal of the Communist Party, if you observe that the former votes for the latter? Nevertheless, they muddle through although laboriously; each goes through the four inevitable stages at varying rates. First stage: "The Communist Party is mistaken, yes, but *just the same* you can't turn against the proletariat." Second stage: "The working class is still my dish, but *just the same* you have to admit it's not very bright. Look at the German workers. They let themselves be taken in by Hitler's claptrap." Third stage: "I lost interest in the working class the moment it could tolerate the Soviet concentration camps without indignation." Fourth and last stage: the Apocalypse: "Arranging alliance with United States. Stop. Pulverizing Russia. Stop. Hanging all Communists. Stop. And rebuilding, on the ruins, the true socialism, international, democratic, and reformist." No doubt about it: American troops will win the finest victory of the working class over Soviet troops. But to dare say it aloud one must be a complete traitor or mad with grief—which amounts to the same thing. In general, they remain in the gray areas and continue to scheme at reactionary social gatherings in order to see the enemy up close; or else they go at it in doses: they'll be for the Indochinese and the Spanish Republicans, against the Chinese and the Greeks; for Lenin, that great liberal, and against Stalin, the autocrat. This doesn't hold up and they know it and they repeat in lowered voices: "If only the damn working class would make up its mind once and for all to dump the Communist Party." Take, for example, Mr. Altman. I know him quite well: he isn't a traitor, not even a bad guy. But the Communists used Charles Boyer's "Gaslight" technique on him: by repeated stratagems, the patient is made to believe he is insane and evil. After three years of this diet, Mr. Altman is already more than half convinced. And this is what he wrote on May 29th, in *Franc-Tireur*: "The incitement against everything 'American' has now taken the form of a murderous and maniacal frenzy. One certainly has the right to criticize American policy if onc thinks it proper. But does one have the right to show, by every means from slander to sabotage, that one will no longer tolerate the idea that some men, allies, can be at our side to ward off a possible aggression? . . . Does one have the right to send men, women and children into the streets with slogans reminiscent of pure and simple racism? It is no longer a question of communism but of Russianism . . . Everything which does not serve Stalin's Russia . . . everything which favors freedom such as it still exists this side of the Iron Curtain, must be brought to naught before being exterminated . . ."

Did you catch that phrase: "If one thinks it proper"? How much finesse, how many undertones are in this little phrase and how willingly one would die for the language and the culture which allow such nuances. "If one thinks it proper" seems simply to mean: "If such is your opinion." But this would ignore the ever so slight discredit that clings to the expression: "Since you have cared to involve me without first asking my advice . . ." You understand: criticize your American *allies* if you think it proper. Mr. Altman doesn't think it proper and although he leaves you free to do so he discreetly warns you that you are about to commit stupidities. I'm afraid these subtleties will be lost: the Americans who will read the article are not yet prepared by a basic education to appreciate these little nuances. In any case, they are our *allies*. Mr. Altman tells it to us straight. Besides he's right, perfectly right: the French government—one might well ask, which one?—signed the Atlantic Pact. In short, the worker enjoys democratic liberties: he can think, speak, vote. Well then? Why does he have to start a brawl like a tough? Ah! it's the Stalinist who is behind it all. This

Stalinist, this evil genius, the eternal manipulator, today's *Russianist,* yesterday's Kraut, squandering English gold in 1789 and Russian gold by 1840, stirring up the discontent of the masses and taking advantage of it to throw them into politics. Made fanatic by his perfidious speeches, they go beyond legal bounds only to become the first victims of their own violence. We now know that it was he who incited the rabble to assault the Bastille; he who profited from the resentment of a few black slaves—punished over severely perhaps—to make us lose Santo Domingo; he who financed the plot of the Four Sergeants, the June days of 1848, the innumerable strikes at the end of the 19th century and, to top it all, the mutinies of 1917. How can we thwart his ruses? How can we reduce him finally to impotence? Mr. Altman tells us how: "If a bold social democracy knew how to rob the Stalinists of their monopoly as champions of the workers we wouldn't be in this fix." That's an old story: for 162 years neither the ill nor the remedy has changed. And Mr. Altman's democratic boldness is somewhat reminiscent of the cautious progressivism advocated by Count Mornay, who as early as January 1898 wrote in the *Revue des Deux Mondes*: "Communism secretly undermines the foundations of societies and governments. Can moderate concessions, intelligent reforms, a conscientious study of financial and social problems, the pious zeal of the wealthy classes on behalf of the poor classes along with a courageous resistance to factions—can these things prevent the ills which threaten us? This is the real question."

So much for bold social democracy: moderate concessions to the unions, employers' pious zeal for the workers, bold resistance to *secessionist* rebels. But where are the essential elements? Where is the political team which will apply the program? Where is the majority who will bring it to power? Mr. Altman is no fool; he knows perfectly well that it takes years before a political group acquires enough influence to be represented in the National Assembly. He is convinced that there will be war *tomorrow,* a war provoked by the Russians and lost by us if we don't immediately find a way of withdrawing the masses from the influence of the

Party. Poor Mr. Altman, you'd think he had known the Communists for 30 years now: he certainly knows they won't let go. So sometimes his favorite reasoning revolves all alone in his head and he says to himself: since the B.S.D. Party (bold, social, democratic) isn't in power yet, shouldn't one acknowledge that the C.P. is, for the present, the only *possible* representative of working class voters? I don't mind telling you that at such times Mr. Altman doesn't sleep soundly. For he belongs to a rather widespread group which is to the next war what the Association of War Veterans (*l'Association des Anciens Combattants*) was to World War I. The Society of Friends of the Yet to Be Shot (*l'Amicale des Futurs Fusillés*). They've often invited me to their banquets, but I haven't been able to bring myself to attend and to share their virile and funereal gaiety. "Come on," they say, "you're one of us!" But if the next war broke out, I see so many reasons why we will all lose our lives that I'm not going to waste time enumerating my personal reasons.

Whereupon, June 4th, great fanfare: the percentage of strikers is two percent. Mr. Altman exults, he feels himself revive. Two percent! At last the worker has understood, he is tired of pulling chestnuts out of the fire for the U.S.S.R. and now he is registering his defiance of the party that wanted to turn him against republican institutions. Surfeited with violence, he is returning to his little proletarian garden, to the much touted pleasantness of his way of life. Immediately everyone offers to guide him. The *Force Ouvrière* opens its arms to him; Mr. Altman goes so far as to seriously wonder whether he could palm off his Bold Social Democracy on him.

My dear slippery customers, you're rushing into war. Take the word of a slippery customer for it. You're rushing into war and you're dragging us along. The workers' indifference won't put the brakes on our slipping gradually into the massacre; on the contrary, it accelerates it; if their indifference were final, you might as well start polishing your boots. In hunting out lice in the Communist Party you have become myopic; you so often deplore the Party's "monopoly as champion of the workers" that you have ended up believing that this privilege came to it by chance. It is, you say, the party of the hysterical, of assassins, of liars; it incites people to hatred and its tricks are so obvious that your newspapers easily expose them every morning. Necessarily then, the whole proletariat must be criminal, lying, and hysterical. If not, how can we explain that it remains Communist? Stalin's nose, perhaps? If it had been shorter . . . ?

Even if it should poison their cowardly comfort, these troubled souls must be brought back to common decency, be reminded of some unpleasant truths: you cannot fight the working class without becoming the enemy of men and of yourself, but if the C.P. chooses to, even though you don't even lift your little finger, the working class will be against you; to be a traitor you don't have to be accused of treason by the Communists; if so accused, however, keep calm; for spite, hate, fear perhaps, and smiles from the Right can turn you into a traitor overnight and, finally, you must not count on the liquidation of the C.P.: it is true that the proletariat is holding a bit aloof from it at the moment, but this is an insignificant matter which will remain strictly between them. Already the Central Committee has learned its lesson. That's the situation: you can't do anything about it, nor can I. If you don't like it, turn on the gas or go fishing; but don't begin to cheat or you'll end up, like someone I know, by preaching war at Carnegie Hall and by disgusting the Americans themselves. When you learned of the demonstration against Ridgway, your indignation was enormous: everything was there, everything! all the intolerable Communist faults: unlawfulness, violence, and that disastrous mania for mobilizing union workers with political directives. Well, I'm afraid you're cheating. I wonder whether this incurable vice of which you accuse the Communist Party isn't simply the particular nature of the proletariat.

The facts speak for themselves: the demonstration, the unsuccessful strike which followed, the by-elections at the Renault factory, then for the National Assembly. The lines are slightly blurred, and contradictory in appearance. Never mind, let the facts speak. They may tell you whether you are traitors or simply slippery customers (*rats visqueux*)*. They will tell you, using other terms, to what extent the C.P. is the *necessary* expression of the working class, and to what extent it is the *exact* expression.

I. THE MAY 28TH DEMONSTRATIONS

Pulling the Chestnuts Out of the Fire for the U.S.S.R.

"The worker is tired of being the plaything of Moscow. He refused to take part in the demonstration because he disapproved of its principle." What do you know about it? Have you heard him complain *with your own ears*? It is *we* who see the hand of Moscow everywhere. I'm not saying we're always wrong, but the worker isn't like us. He is a "great interpreter" like the bourgeois, but his Manicheism is the reverse of ours: *he* discovers American gold behind all our actions. To say that he *has become* aware of being misused is to assume that our system of interpretation has replaced his. Has Mr. Robinet *become aware* of being a pawn of the United States? Has Mr. Altman? Besides, the French Communist Party has never hidden the fact that it aligns its policy with a general policy whose directives were formulated by the Komintern and then by the Kominform. The resolutions passed by the Third World Congress of the Third International include the following: "The Party as a whole is under the direction of the Communist International . . . the decisions of the Communist International are binding on the Party and on each of its members." Now, at that time (1921), of the five members of the "Presidium of the Executive Committee" three were Russian, one was German, and one Hungarian. That didn't prevent 130,000 French socialists, after the Congress of Tours, from forming the Communist Party while 30,000 stayed with Blum. Moreover, the profound differences between the Italian and the French Parties prove that a wide margin

**Le rat visqueux* has not betrayed. But the Party is sure that he would have been able to if the occasion had arisen. In brief, the word designates this—unfortunately very widespread—category of individual in our society: the culprit who has done nothing for which to be reproached.

of initiative is left to the regional leaders. You claim that this policy serves the interests of the U.S.S.R. exclusively. But it's easy for you to say so. You should, as a matter of fact, see that the Third International was born of a need for authority. The failure of the pacifist movement of 1914, the powerlessness of the workers and the collusion of the socialist leaders with the bourgeois Government of National Union influenced the militants in favor of rigorism. The congresses of the Second International "were only academic assemblies concluding with worthless resolutions." Anarchy reigned at every level of the S.F.I.O. Now most of the militants were convinced that "the class struggle was entering its period of civil war." They therefore wanted to forge a new party which would be a weapon. Authority, efficacy, and hierarchy were what they asked of the Third International; and doubtless they preferred to follow the directives of foreigners who had conquered the bourgeoisie of their own country rather than to obey Frenchmen who had collaborated with the French bourgeoisie. What the 130,000 adherents of the C.P. wanted, what they achieved, was *democratic centralization,* a kind of total and permanent mobilization which assured maximum efficacy to each one. Ever since, the leaders have been defending themselves against two constant criticisms: "Centralization must be carried out in such a way as to be a reinforcement of the activity of Party members . . . Otherwise, it would simply appear to the masses as a bureaucratization of the Party." And "the outcries about the Moscow dictatorship are a commonplace means of diversion."* However the apparatus thus conceived is by its very essence ambiguous. For if the workers' action is conceived and led at the international level by a centralized party, its directives, whatever their goals, will look to this or that local sector like abstract imperatives. Every regional proletariat will be treated as the means to that unconditional end which is world revolution; and lacking a minutely detailed knowledge of all events—possible only for the historian and in retrospect—it is confidence alone which will persuade a worker that he has not been fooled and that the

* Message to the German and French workers. (Lenin)

sacrifices accepted were legitimate. As always, the facts say neither yes nor no: after Pearl Harbor, the Communist Party of the United States asked its Negro members to tone down their anti-racist campaign: no point in feeding Nazi propaganda. Many Negroes had entered the Party because it was the only organization defending them: after Pearl Harbor they felt they were being sacrificed and so they left. No one can blame them: but what was the ultimate purpose of the directive? Was it aimed solely at the interests of the U.S.S.R., or at those of Europe and the rest of the world? To decide, it would be necessary, first of all, to maintain that World War II was only an imperialist war. That, indeed, is what the Trotskyists think and they are consistent since they condemned the Resistance in 1942. But the left-wing *Résistants* would have a hard time following them. In any case, one will come to a decision on the question only after taking a position on much vaster questions, ultimately, on the question of the worth of the Russian revolution and Marxism. It was precisely this that was evident in 1921. Since World War I, the French socialists had tended to come back to the absolute pacifism which, despite the setback of 1914, had remained in the French tradition. Lenin wanted them to distinguish between imperialist wars and revolutionary wars. The extreme left-wing anarchists refused to do so for a long time: being integral pacifists they demanded the right to shout, "Down with all armies, including the Red Army." Who was right? It obviously depends on the *worth* of the U.S.S.R. for the Revolution, hence on the worth of the Revolution in the U.S.S.R. And you will be able, according to your convictions, to show either that Lenin's demand breaks a deeply entrenched tradition of French socialist life and introduces, by force, an absurd exception into the center of a coherent system, or that the situation which made absolute pacifism legitimate before the war was left far behind since the October Revolution. One would think oneself involved in one of those interminable discussions which pit optimistic philosophers against the disciples of La Rochefoucauld: human actions are passed in review and each man explains them according to his own views: one by altruistic motives, the other by self-interest. If these disputants can't agree with each other it's because they have decided *a priori* on human worth. And if you cannot agree with the Communists it's because you have adopted *a priori* an opinion on the worth of the Russian experiment.

In January 1918, Lenin wrote: "The Soviet Republic will remain a living example in the eyes of the people of every country, and the power of this example's revolutionary penetration will be prodigious." And in March, 1923: "What interests us is not the *inevitable* final victory of socialism. What interests us is the tactic that we must follow, we the *Communist Party of Russia,* we, the power of the Russian Soviets, in order to prevent the Western counter-revolutionary states from crushing us." The entire problem is contained in these two texts. For a committed communist, of course, socialism must necessarily triumph since capitalism carries its death within it. That means that Russia is not the sole path leading to the final outcome. Born of the antagonisms which provoked the war of 1914, Russia can disappear: the antagonisms will survive her and the capitalist nations will ultimately collapse. In this very precise sense the safeguarding of the U.S.S.R. is not the *necessary* condition for the World Revolution. But these considerations are not *historical*: historically the proletariat's chance, its "example" and the source of "the power of revolutionary penetration" is the U.S.S.R. Moreover, the Soviet Union is *in itself* a historic value to be defended, since it is the first State that without yet achieving socialism "contains its premises." For these two reasons, the revolutionary who lives in our epoch, and whose task is to prepare for the Revolution with the means at hand and in his historical situation, without losing himself in the apocalyptic hopes which will ultimately turn him away from action, must indissolubly associate the Soviet cause with that of the proletariat. At least this is what Lenin thought and this is what comes through clearly in the texts. But, on the other hand, the U.S.S.R. appears as the Revolution's *historic opportunity* and not as its *necessary* condition (in the mathematical sense); thus it seems, in any case, that the U.S.S.R. could have been other than she is without jeopardizing the future of the Revolution; she could, for example, have demanded fewer sacrifices from the eastern democracies. The more perilous her situation, the more the aid she asks of the European proletariats is necessary *to her*. But the more exigent her demands, the more she tends to appear in the eyes of the People's Democracies and the proletariats simply as an individual nation. Thus, at best, the identification of the U.S.S.R. with the revolutionary cause will never be complete and the anti-Communists will always be able to point out to the French worker that he "is pulling the chestnuts out of the fire for Moscow." But, inversely, the worker will be able to prove it *in only one case*: by showing that the Soviet leaders no longer believe in the Russian Revolution or that they think the experiment has failed. It goes without saying that even if this were true, which I strongly doubt, to prove it would not be possible today.* In any other hypothesis the Politburo can be mistaken, can be on the wrong track, commit grievous errors (the Revolution is ineluctable, but the U.S.S.R. may disappear); whatever the Politburo may do, it will not sacrifice the worker to the *Russian nation.*

In the May 28th demonstration, we find a perfect illustration of the conflict of opinion which irreconcilably pits anti-Communists and Communists against each other: both are unaffected by the experience because their minds were already made up, but the former, sensitive to the bloodshed, saw only a cruel and warlike violence; the latter could deem it inopportune and clumsy: nonetheless, the demonstration remains, in their eyes, a move in the great chess game which the proletariat is playing against international capitalism.

"Moscow Wants War"

In any case, the real problem lies elsewhere, and those who talk of Moscow merely want to mislead us. For it certainly was not the U.S.S.R. that ordered this demonstration. I am perfectly willing to grant that she inspires the policies of national parties, but in a very general way. Billoux,† upon returning from Moscow, wrote

* I will come back to this in the second part.
† In fact it was he who was to be the most severely condemned in Fajon's report.

an article to announce the Communist Party's break with "the bourgeoisie, which is delivering the country to colonization by the new occupying power." But admitting even that the article was dictated to him—which seems simplistic to me—the actions it heralds are much more serious than a simple parade, even one accompanied by head-on clashes. The demonstration must have been decided upon, along with routine affairs, by the Political Bureau and on its own responsibility.

And just what is its goal? The press speaks of disturbances, of disorder, of hatred but without giving a reason for all this uproar. "Its goal?"—the anti-Communist is amused by my candor—"to prepare war of course!" Obviously! Why hadn't I thought of it: the Communist Party and the Peace Fighters (*Combattants de la Paix*) call upon the population of Paris to demonstrate against war: and this is irresistible proof that the U.S.S.R. wants to attack us. Irresistible indeed for those who rely on the doctrine of our ministers: *si vis pacem para bellum* (if you want peace prepare for war), from which by logical consequence one deduces: *si vis bellum para pacem* (if you want war prepare for peace). Since the signing of the Atlantic Pact, scenes of pastoral tranquility are commonly associated with the sight of a military uniform; and the unexpected encounter with a tank has the effect of a tranquilizer on the jittery. Conversely, the civilian is suspect for not wearing a uniform. Doesn't he want peace? Why, he's shouting for it: so obviously he's a subversive. He's clearly chosen his get-up to offer us the discouraging picture of disarmament; and his appeals for reconciliation have no other purpose than to disorganize our defense. Remember our uneasiness whenever the cold war gave us occasional respite? Everybody wondered: what's behind it? And only yesterday, General Clark was seized with anguish when he saw that things were quiet on the Korean front: it took five massive bombings to calm him down. For some time such strange silences have been making the world tremble. Communist or not, for us the man who wants peace is the one responsible for these periods of uneasiness: he must be in the pay of the enemy. What if his conduct is inspired by the very violence he rejects? And I admit the

C.P. has a loud voice: it shouts its desire for peace so loudly that everyone believes that the last hour has come.

But you who pretend to be indignant, are you doing anything different? Don't you also claim to want peace? Well, I look for your olive branches and I see only bombs. You say you display your strength so that you won't have to use it. But a show of force is violent in itself. To make an African chieftain surrender, you cover the African sky with your bombers; this white violence is worse than the other: he will surrender without your firing a shot but you will have broken his will by terror. Just take a look at the result of your very peaceful threats: they elicit some very peaceful responses in the form of massacres. You publish the result of your atomic experiments and you boast of being able to level Moscow in 24 hours: for the sake of peace, naturally, and to discourage a possible aggressor. But the Soviet government is equally anxious to discourage the aggressor: it shoots down a Swedish plane to show that its air space is inviolable. From one discouraged aggression to another, in Greece, Berlin, Korea, even in Paris, men are dying every day. And there it is, your Peace! Peace by fear. If the U.S.S.R. were as afraid as you are, your peace would be war by now.

For the Soviet Union wants peace and proves it daily. Your American allies repeat that the conflict will be avoided only by arming to the hilt. "The U.S.S.R. won't worry us any more when we're stronger than she is." Stronger: capable of crushing her if she so much as stirs. Supposing you attain this degree of power: who will decide that she has stirred? What will define the limits of your patience? Will she have to invade an allied country or will it be enough that a satellite state imprisons a cardinal? The American government asserts that it will not attack without very serious grounds. I'd like to believe it. But what about the Russians? How can they believe it? How can they trust the promises of a Democratic government which isn't even able to restrain its generals and which, in six months, may be replaced by a Republican government? Naturally, I don't doubt the purity of American intentions, but unfortunately I know that a change of military potential necessarily produces a change in minds. We don't have to apply Marxist analyses to know that any nation whatsoever follows the foreign policy of its armament: the greatly regretted era when Americans detested war because they didn't have cannons isn't very long past. Now, you claim that the Soviet leaders are monsters who have no regard for human life and who can unleash war by snapping their fingers. Then *why don't they attack*? Why don't they attack now, while there is still time, while their fighter planes are superior to those of the enemy and their armies could overrun Europe in a week? "Because," you say, "they're afraid of our atomic bombs." I understand: they're waiting for the nuclear stock to be tripled and the Atlantic army to be ready. What marvelous figuring! The U.S.S.R. wants to wage war; in three years she will surely lose but she won't attack now while she can still win. The Russians must be mad. Unless, quite simply, they want peace.

Peace? I see you suppressing a smile: another neutralist, one who believes in Santa Claus. —OK: you're a realist. During the Second World War, people applied the term *realist* to any Frenchman who collaborated with the German Army; today, a *realist* is a Frenchman who believes that the U.S.S.R. is the devil and who runs yelling for shelter in America's skirts. Therefore, *you know* that the members of the Politburo are mad dogs. And who told you so? What are your proofs? I choose the smartest of *Le Figaro's* writers, Mr. Raymond Aron, and I read this: "[the neutralist] . . . likes to envision a Soviet Union strictly on the defensive, worried by American preparedness, desirous solely of assuring her own security. One need only recall Soviet diplomacy between 1943 and 1947, while the Western powers were multiplying efforts for cooperation, in order to understand the illusion on which the neutralist attitude is founded."[1] "*One need only . . .*" Aron can't be serious: for after all, no matter how much I reflect on Soviet "diplomacy," as he invites me to do, I can't manage to cast off my illusions. This diplomacy was not polite; it was brutal, unscrupulous, it smacked of distrust and hatred. The U.S.S.R., no doubt ill-informed, did not take

[1] Aron: "Les Deux Tentations de L'Européen," *Preuves,* June, 1952.

seriously the Europeans' efforts toward cooperation. She demands pledges wherever possible, sometimes at the risk of dangerously increasing international tension.* No: I won't give the U.S.S.R. a good-conduct medal. But she was invincible in Europe; American rearmament—even Aron admits this—hadn't begun and the U.S.S.R. *never* made a gesture liable to unleash war. Moreover, the Communist Party collaborated with the bourgeois parties in the Western democracies and its slogan was: *Produce.* If you accuse the U.S.S.R. of having sabotaged European reconstruction from 1947 on, at least admit that she stimulated it *beforehand.* And if you view this sabotage as proof of her bellicose intentions, then, for the love of logic, look upon Marcel Paul's Stakhanovism as proof of her peaceful intentions.

It seems to me, on the contrary, that the current attitude of the U.S.S.R., her hesitations and the ambiguity of her diplomacy were perfectly defined thirty years ago in an article by Lenin published in *Pravda,* March 2, 1923 (*Oeuvres complètes,* II, 1041):

> . . . It will not be easy for us to hold on until the victory of the socialist revolution in the most advanced countries . . . This system of international relations is now such that in Europe one of the states—Germany—is enslaved by the victor states. Next, a group of states and—to call a spade a spade—some of the oldest in the West, find themselves, following their victory, in conditions which enable them to use this victory to make a series of concessions which, though piddling, retard the revolutionary movement in these countries and create a semblance of "social peace."
>
> At the same time a whole group of countries—the Near East, India, China—were definitively thrown out of the rut as a consequence of the last imperialist war. Their development has gone the way of European capitalism. The fermentation affecting all of Europe has begun in these countries. And it is clear now to the whole world, that they have embarked on a path of development which cannot help but end in a crisis for the whole of world capital.

---

* I'm thinking particularly of the Iranian affair.

We are, consequently, now confronted with the following question: Will we be able to hold on with our small-scale peasant production, with the ruined state of our country, until the capitalist nations of Western Europe have completed their development towards socialism? But they are not completing their development as we previously thought they would. They will complete it, not by a steady "maturation" of socialism within their country, but by the exploitation of certain states by certain others, by the exploitation of the first state conquered in the imperialist war, an exploitation joined to that of the whole Orient . . . The Orient has entered . . . definitively the orbit of the world revolutionary movement.

What tactic does this situation impose on our country? Clearly, the following: we must display great prudence in order to preserve our workers' power, in order to maintain within its authority and under its direction our small-scale peasantry . . . We are faced with the disadvantage that the imperialists have succeeded in splitting the world into two camps; and this split is complicated by the fact that Germany, a country where capitalist culture is really advanced, will have a difficult time rebuilding herself today. . . On the other hand, in the entire Orient conditions are such that the physical and material forces could in no way be compared to the physical, material, and military forces of any much smaller state in Western Europe.

Can we avert the future clash with these imperialist countries? Can we hope that the antagonisms and the internal conflicts between the prosperous imperialist countries of the West and the prosperous imperialist countries of the East will allow us a second respite, as they did when the first crusade undertaken by Western counter-revolution to aid the Russian counter-revolution failed because of the contradictions in the counter-revolutionary camp? . . .

It seems to me that we must answer this question in the following way: the solution depends on too large a number of factors; predicting the outcome of the struggle is possible only because the immense majority of the world's population is, ultimately, trained and educated for the struggle by capitalism itself.

The outcome of the struggle depends finally on the fact that Russia, India, China, etc., form the immense majority of the world's population . . . in this respect there could be no shadow of a doubt as to the final outcome . . .

But what concerns us is not this inevitable victory of socialism. What concerns us is the new tactic necessary to prevent the Western counter-revolutionary states from crushing us. In order for us to survive until the next military conflict between the imperialist counter-revolutionary West and the revolutionary and nationalist East, between the most civilized countries in the world and the most backward, e.g. those of the Orient which nevertheless constitute the majority —it is necessary that this majority have time to become civilized. We too lack the necessary civilization to pass directly into socialism even though we have its political premises . . .

(This is followed by a comprehensive plan for the internal economy of the U.S.S.R.)

What has changed since this admirably lucid text?

—The U.S.S.R. has been industrialized. But the colossal effort of the United States tends to maintain the production gap between West and East.

—The Chinese revolutionary movement has been completed by a revolution. But the industrialization of China has not even begun. India has stayed outside of the movement: at any moment conflicts may arise there which will benefit the U.S.S.R.; but so far they haven't.

—One cannot, in 1952, speak of "prosperity" as one could after 1918. Or of social peace either. But the working class is at an ebb and the bourgeois governments are firmly resolved to put down social disturbances by any means. The centralizing action of American imperialism is temporarily preventing national and international conflicts from growing worse. It seems that the Russians were counting on an economic crisis in the United States which has not yet occurred.

On the whole, a real disproportion remains between the Eastern and Western blocs. Although the United States and China are practically in a state of war, this conflict between an economically backward country and the most "civilized" of the capitalist states in no way resembles the one that Lenin predicted and which he expected to deal decisive blows to capitalism. In a word, if one tries to imagine, on the basis of this article, what policy its author might prescribe for the U.S.S.R. today, it seems obvious that he would repeat the key phrases: "We must display great prudence. . . . Can we avert the future clash with the imperialist countries? Can we hope that their antagonisms will allow us a respite for the third time? . . . The solution depends on too great a number of factors for anyone to predict anything . . . But the outcome of the struggle leaves no room for doubt."

I don't see that Stalin followed any other policy. First of all, the Soviet government scorned the League of Nations, that instrument of bourgeois imperialism; then, alarmed by Japan and Nazi Germany, the Kremlin became reconciled to the League of Nations, supported the theory of indivisible peace, and lined up on the side of the "conservative" nations against the "proletarian" ones. This was the period during which Stalin declared: "We do not want an inch of anyone else's territory and we will not allow anyone to seize an inch of our territory." The U.S.S.R. went so far as to sign a mutual assistance pact with France. Until Munich, she played the game of the democracies, limiting herself to recommending greater firmness on their part. The attitude of the French Communist Party, considered in connection with the foreign policy of the U.S.S.R., was highly significant. From 1928 to 1930, fearing that the capitalist powers would attack Soviet Russia, it drew up its program of struggle against the imperialist war and determined the principal measures to be taken in case of conflict. As of 1935 and up to 1938, in the face of the internal and external threat of fascism, unity of action with the Socialists was envisaged and then realized. We remember the anger and the apprehensions of the U.S.S.R. after Munich, "the attempt by the reactionaries of England and Rome to unite with the fascists of Germany and Italy behind the back of the Soviet Union." It is certain that the U.S.S.R. feared encirclement and war. The British and French governments, faced with immediate danger, tried in vain to bring about an alliance with Russia in 1938-1939. Soviet distrust would not relent: they were convinced that Germany was at a crossroads and that, depending on the play of alliances, she would attack either her Eastern or her Western neighbors. Ribbentrop and Molotov signed the German-Russian pact, of which no more need be said; it certainly showed a want of tact. But who can deny that Russia, in the absence of world peace, meant to preserve *her* peace? Germany of course attacked her in 1941, and the first operations seemed to indicate that the Soviet Army was not entirely prepared for the shock. After 1944, the collapse of Germany revived the obsession of the anti-Soviet crusade. The U.S.S.R. tried, by every means, by every policy, to protect herself. Starting in 1947, the Communist Parties of Europe were eliminated from command posts; the Soviets grew rigid again. Search as I may, I find in the course of these three decades no evidence of aggression on the part of the Russians; I see a distrustful and hemmed-in nation that still remembers the Allied intervention of 1918 and the quarantine which followed, a nation which would prefer anything to being crushed, even a world war, but which tries by every means to avoid having this war; crude and distrustful and irritable and mean on occasion: but what can you expect when the revolutionary parties, justifying their own policies by hers, scarcely help to calm tempers; inversely, the insults heaped on them in the bourgeois democracies, the police repressions, and, in the fascist countries, the systematic extermination of Communist leaders only increase tension. For it is the U.S.S.R. that the bourgeois detest in the Communists and it is the Communists that they detest in the U.S.S.R. One thing is certain in any case: our obsession with Russian aggression corresponds exactly to the Russian obsession with encirclement.

Make no mistake about it: if the U.S.S.R. were ever to lose all hope of avoiding war, she would unleash the conflict herself. And who could blame her? But her leaders are as divided as ours. As early as 1946, Molotov thought war inevitable. The Yugoslav affair showed that he hadn't entirely convinced his colleagues, some of whom, it seems, continue to think that the conflict can be postponed until a decisive crisis shakes the Western world; German obstreperousness, British reserve, fluctuations of opinion in France and Italy, the bogging down of the Americans in Korea, agitation in the Arab world, the war of the Viet-Minh are so many cards left to play. Depending on the international confluence of events and perhaps also on the relations of forces inside the Politburo, one of these conceptions or the other prevails, always tempered by that of the minority.

These alternations are reflected in the policy of the Communist Party, and it is in this climate that the May 28th demonstration must be viewed. It has frequently been connected with the article published by Billoux after his trip to the U.S.S.R. Now, this article, as Gilles Marinet clearly demonstrated in *L'Observateur,* did not so much indicate a "change" in the line of the Party as a return to the 1950 line. That year, at the Twelfth Party Congress, Thorez denounced "the Marshallized rulers who are in bond to the American capitalists . . . and . . . who resort to methods of murder and terror against the working class." In September 1951, on the other hand, Jacques Duclos declared in the Central Committee: "Employers and workers can perfectly well find themselves allied in regaining French independence." And, in May 1952, Billoux took up Thorez's themes again: "The defense of French industry cannot be undertaken by a 'national union' of workers, middle-classes and industrialists." Thus they simply returned to the hard line of 1950, only to do an about-face a month later in Fajon's report to the Central Committee (June 19, 1952), back to the Duclos line: management is not homogeneous, many French industrialists are threatened with ruin because of the armament policy; Billoux's article was misunderstood; it is necessary to abandon sectarianism, extend our hands to the farm masses, to the middle classes, to the intellectuals, and "to those employers hurt by American domination." This time the oscillation was faster and wider: Billoux had gone further than Thorez, Fajon goes further than Duclos. The pendulum seems to be running wild. It has been said that its phases corresponded to the erratic rhythm of the international situation; but this isn't quite correct: in April, 1950 Thorez did declare that "peace hangs only by a thread," but the war in Korea had not then broken out (did he know that it was near?) and American rearmament dates from the following autumn; in September, 1951, a slight détente could be noted in comparison with January, yet the same threats hung over the world: German rearmament was decided upon, the armistice negotiations in Korea were dragging out, the victory of the Conservatives in the British elections was taken for granted, the Ottawa conference was about to open. The last two oscillations occurred in the same tense and threatening atmosphere, and this double sensation was not accompanied by any noticeable modification of the Soviet atmosphere, which remains rather ambiguous. Besides, there is nothing analogous to be found in Italy during the same period and it is striking that Togliatti, several days after the publication of Billoux's article, had Nenni propose to DeGasperi a common front against the monarchists and neo-fascists. That alone would suffice to rule out the idea of an orchestration of national Communist movements.* The oscillations of Communist policy in France are characteristic of the French C.P. For reasons that I'll explain further on, they match and step up the Russian alternations; their rhythm, their periodicity, their proportions depend on at least three factors: the international confluence of events, the internal life of the Politburo, the internal life of the French Central Committee. The May 28th demonstration was decided upon in a climate of pessimism. It was a supreme effort toward peace; but few really believed in it, which explains the will to failure and the recourse to violence. The C.P. expected the worst: "No capitalist

* In his speech of June, under the pretext of attacking DeGasperi, Togliatti hauled the French C.P. over the coals: "We are no fools!" he said in substance. "You have massed your police and your troops in the streets of Rome but we haven't fallen into the trap and we haven't responded to your provocations." It is not very difficult to infer his opinion of the May 28th demonstration.

country," said Stalin in 1927, "could throw itself into a large-scale war without having first secured its rear, without having 'brought to heel' its workers, its colonies." Convinced that it would be dissolved, the Party already envisaged going back to a clandestine existence. The Fajon report clearly alluded to this defeatism: "All Party activities must openly pursue their mass work," he said, as if he wished simultaneously to reassure the militants and disavow the too-hastily drawn conclusions. When the Political Bureau decided to demonstrate, it little cared whether the Parisian populace would participate; it already knew that the order would not be followed: * "It was," says Pierre Thibault in *France-Soir,* "a concerted action by commandos who were proceeding on orders to a battle that was lost in advance." A battle lost in advance: it's true the demonstration was *expected to fail.* But it is also true that the victories of the proletariat are long-range victories and are often born of present defeats. What we can hardly understand—we bourgeois who wish to preserve only the memory of our partial victories—is the enduring patience of the worker and his mixture of fatalism, despair, and courage which, under the pressure of an intolerable situation, sometimes makes him attempt a battle which he is almost sure to lose. In deciding, against all odds, on this absurd "day of action," the Party drew inspiration from the workers' tradition after all.

But above all it *was acting out* the deep-seated pacifism of the masses, and you lie deliberately when you congratulate the worker on not allowing himself to be mobilized for interests that are not his own. One of the deepest and simplest feelings of the proletariat, one of the factors of his class consciousness, is this recognition of himself as pure *presence* (*être-là*) without any relation of solidarity with the social whole. He is not integrated into society, he *lives alongside it,* in a semi-segregation which is first imposed on him and which he eventually demands. In a period of

* How could it not know since it had, as Duverger says, "constructed a scientific method enabling it . . . to 'tune in on the masses' "? It is said that the local leaders inadequately inform the top leaders. It's possible: in that case the truth would be twisted, but not totally hidden.

international tension, his social ties grow looser, while everywhere else they are being drawn tighter; how could he put himself on the level of the psychic and social tension of the petty bourgeoisie surrounding him? This contrast between absence of interest and the general over-excitement influences him in favor of pacifism. And pacifism, inversely, is *first of all* the reaffirmation of the worker's seclusion in the midst of a society of *exploitation,* and *only secondarily* a declaration of solidarity with the working class of the enemy nation. While other classes project their own society onto the other side of the border, only changing the plus to minus and representing that Society as diabolical, the worker projects himself without a minus-sign; for the negation of himself is the bourgeois class of his own country. Thus, the simplest attitude, the nearest to spontaneity, that which best expresses his feeling, is internationalism. The oldest workers may still remember the appeal issued in January 1906 by the National Committee of the C.G.T.: *"War on war.* Workers . . . a trifle can start off a war. The press knows this . . . and it is silent. Because they want to make us feel obliged to go along, they use as their pretexts national honor, the inevitability of a defensive war. The people, however, do not want war . . . The working class has no interest in war. It alone pays the price—with its work and blood. Hence, it is the workers who must say loudly that they *want peace."*

As we have seen, establishing the Russian Revolution as a Nation complicated things somewhat. In asking the proletariat to make one exception to its anti-militarism, the Party introduced a contradiction which, finally, spread total confusion and prevented the expression of spontaneous feeling. As early as 1928, they sought to turn to the advantage of the U.S.S.R. the *sacred* power of certain words and situations. Instead of explaining to the worker the bonds of real and indissoluble solidarity which united him to the U.S.S.R., they made Russia the socialist fatherland of the worker, and they made the worker a soldier fighting behind the lines for the Soviet Union. At the same time, the techniques of waging war against war were perfected and in the process militarized: in place of the vague and solemn "general strike," the C.P., having learned something from the setback of 1914, sought to substitute acts of sabotage, defeatist and underground propaganda, etc. Around 1928-1930, the working class already seemed disconcerted, and the "Red International Day against War" was a failure (August 1, 1929) rather similar to that of May 28, 1952. Today, as might be expected, internationalism, which presupposes the inorganic juxtaposition of the masses (they are *alongside* each other and separated by borders, none is in command, the assemblies of their representatives are parliamentary), has been shattered by *centralization.* The gist of the 57th "thesis of September, 1921" was "The Central Committee of the Party is responsible to the Party Congress *and* to the Executive Committee of the Communist International." This principle could be expressed symbolically by the sentence: The worker has two homelands, his own and the Republic of Russian Soviets. Fundamentally, the emergence of homelands completes the horizontal partitioning. The Party, on the international level, provides itself with as strong a system of links as it does in each individual country: like cells, nations communicate with each other only by the intermediary of the higher echelon. But beyond this partitioning destined to tighten the bonds and establish the authority of the central Power, the self-interest of the proletariat and that of the U.S.S.R. remain identical: the Party abstains from the arguments of Greffuelhe, which so touched the hearts of the trade unionists. ("Defend the soil of the Fatherland? I see no objection, on condition that whoever defends this soil shall be its owner." —Survey of the Socialist Movement, August 1905.) But we must also realize that the new propaganda aims at emancipating the worker, at furnishing him with an immediate means of getting outside of himself, a transcendent bond with the Other—unfortunately in the form of the Kantian imperative and of military duty. The language itself is military: "[This day of action of 1929] will mark the passing of the proletariat to the counter-offensive on the international front . . ." But behind this kind of communique language and with words borrowed from nationalist propaganda, a kind of sub-dialogue continues between a proletariat still thoroughly pacifist—simply because its situation is to be pacifist—and militants who, behind their ideological and verbal apparatus, have perhaps remained so also. In short, this is one of the serious symptoms of *aphasia* as an international phenomenon: people communicate by language; but against it, the cadres and the troops make use of words that lie but tacitly conspire to restore the truth. The old trade unionists are told of the counter-offensive of the proletariat and they hear an old pre-1914 voice murmuring: "Workers . . . in Germany as in France the communion of ideas is categorical on this point: the proletariat of both countries refuses to wage war. Therefore, by common and simultaneous action, let us force our respective governments to take our will into account." In a certain sense, the demonstration of May 28—which was much more the doing of disciplined militants than a spontaneous demonstration—aimed at giving the masses a tragic representation of their profound aspirations, somewhat as, according to Nietzsche, the "symbolic" performance in Greek tragedy reflects the innermost instincts of the chorus.

In short, our fine gentlemen must realize once and for all that the proletariat has no reason to fight. You tell the worker daily that the U.S.S.R. has betrayed the Revolution; he is surprised, he would never have thought that that could cause you so much distress; and to tell you the truth, he doesn't believe a word of what you say. When *Le Figaro* publishes pantry gossip about the Roumanian Embassy, it may amuse the dowagers; but that's because dowagers like valets. The workers don't. Even if, by some stroke of madness, a worker happened to read this sheet regularly and let himself be convinced of the Soviet betrayal, it might be a reason not to fight in the ranks of the Red Army; it would certainly not be a reason to fight against it. Oh, but it is! you will say: to free the unfortunate Russian proletariat. Yes. Well, I have the impression that the propaganda isn't perfected yet; and I don't think that you will enroll many people if you ask them to take up the anti-Bolshevik crusade that Hitler preached, to line up with Chiang Kai-shek against Mao Tse-tung's Chinese, with France against the Spanish Republicans, with Syngman Rhee against the entire Korean people, with the assassins of Beloyannis against the fathers and brothers of Makronisos deportees, with an oligarchy of colonialists against the Tunisians, the Madagascans and the Vietnamese.

I think you've realized that that was asking a lot; and you've given up indoctrinating. When you simply must, to satisfy your conscience, produce some reason to die for the United States, you organize art exhibits, lectures and concerts; in short, you wage what has been only recently labeled a "cultural battle." But you always make sure to double the price of admission: to be certain, at least, that the "wrong people" are kept out. Or else you marshal out, from Paris to London and on to Berlin, a handful of pale intellectuals, gentle as girls, who recite memorized compliments on culture and freedom. But whom do you really expect this womanish orchestra to convince, aside from the readers of *Annales*? Culture is quite dead when writers begin to *defend* it instead of *creating* it. As for the worker, he couldn't care less. It might interest him if it were given to him and if it were concerned with his interests. A woman working in a refinery has to take care of a group of four machines, and each machine fills thirty plates in two and a half minutes; a plate weighs almost two pounds. Thus she transports two hundred and twenty pounds every two minutes, which adds up to about twenty tons a day. Go ask her for her son and her husband, explain to her that it's to liberate the poor Russian "women refinery workers" who don't have the right to express their opinion on abstract painting or on the theories of Lysenko; make her understand that the United States is perfecting a hydrogen bomb and quietly preparing the admission of Spain to the U.N. just so that the "women refinery workers" in the Western democracies can continue to think and to express their thoughts freely. Don't be afraid: she won't hit you; she's too tired. It's *you* who will be incensed at *her,* and you'll go off deploring the fact that the sense of liberty has been lost in Europe. And yet she, too, wants liberation. But her freedom doesn't resemble yours; and I think that she would gladly do without the freedom of expression of which such fine use is made in the Salle Gaveau if she were freed from the throbbing rhythm of the machines, from the heteronomy of tasks, from cold, from the dismal setting of the factory. Why, for her to feel free, freer than she has ever been, it would suffice—for the time being—for her to have, in the same time and for the same salary, to transport ten tons instead of twenty. What are you waiting for? You would be serving culture. You say that you can't, that patience is necessary and that the grandchildren of the women refinery workers will be freed by technical progress. Fine: then, if you want to go to war, wait until they're born. And don't think you can convince their grandmother-to-be by praising high wages and the superiority of material life in America. What do these perpetual comparisons between the U.S.S.R. and the U.S.A. matter to her? For it is not a question for her of working in Stalingrad or Chicago, but in a France at peace or at war. You nincompoops, you are so afraid of the Soviet regime that you're doing your best to sample it. For today we have peace; the Americans are in our country and the Russians are in Russia, but if there's war tomorrow, the Americans will be in America and it's the Russians who will be here. The workers know it: right at the outbreak of hostilities they'll lose their miserable salary, the so-called "subsistence minimum"; they have no interest in being "occupied," even by the Red Armies; they want the Russians in the U.S.S.R. and the Americans in the U.S.A. If they didn't bother to turn out on the 28th of May, it's because they felt—for reasons which I will examine further on—that the game wasn't worth it; but the disagreement was not over the principle of the demonstration. And take my word that they have no great love for Ridgway, or for any other American. For you slippery customers know it, and even *Le Figaro* is beginning to suspect it: the Americans are admirable propagandists; but their best propaganda is made for the Russians.

"The C.P. and the C.G.T. Tire the Workers Out by Imposing Political Demonstrations on Them"

Why, here's a new argument: the workers are supposedly accusing the Party of having perverted their sole instrument of defense by misusing it; apparently they evinced good sense and showed the "Russianist" agitators that they intended to maintain a separation between politics and economics.

If what you say is true, they have given management the best possible gift: for the employers prize this separation; even more, perhaps, than the men of 1789 prized the separation of powers. When the Puritans had secularized commerce and industry, God had to be replaced by an iron law of wages, an inflexible law that whitewashed the exploiters; a divine law that justified success; one could always invoke it to prove that the rich man was good and the poor man bad.

This was the law of supply and demand, "a true, regulating mechanism, adjusting prices, eliminating some would-be sellers and some would-be buyers . . . stimulating production in case of undersupply, discouraging it in case of oversupply."[2] Establishing that wealth is in proportion to social utility, that the best merchant is he who sells cheapest, hence the elect of God and the benefactor of humanity, this law permitted a return to optimism. The law applied marvelously to relations between employer and employee: labor was a commodity and wages its price. No one could blame the employers: the wage was at every moment whatever it *could be,* nothing more and nothing less, since the regulation was automatic. Thus the economic domain became that of necessity, while the political domain remained that of freedom. All goes smoothly as long as the two domains remain separate; people will admit, if need be, that the economy influences politics, but the intrusion of politics into the economy troubles consciences and scandalizes people: political action tends to prove that economic necessity may not be autonomous and that we modify its course by acting on other factors. Some theorists suggested reducing politics to economics: but the bourgeoisie refused; it prefers compartmentalization. Divide and rule. People simply got into the habit of labeling as demagogic every concession which politics makes to the poor classes without having been forced to do so. Generosity, on principle, is *false* generosity. "This reform, generous in appearance . . ." This means

[2] Robert Mossé: *Les Salaires,* Rivière, 1952, p. 40.

that every attempt to substitute a human order for mechanical order is doomed to failure. There is only one way to be good: adjust to the natural order, obey the law, make each person work as much as possible and pay him as little as possible; all of society will be served by producing goods at the lowest possible price. This praiseworthy concern to justify profit is at the bottom of a rather comical theory: that of "*terrible goodness*" (*la bonté terrible*), which one finds in Claudel and in the Nazis. If the worker makes use of his trade-union right to mix economics with politics, he will only end up throwing the whole harmonious mechanism out of gear. All is well if he restricts union activity to defending his interests. After all, we must realize that market fluctuations tend to make the average wage deviate slightly from what in the eighteenth century was piously called the *natural* wage and what Turgot defined as "that which is necessary to the worker for his subsistence." The trade union may intervene only by replacing multiple sellers with a single bargaining agent. It cannot modify eternal laws of economy; but a certain power has fallen to it by virtue of its functioning simply as a monopoly. It will take advantage of this to better the gross wage, determined solely by the play of economic forces, and to bring it as close as possible to the natural wage.

Thus classical economic theory describes what would happen if relations among men were strictly similar to relations among things. In other words, it establishes the laws of a universe where man is completely inhuman to man. The union is tolerable if it submits itself, as an individual case (that of a single seller and multiple buyers), to the framework of these rigorous laws. It will not be tolerated if it aims to humanize them. But, while the bourgeois point of view is clear enough in itself, I cease to understand it as soon as I try to envisage things from the wage earner's point of view, where the distinction between economics and politics becomes so vague and fugitive that I have difficulty believing it exists. First of all, I really don't know what people mean when they say they want the worker to limit himself to defending his interests. Is there a worker's interest? It seems to me that the interest of the worker is to be no longer a worker. As Marx puts it:

"The real task of the proletarian is to revolutionize his living conditions." I can see the anti-Communist shrugging his shoulders to indicate that I'm not serious and that these Byzantine games spelled the doom of France in 1939. Very well. Let's be serious then. There is an interest of the worker *as a worker.* That is, *to begin with,* he must accept his condition as a whole. Only then will society grant him the right to improve minor details of his condition. Thus, the bourgeois thesis (both in the rather crude form of classical economics and in the modern form of class collaboration) is that the worker must remain a worker. This is not surprising since he was created a worker, just as the employer was created an employer. A strike is called subversive when the demands of the strikers are inspired by a conception of man. When the employer declares that the proletarian is proletarian by birth and must remain so, he is not acting politically: he is establishing the principles of the economy. The worker, on the other hand, *is* acting politically, when he seeks to do away with the proletariat. The whole history of labor legislation reveals the bourgeois magistracy's concern for distinguishing good strikes from bad. As early as 1872 Depeyre, defending in the Assembly a bill to punish affiliation with the International, declared that the legislator's intention had been "to protect the working population" against any attempt to strike "resulting from an evil intention, a plot against the social order." And even today, in more subdued terms, the Seine Labor Arbitration Council (*Conseil des Prudhommes*) (decision of March 26, 1947) accepts the theory of the "improper strike": "It is fitting to apply this right [to strike] while taking into account the absolute principle that the exericse of a right is limited by the abuse which might be made of it; that no right is, in fact, unlimited, in an organized society; that it finds its natural limit, in the absence of specific regulation, in the rights of others and of the collective. . . ." Fine words: the only trouble is that the "organized society" in which the worker lives and whose rights he must respect happens to be the capitalist society which is oppressing him. Thus the bourgeois decision to limit grounds for a strike to occupational grievances is *political* in itself and rests on a particular conception of the world and of man.

Even accepting this conception, even defining *with* the employers the interests of the worker, I still don't understand what these interests are. A factory makes a sink available to its personnel: the *interest* of the personnel is that the drain pipe doesn't get stopped up. The country of these workers is swept along towards war by political stupidity: their *interest* is that the war not take place. Between the first example and the second, there is room for the whole of social life. You say that the second is of a *political* nature? Is that so certain? In case of war, the peasant class furnishes the "human material" and in return benefits from higher food prices; in short, quarts of blood are bought from it. The situation of the proletariat is exactly the opposite: its losses in human lives are fewer: but it suffers *economically*. Not at first, but later, when the hypertrophy of heavy industry and the difficulties of reconversion cause recession and unemployment. In 1938, total wages were worth twice total taxes; in 1950 total taxes are equal to total wages. The worker can declare with good reason that military conflicts prove prejudicial to his material interests. Furthermore: if you claim that war is a political fact you reject the socialist explanation of war and the vicious circle: overproduction—the search for markets—wars. I am not saying that you are wrong or that this theory is true: that's not the point. I am merely saying that you bring value judgments, presuppositions, an ideology into your definition of what is political and what is not. The Marxist theory of cyclical crisis, Lenin's theses on capitalist imperialism may be true or false. But the burden of proof rests with the specialists. Most people reject or accept those theories without really understanding them and would have a difficult time arguing about them. Nevertheless, Merrheim declared, in a resolution which was passed in Marseilles in 1908, that "every war is only an attack on the working class, a gory and terrible means of distracting it from its demands," and all the union members repeated the formula after him *as though they understood it*. And the nationalists retorted by accusing these "defeatists" of having sold out to the enemy *as though they knew it.* These are two clashing conceptions of the world, and they are lived and felt more than they are thought out. Any reconciliation of the two seems impossible: "reformism" in particular, brings to workers' demands an abrupt and wilful stop which seems perfectly unjustifiable. We can judge it by what happened in 1908: two years before, a congress had passed a resolution advocating "anti-militarist and anti-patriotic propaganda." Niel, reformist trade unionist and leader of the minority, expounded his point of view at Marseilles: he was against an anti-patriotism which groups the militants *politically*. Janvion maintained the same point of view: a victorious Germany would easily impose reparations of which the workers would pay the lion's share. One would be tempted to believe that the two orators were against anti-militarism *for the same reasons*. Not at all. According to Niel: the goal of anti-militarism which remains on trade union terrain is "to struggle against Army intervention in strikes." Which will seem neither abstract nor absurd to those who remember the massacres at Fourmies (1891), Martinique (1900), Chalons-sur-Marne (1900), Raon-l'Etape (1907), Draveil-Vigneux and Villeneuve-Saint-Georges (1908). The workers had to fight against the Army because the Army was the repression. But such reasoning is no less untenable for that: inciting the military to disobedience is a political action. And, if the anti-militarist trend had been strong enough, it could have weakened national defense, thus Germany would have won the war and the workers would have had to make reparations which Janvion wanted to spare them.

No, we must accept it: trade unionism has only two coherent positions. Either it limits itself to supporting immediate demands or it will defend the workers in all areas of national activity. But we must realize that the worker who confines himself to elementary demands has *already* taken a political stance: he not only rejects the Revolution but things like solidarity strikes as well; he resigns himself to his fate and betrays the working class.

The truth is that we cannot confine ourselves to immediate demands: Marx put it very well: "A struggle for a wage increase only follows *previous* changes. It is the necessary result of previous changes in the amount of production, the productive powers of labor, the value of labor, the value of money, the extent or the intensity of extracted labor, the fluctuations of market prices, which depend upon the fluctuations of supply and demand, and which occur in accordance with the different phases of the industrial cycle; in short, reactions of labor against previous actions of capital." But in this case the worker intervenes *too late* and "in 99 cases out of 100 his efforts at raising wages are only efforts at maintaining the given value of labor. In order for the proletariat to be able to defend itself the trade union would have to be able to act *on the causes* rather than on the effects. If you refuse it the right to influence the market with all its political and economic, national and international implications, you reduce its demands to the level of blind impulse, you deprive it of the *human* possibility of foreseeing and forestalling. You turn the worker into a starving belly and a mouth which cries out. In short, with regard to the company, the union's "real task" is to demand and obtain the right to participate in management; with regard to the nation, to check the economic consequences of government policy. And this holds true whether the union be reformist or revolutionary; that is to say, solely from the point of view of the interests "of the worker as such."

The truth is that *economic data,* as well as *homo oeconomicus,* is a merely arbitrary abstraction. Or rather it correctly symbolizes certain extreme situations, in which the oppressor is in a position to treat the oppressed like a dupe. In French West Africa, for example, racism and the inadequacy of black trade unionism have created a native subproletariat, which is systematically maintained and, in all domains, at a standard of living inferior to that of the least favored white.* Concomitantly, "In practice, remuneration tends to

* The family allowances are distributed as follows: Europeans: 1st child, 175, 2nd child, 550, etc.; 6th child, 2,350 francs. Africans: 1st child, 93.72, 2nd child, 137.50, etc.; 6th child, 597 francs. The French are compensated for every kind of accident; the blacks have compensation only in a case where the accident is caused by an explosive or by a machine "driven by a force other than that of men or animals." To acquire 2.2 lbs. of white bread an unskilled laborer in Dakar must work 1 hour 27 minutes, a Parisian unskilled laborer 25 minutes. To acquire an egg the black of Dakar works 29 minutes, the Parisian 11 minutes.

be determined by the interplay of supply and demand."[3] In other words, racial ideology permits reducing the native worker to the level of pure economic data. Not entirely, however: for obvious reasons, the administrative authority fixes the rate of minimum wages. Thus, the political ideology of racism (with its economic infrastructures) and the political ideology of paternalism (metropolis-bureaucracy) combine to determine the standard of living which is considered "just" and "sufficient" for a black. Now it so happens that in the mother country the bourgeois economists have stopped basing wage theory on the law of supply and demand. "Labor," writes Mossé, "is not a commodity. A wage is not a price which takes form in the market. . . . It is impossible to state positively the nature of the relationship, if indeed one exists, between a worker's wage and his productivity, between the general level of wages and the level of employment, production, prices, money, etc." They think today that the problem of wages has become a problem of the distribution of national income among individuals and social groups. And what will determine the rates? A complex array of factors, including the collective demands and the values, ideologies, relationships of forces among the groups, as well as strictly economic data. "Rather than being a price," writes Mossé, "the wage is a *participation* in a total result within which an apportionment among the component units imputable to this or that factor is impossible. Or perhaps it is a *deduction* comparable to a tax by its method of establishment and by its incidences. Or perhaps it is the wellspring which supplies individual and family needs. If this is the case, the problem of wages becomes one of human relations, of psychology, of relationships of forces: *in short, a political problem, dominated by ideologies, beliefs concerning justice, equity, and the social hierarchy.*"[4] The economists are getting sentimental: "We have passed," says one, "from neutrality to humanism." And another: "From objective economic theory to normative, political economic theory." What has happened? Simply

[3] William Top: "Valeur du travail des salariés africains," "Le Travail en Afrique noire." *Présence Africaine,* No. 13, p. 252.

[4] Mossé: *Les Salaires,* p. 128. (My emphasis.)

this: the proletariat has broken into the human race like a burglar. Until 1848, the factory worker was isolated, was not ready for a test of strength. *Therefore,* he was nothing more than a beast; his relationship with the employer could be identified as a purely economic relation. During the second half of the nineteenth century, the proletariat came to constitute an independent social force. Now at last the bourgeoisie *acknowledged* human dignity in the workers. From then on, the *humanism* of which it was so proud was marked by a contradiction: the worker is a man because he inspires fear, but the social order requires that he be kept in his bestial condition. The contradiction lived and suffered by the proletariat becomes the contradiction of bourgeois thought. Everyone suggests a solution. And everyone, in the name of one of the teeming humanisms (reformism, class collaboration, corporatism, radicalism, Christian socialism, etc.) seeks the measures that enable bourgeois society to digest its proletariat. The problem was simple, but difficult to solve: to what conditions must a creature of human appearance adapt so that we can call him human and still treat him like an animal? No solution has yet been found. Thus, by their silent presence alone, by the calm menace which their admitted strict discipline brings to bear on the established system, by their very look, these men, appearing all at once as a society within society, stir up trouble in paradise and blow humanism apart. Isn't this a *political act,* and the most important one, perhaps, since 1789? Obviously, every common action of the oppressed, even if kept within the strict limits of occupational grievances, is *by itself,* and as an event of a certain order occurring in a certain society, a political action. For it reveals the degree of cohesion of the workers' troops, their moral climate, and the force and extent of the labor movement. According to the outcome of the battle, this force will increase by becoming conscious of itself, or will diminish; the ties between union members will become stronger or weaker, the relationship between the employer and the wage earner will evolve in one direction or another. The workers are profoundly aware of this deep connection which attaches them to the working class as a whole and which sets them against the bourgeois class.

Thus any kind of strike is always something more and something other than a strike. A great workers' association does not limit itself to confronting the chiefs of industry; it also concentrates on the consumers, the *public*. Labor has to get the public on its side, avoid becoming unpopular, make people appreciate its importance in the national economy, and bring the pressure of public opinion to bear on the employers. Very often the improvement of living conditions is not the end *in itself* of union activity: the union wants to win for the sake of prestige, to hold on to its members, and to increase their numbers. As for the striker himself, he is after something more than his immediate interest: more than want, more than misery, it is anger that impels him, his confidence in the leaders, the need to assert that he is a man in the face of those who treat him like a thing. We can say that trade unionism is a *way of being a man*.

Objectively, trade unionism is political. It's a matter of course for it to take in hand the totality of *factors affecting the worker;* the limitations imposed on it originate, without exception, in ulterior political motives. Quite obviously, the reformist is timid, conservative, secretly tempted by the bourgeoisie: the limits to union action which he prescribes have to emerge from secret compromises since they could not possibly be explained by the objective situation; and it is obvious that Niel's aversion to all anti-patriotic demonstration was rooted in an unacknowledged chauvinism. But it must be added that the trade-union militants have always been aware of the *political* importance of the union. Of course, in the heroic times of anarcho-syndicalism, they displayed defiance of parties, but it was "from a feeling of savage opposition to the bourgeoisie." Greffuelhe tells us that they "*fiercely* wish to be led by workers." They wished it precisely because "for them bourgeois reactionaries and socialists are charlatans of the same stripe; the workers *will make the Revolution by themselves.*" The same congress in 1888 urged the workers "to separate themselves from the politicians who deceive them" and to place their hopes in the general strike which alone "can carry them towards their emancipation." As a result, one can note within the C.G.T. a certain alternation between reformism and revolutionary syndicalism. But the militants of both sides agreed to develop union action *in all directions.* For the revolutionary, the worker is in himself the major contradiction of bourgeois society; he is the negation of the property system. His demands will have a double goal: if they are satisfied, they will improve his lot by achieving the progressive disruption of the capitalist order. The general strike will finish the job. The reformist fundamentally wishes to reach the same final goal, but by gradual progress. In any case, he will be "everywhere that the interests of the worker are being discussed" and will claim "direct and ubiquitous participation in economic matters."

Both sides would have approved *without reservation* the C.G.T.'s "Program of 1949," which stated among other things, that "The fundamental condition is dictated by the experience of the first plan for the modernization and retooling of industry and of what became of it through the intervention of the Marshall Plan. [We must] get rid of the Marshall Plan . . . denounce the military agreements of the Western bloc, reestablish normal relations between states, demand that reparations be paid to us . . . *So many decisions which condition the implementation of the C.G.T. program for economic and social recovery, which implementation in turn conditions their total achievement . . .*"

For your hatred of communism, my slippery friends, has made you forget how restrained it is in comparison with the old days. Between 1905 and 1910 your fathers lived in fear of a *coup de force.* As May 1st, 1906 drew near, their capital fled where yours flees today. In order to bring back gold and restore confidence, it was necessary to fabricate a conspiracy and jail a few unionists. Our Communists are nationalists, don't forget. They are against *a certain policy* but not against national defense. We sentenced Henri Martin to five years of prison for distributing leaflets against the abject stupidity of the war in Vietnam: but he was not inciting the soldiers to disobedience. In the early part of the century anti-militarist propaganda was a daily occurrence. There was a lot of shouting because some leaders of the Communist Party had publicly declared that the proletariat would not fight against the U.S.S.R. But the French trade unionists, believing themselves in agreement with the German workers, had also made public declarations and let the country know by way of posters that they would resort to a general strike in order to prevent war. And, even though this type of fantasy is scarcely of interest, if one can imagine the Greffuelhes and the Merrheims placed in a situation analogous to ours, one cannot doubt that they would have led the federal Congress to condemn any anti-Soviet crusade in advance. Thus, when our respectable newspapers speak nostalgically of a golden age when the unions offered their demands to the employers like a New Year's greeting, they are dreaming. They wish to cover up the fact of exploitation, which the union militants never lose sight of; they think that unionism is a weapon which the employers have freely given the workers so that equitable discussions might take place. But the workers know that their organizations have been prohibited and hounded; they know that the trade union, with or without the help of the C.P., aims above all "to change the world." It is this apparent misunderstanding which makes the trade union phenomenon ambiguous. But the employers are not misled, and they know how to sing two very different songs. When the organizations of the working class seem to be opposing rearmament or a war policy, the employers raise their eyebrows, painfully surprised. "Is this the way you thank us?" they say. "Politics has nothing to do with unionism." But when a strike worries or annoys them, even if it is purely economic, they invoke the name of politics in order to break it. In 1910 the railroad workers stopped work. Briand had the strike committtee arrested. Called on the carpet by the Socialists, he declared: "There is one right superior to all others, it is the right of a national collective to maintain its independence and its pride. A country simply cannot keep its borders wide open; if, to maintain security, it had been necessary to resort to illegal means, I would not have hesitated." Thus the principle was established: any strike can be prohibited for the sake of higher interests. Unions don't have the right to resist war; but for the good of the war effort, unions can be suppressed. On January 13, 1915, Millerand declared before the Metalworkers' delegation: "There are no more workers' rights, no more social laws, there is only the war." Thus the rights of unions are suppressed in the name of a war which the unions did not have the right to reject.*

"They did have the right to do so," the indignant anti-Communist tells me. "They had the right. Did they or did they not vote?" The argument is taken up in all good faith, I'm sure, by Mr. Thibault, the political editor of *France-Soir*: "Free elections, such as the Muscovite paradises are far from knowing, have taken place in all the countries of Western Europe since the signing of the Atlantic Pact. The majority of electors have clearly expressed themselves everywhere, and it is an imposture on the part of Communist agitators to claim to speak in the name of the French people, who have emphatically defined their position."

Who knows whether to find heartening or ominous these deaf men's dialogues which the blocs and the classes have been carrying on for the past seven years and which almost all men rediscover deep within themselves when they have closed their newspapers. For after all, Mr. Thibault does not expect to bother a Marxist by this evocation of universal suffrage. In case he really believes his argument unanswerable, may I remind him of the following text of Lenin, chosen almost at random among a hundred similar ones: "The bourgeois parliaments are all the more dependent on the Stock Exchange and the bankers the more democracy develops there. It does not follow that bourgeois parliamentarianism must not be used, the Bolsheviks have used it more successfully than any other party in the world . . . But it follows that only a liberal is capable of forgetting the *narrowness* and the *relativeness* of bourgeois parliamentarianism. In the most democratic bourgeois

* It is necessary to add that if in a *liberal* economy it is absurd to restrict union activity to the defense of occupational interests, it is utterly idiotic to seek to maintain these restrictions today when the state has assumed new economic and social functions. How can one distinguish politics from economics when it is *with the State* that the worker will have to deal?

state, the oppressed masses at every step run up against a flagrant contradiction between *formal* equality, proclaimed by the 'democracy' of the capitalists, and the thousands of *real* restrictions and stratagems that make the proletarians paid slaves."

Between 1944 and 1947, the C.P. helped the bourgeois class reconstruct its state apparatus because it was counting on using parliamentarianism to seize power and, by this very means, to transform the parliamentary system; but it remained faithful to the Leninist doctrine according to which the power of the working class manifests itself truly only on the terrain of class struggle. From 1946 on, the Party found itself torn between its parliamentary policy and the social conflicts: its ministers were like hostages in the bourgeois state, and the Party rediscovered within itself, in the shape of a growing tension between its deputies and its militants, the conflict between the propertied classes and the proletariat. After the Party's eviction from the Government, the state apparatus fell entirely into the hands of the bourgeoisie, who proceeded to replace the Communists at all command posts with its own creatures; all republican institutions now functioned against the Party. It therefore made itself the spokesman for the popular will on another terrain, that of street demonstrations.

That, in any case, is how a Communist would answer. But this answer would not satisfy Mr. Thibault any more than his question would have bothered Mr. Fajon. I will try to set forth the facts without any dogmatism and to explain as simply as possible why today a worker voting Communist has just cause to consider his ballot worthless.

Let me, incidentally, remind you what you have made of him: a second-class citizen. No sooner did he decide to vote Communist, than his vote underwent a mysterious degradation; it acquired *ipso facto* a smaller electoral potential than that of his neighbor. To send 103 Communists to the National Assembly, 5 million votes are necessary; to send 104 Socialists, only 2,750,000 are needed—what a bargain—and for 95 M.R.P.'s, 2,300,000. A loss of 400,-000 votes for the Party means a loss of 79 seats; the Socialist Party gains 5 when it loses 600,000 votes. Roughly—quite roughly

—a longshoreman's vote is worth half a druggist's, or half a sexton's, or half a vote of his brother-in-law. a city-hall clerk. We must admit that the R.P.F. doesn't look too healthy either. But with 900,000 fewer votes than the Communists, they have 15 more seats. That's not such a bad bargain; the operation was brilliantly directed against the two extremes, but one of the two is more extremist than the other. "So," says our longshoreman, "does that make me subhuman?" Right: he's a "political have-not." And, entirely by chance, he just happens to be a worker. Oh, I know: it's legal; and that's that. An electoral law had to be made, didn't it? And then, after all, the C.P. had only to form an electoral alliance. The final motion of the M.R.P. Congress states explicitly: "Those who refuse to respect democratic rules and the diverse political families debar themselves from this union and bear the responsibility themselves." In short, if anyone holds aloof, so much the worse for him! But *with whom* do you want the C.P. to ally itself? With the M.R.P.? With the R.G.R.? And as for a rapprochement with the S.F.I.O., Mr. Guy Mollet has come right out with it: with a *French* Communist Party, unity of action. And right away. With the Russian Party, never! In short, the trick has been played: within the framework of the universal institutions of democracy we have quite legally passed an antidemocratic law which applies to a specific party. Frankly there's plenty of reason to go out into the streets and smash a few windows or a few faces. Just a century ago, on May 31, 1850, the longshoremen of the period had been tricked by a similar scheme. Univeral suffrage wasn't abolished. There was simply a three year's residence requirement for voting. Since the workers had moved around a great deal in search of work during the critical years of 1847-1849, this measure amounted to depriving the industrial proletariat of its right to vote. One stroke of the pen eliminated 2,600,000 voters. The 1951 method is much more sophisticated: it also eliminates two and a half million Communist votes, since it takes 5 million to elect 103 deputies. Only no one knows which of these five million men are doomed to have a void ballot. Of two Communist voters, there is always one who really counts, but who knows which one? And besides, the proletariat is not grossly marked by external characteristics: the C.P. marks itself as the Party of the spiteful by refusing to make alliances, and the voter marks himself as a proletarian by voting Communist.

The longshoreman can still be hopeful. After all, the C.P. is the largest party in France. Maybe these 103 deputies will do a good job of it. They won't ever, of course, enter a government coalition. But the opposition has its role to play: it criticizes, it restrains or stimulates, it influences. It may even give the Government the courage to say no to Washington occasionally. Unfortunately, the same holds true for the opposition as for the members of the Communist Party: there are two oppositions in the National Assembly, one that counts and one that doesn't. The R.P.F. has some influence at a distance—on the policy in Indochina, for example—where the C.P. has none. The votes of its elected representatives are thus practically neutralized: the Government takes them into account as a negative constant in the calculation of its majority. They complicate the parliamentary game a little and precautions must be taken before the question of confidence is put, but that's all: instead of playing classical billiards, our champions play pocket billiards. So when Mr. Brune reproaches Duclos for resorting to agitation rather than setting forth his opinion in the Assembly, when Mr. Bony loudly proclaims in *L'Aurore* that every French citizen has the right to persuade others, I can only assume that they must be joking. Just tell me, really, *with whom* Jacques Duclos can debate in the Assembly? Imagine that an inspiration of genius carries him to the rostrum. He speaks, he is fired up, he lashes out, he makes the gallery weep. And afterwards? He will collect the monotonous applause of his partisans and the even more monotonous insults of his adversaries. He hasn't moved the deputies? Not one: they weren't even listening. It has happened in parliamentary history that the speech of a member of the opposition has brought down a Minister. But that was because people still believed that a member of the opposition could speak the truth. Today people *know* that the member of the opposition is a liar: after all he's a Communist! The largest party in France is separated from the other parties by an invisible barrier; the deputies of the proletariat never fail to give their advice on the business under consideration, but it's pure ceremony. Of the two longshoremen walking along the docks of Le Havre, one has no right to vote and the other voted in vain. Do you think the Communist Party was so far from expressing the opinion of its voters, when, on the day after the elections, it implicitly gave notice of the May 28th demonstration by saying: "The Party will have to resort to other forms of action which are indispensable in order to struggle against a ferociously reactionary majority." To punish these second-class deputies, the majority resolved to deprive them of their parliamentary immunity.

But our longshoreman hasn't had it all yet. Fifteen years earlier, he could still hope that his government, in a sudden upsurge of independence or pride, would stop following England for a moment. Today he knows definitely that the "continuity of our policy" is the tranquil continuity of enslavement. We show our spirit only with Madagascans and Tunisians. Sold out? No, not even: it's much worse. The Americans got us for nothing. If, at that moment, the longshoreman remembers Lenin's phrase: "In the most democratic bourgeois state, the oppressed masses at every step run up against a flagrant contradiction between the *formal* equality proclaimed by the democracy of the capitalists and the thousands of *real* restrictions and stratagems which make the proletarians paid slaves," and if he then says to himself: "Lenin is right again," whose fault will it be, O great family of Petsches, Bidaults, Lussys, Pinays and affiliates? One day he will get fed up; and so will his buddy. The two of them, instead of unloading American machine guns, will heave them into the water. And the cops who arrest them will say indignantly: "You skunks! If you were against the Atlantic Pact, couldn't you have said so instead of damaging the materiel? Everyone's free here. Everyone has the right to vote."

"The Communist Party Sets the Workers on a Course of Illegality and Violence"

The May 28th demonstration was deliberately, insolently illegal: with what arrogance they disdained to request authorization! Wednesday, the 27th, the Prefecture issued a communiqué in the newspapers: "No authorization having been requested, all illegal assembly on public streets remains forbidden." At the same time, by means of posters, the Party calmly urged Parisians "to respond en masse to the call of the Peace Council."

Shall I say that this blatant flouting of the law hardly bothers me? This admission would deeply grieve certain professional thinkers in the United States. They would diagnose it as a "weakening of the democratic consciousness among European intellectuals." It would be unsporting, however, to demand that French intellectuals be surprised by the illegal doings of the C.P. since, as early as 1920, in "The Address of July 26th to the Members of the French Socialist Party," the Third International demanded that "wherever propaganda is difficult as a result of discriminatory legislation, it should be conducted illegally." The text added: "To refuse to do so would be a betrayal of one's revolutionary duty." The socialists were frightened by neither the word nor the deed itself. And Léon Blum, at the Congress of Tours, made a curious distinction on this subject: "There is not a single socialist who consents to let himself be cooped up in legality . . . But illegality is one thing and clandestine activity is another."* So far I don't see any problem: a party declares that it will if necessary resort to illegality. The democracy tolerates it in the name of freedom of thought. This party organizes a forbidden demonstration. The police suppress it by force and arrest those demonstrators who resist them. All this is *normal* and Mr. Cachin wasn't even born when the first clashes between demonstrators and the cops of the

* Unfortunately, illegality could not be *maintained* without decisions having been taken clandestinely. And anyway, in the case which concerns us, the illegality didn't rely on clandestineness: it was proclaimed and deliberately sought.

Second Republic occurred. On the other hand, you will have a hard time getting me to deplore in good faith, the illegality of the demonstration without at the same time denouncing the equally blatant arbitrariness of the repression. What justifies the arrest of Duclos? Being caught in a plot against the security of the state? That doen't exist. And even if it were conceivable, how could anyone have been caught in the act two hours after the demonstration? How about illegal possession of weapons? A deputy has a billy-club and a revolver in his car, and for this offense you arrest him in spite of parliamentary immunity, you throw him in prison and you keep him there without even letting him out on bail. Come now! You arrested Mr. Duclos because he was serving as General Secretary of the Party and because the Party had organized the demonstration: the government abandoned all the precautions taken in the last century and a half by magistrates and jurists to temper public vengeance. In fact, it returned to the crudest conception of responsibility. Its lack of concern for justifying its acts is even more disturbing: it knew that public opinion would be in its favor. No, it's not just the Western intellectual who is disgusted with the Republic, it's all of society. The fact that for the past thirty years the Communist Party has been asserting its scorn for bourgeois legality, and that it has been doing so with impunity, proves the strength of our institutions; find in that, according to your taste, reason to admire the greatness of democracy or to denounce its contradictions. Let Mr. Pinay toy somewhat brutally with republican institutions and nearly wreck them—no great harm has been done as yet: this gentleman is insignificant; he emerged from the shadows only a few weeks ago; the governmental apparatus will be repaired when he has gone back into his darkness. But France caught its Prime Minister in the act of violating the law and didn't even wince! It seems to prove that the Republic really has been winged. And what arguments are trotted out to justify this arrest! Look at Mr. Robinet and Mr. Brisson: Mr. Duverger was calmly explaining in *Le Monde* that perhaps there was no urgent need to dissolve the C.P., whereupon these two gentlemen lost patience and attacked him: "A plot? What plot? The whole Communist Party is a plot! For thirty years it's been boasting of it! What more do you want?" But, you will say, these big guns are obliged to practice shock-type anti-Sovietism. Fine. But Mr. Duverger, as he lets us know in another article, received a great number of letters which prove that the general opinion of the peaceable readers of *Le Monde* is completely antidemocratic. "What are you complaining about? Don't prevent the Government from carrying out its policy: it's getting rid of Duclos for us." Or else: "The leaders have to pay like their troops." Or again: "Pinay was right, since the Communists haven't stirred." Or: "You can't go by the law when you're dealing with outlaws." To tell the truth, Mr. Duverger doesn't quote the letters precisely in *these* terms: I've edited them, because the same answers have been given to me and I recognized them while reading his article. A serious warning to the Communist Party: all this proves that it has frightened the petty bourgeoisie and the middle classes. It's well known that the leaders of industry are quite unconcerned about democratic freedoms: what do you expect them to do with freedom of thought? When they have it, they don't enjoy it any more than a woman refinery worker does: they pay fools to enjoy it in their stead. The freedom they demand, the only one, is the freedom to direct, at will, the battles of production: this is called liberalism. For them Pinay's advantage over de Gaulle is that he juggles away freedoms without touching liberalism, whereas the Gaullists, according to Mr. Vallon, are thinking of "substituting a conscious economy for a blind economy." Between the upper bourgeoisie, which demands concrete power to make, acquire, and take profits, and the proletariat, which demands above all the right to live, only the petty bourgeoisie defends the formal freedoms of our democracies. These freedoms may be negative and restrictive, they may separate men much more than they unite them. But precisely because of that, they protect the *status quo* and permit a certain expectation, establish a sort of open window within a society which is becoming more integrated each day. It was the petty bourgeoisie that accelerated the coming of universal suffrage, and that largely provided the opposition cadres for the Second Empire and the personnel of the Radical and Radical-Socialist Parties after 1880. This class made the Republic; republican institutions are violated before its very eyes and it remains silent. Is it so frightened? We will come back to this. But what seems clear, in any case, is that today's democratic regime is no more than a façade: all the real conflicts take place outside it. In his last article, Duverger puts the question very well, and in statistical terms. When the C.P., he tells us, has won a fifth or a fourth of the electoral body, its adversaries can still do without fascism: we can still get by in a republic. But if it gathers fifty or fifty-one percent of the votes: "There is no longer a question of maintaining democracy but only of choosing the regimes to follow." The C.P. in France gathers a majority of the workers' votes: the nature of the political regime therefore depends solely upon the importance which the organizations of the proletariat can take on in the life of the nation. What's being played here is a bridge game with "danger zones": if you pass a certain limit, you get reaction and fascism. But if the "danger zone" is rapidly crossed, the workers' parties will take power and establish a "People's Democracy." As we can see, the reproach of illegality doesn't get at the heart of the question. It's simply that we are on the threshold of the danger zone and these skirmishes around the old legality are also the first notices of a new legality, based on the sovereignty of the masses, the notables, or the Party.

The reality hidden beneath these indignations is the class struggle. If you have understood it, you may be embarrassed about reproaching the Communist Party for its violence and its illegal activities: today, all violence comes directly or indirectly from the proletariat, which is merely paying us back. All workers' rights, even those which were "freely consented to," had to be violently fought for. In the midst of the tidy rights of bourgeois jurisprudence, they look like parvenus, they are held in quarantine and the purists gingerly handle the right to strike even though the Constitution of 1946 recognizes it expressly. On what do you want to base the right to strike? On the excellence of human nature? In that case, it would be superfluous. On freedom? But the striker exercises a constraint. On equality? But it is, on the contrary, the implicit recognition of inequality. "By its very definition, a strike has the right to do harm; it's more than a right, it's a weapon." And you give some men the right to harm others? "It's the right of legitimate self-defense applied to a group." Is a contract thereby an aggression? Society cannot justify a strike without recognizing first of all and openly that ours is a society of oppression. "For half a century, the regulation of the right to strike has been a foremost issue in each wave of social conflict." Of course! They have recognized this practice the better to channel and limit it. To top it all, a jurist confesses with a sigh that "the fact of the strike (is) a phenomenon akin to a volcanic eruption . . . unwilling by nature to appear within the framework of the law." A strange function for the worker: he is the illegal source of legality. In May, 1936, Blum declared: "I do not consider the occupation of the factories as something legal . . . It is inconsistent with the rules and principles of French civil law." In fact, it is an attack on the right of property. To which Thorez quite rightly replied: "They call it illegality. On the contrary! A new legality is taking form." One could, however, object that this new legality is not conceivable in any regime: it contradicts the fundamental principle of bourgeois society and, in a socialist society, no longer has a *raison d'être.* Irrationally and hastily sanctioning working-class *practice,* it makes sense only in our transitional and contradictory world; it is the very image of the worker, negation of himself and of society, his *real* function being to destroy the order which crushes him by destroying his own condition as proletarian. Even when he does not envisage stopping work, a worker knows that he *can* strike and that this permanent threat has a regulative effect on wages. He *is* this threat and he senses his own violence: in a society based on oppression, a supreme injustice requires that violence be in the first instance the oppressed person's role. How much clearer everything would be if, in fighting oppressors, one could count on their being just. Unfortunately, the oppressor is calm and strong; he places his strength in the service of law; if he kills, he does so legally. Naturally! He's the one who makes the laws. And then, as Engels has shown: "The bourgeoisie created the proletariat, without any cabalistic intervention of violence, by purely economic means." And he adds: "Even supposing that all private ownership is based on the personal work of the possessor and that, in the further course of things, only equal values are exchanged, we nevertheless necessarily arrive, by the progressive development of production and exchange, at the present mode of capitalist production, at the monopolization of the means of production and subsistence in the hands of a not very large class; at the reduction of the other class, which forms the vast majority, to the state of propertyless proletarians." In short, the worker has a good chance of being duped. He is oppressed, overworked; and yet if he reflects on the causal links, he finds neither theft nor constraint: everything has come about ever so gently. Furthermore, he has even *accepted* his condition, at least for a while: "So long as a mode of production is in the ascending stage of its evolution, it is acclaimed even by those who are handicapped by the corresponding mode of distribution. This is what happened to the British workers at the advent of large-scale industry." When the crisis comes and the mode of distribution suddenly seems unjust, *who then* is responsible? The worker, no matter how far he goes back in the past, finds himself *already committed to and enlisted in* a society which has its code and its jurisprudence, its government, its notion of what is just and what is unjust, and (a more serious fact still) whose ideology he spontaneously shares.[5] Society imposes on him a destiny, limits: it systematically inflicts on him both fragmented and semi-automatic tasks, the sense and the law of which escape him, and occupational diseases. By fatigue and misery, by obliging him to reiterate the same gestures a thousand times a day, society discourages him from exercising his human qualities. He is enclosed in the insipid world of repetition; little by little he becomes a *thing*. But when he looks for those who are responsible, there is no one: everything is right, he has been paid his due. In 1930, many American workers refused to register

[5] "The spontaneous development of the workers' movement quickly ends up by subordinating it to bourgeois ideology." (Lenin: "Que Faire?", *Oeuvres,* Edition de Moscou, 1948, I, p. 206.)

at the hastily improvised unemployment compensation offices: they were ashamed to be unemployed and felt guilty. The European worker, more enlightened, lives out this intolerable situation in ambiguity; he may reject it with all his might, but he accepts it in spite of himself because he was born into it, accepts it to the very extent that he simply seeks to ameliorate it. The semiskilled worker increases his pace in order to earn as much as the skilled worker, hence in order to compensate for humiliating inequalities and to feel more like a man, but he succeeds only by making himself more of a thing. He may prefer working on an assembly line, he may refuse to support union locals which try to limit or regulate the pace. And when he finds himself at his work, exhausted, subjugated to laws which come from the outside, his spontaneous refusal, a tacit but constant refusal to be reduced to the state of a piece of machinery, clashes with his desire to maintain a mode of production more lucrative to him. In short, he doesn't know at first whether or not he is responsible for the society in which he was born, a society devoid of institutions to protect him or words to name the wrong being done to him. The other classes courageously put up with his misery and explain to him that it is necessary for the collective equilibrium. He is the object of the government's solicitude. The state pays him a wage supplement and Social Security benefits; and yet he can't convince himself that he is entirely one with a community which daily, secretly, hands down death sentences for economic reasons and which will let two babies of the poor die for one of the rich.[6] Half accomplice, half victim, participant and martyr, he wants what he doesn't want, and rejects with his whole body what he accepts with all his will to live; he detests the

---

[6] *Infant mortality in France, in 1939:*

	Mortality per 1,000 children born alive but under 1 year of age.
A. Upper middle class, high civil servants, managers	26.8%
B. Farmers, employees, civil servants, shopkeepers	34.4%
C. Artisans, skilled workers	44.4%
D. Semiskilled workers	51.4%
E. Unskilled workers	60.1%

monster that mechanization makes of him and yet he knows he can't be different without changing the universe. The contradiction is not only *in* him: it is imposed on him; mass production requires that he be contradictory. He is simultaneously a man and a piece of machinery: people can demand his services whenever it is too difficult or too costly to build an automatically controlled machine; the progress of cybernetics will render him useless. Thus he is asked to combine equity of mind with a certain diffuse vigilance, to be present and absent at the same time. He is human *up to a certain point*: for the industrialists will make no bones about telling you that general education is prejudicial to the output of a semiskilled worker, and yet, his human eyes still can't be replaced by photoelectric cells. Thus the original violence is not the oppression: the latter merges with justice and order; it's the *interiorized oppression,* the oppression *lived* as an internal conflict, as constraint exercised by one half of one's self on the other half. The worker commits the first violence against himself to the extent that he *makes himself* a worker. The hunger and the anxiety of the unemployed worker are not suffered violence until he *takes them on his own back,* until he makes himself their accomplice in order to force himself to accept a salary below the union rate. An employer needs a typist. A crisis: thirty persons apply, equally capable, all with identical diplomas. He calls them all together and asks them simply to let him know what salary they want. A horrible bidding-down commences: the employer has—in appearance—merely let the law of supply and demand go into effect, but each typist, by asking *the lowest* salary, does violence to the others and to herself, and contributes, in humiliation, to lowering a bit more the standard of living of the working class. The employer will finally hire the one who, having the advantage of a very small outside income (a widow with a pension—or else a girl who lives with her family), will ask for a salary *below* the subsistence level; that is to say the one who will exercise on herself and on all the others the destructive action which the employer would take care not to exercise himself. To be a worker is *to force oneself to be one* while making the workers' condition more and more unlivable for oneself and for everyone else. People pretend to believe that violence is born suddenly, at the very moment of the riot or the strike. Not so! In periods of crisis violence is *exteriorized,* that is all. The contradiction is inverted: the docile worker rejects the human in himself; the rebelling worker rejects the inhuman. This refusal is itself a humanism—it contains the urgent demand for a new justice. But since oppression is not a visible offense, since the ideology of the dominant class defines the just and the unjust, since nothing will be obtained without smashing a sacred order, the affirmation by the worker of his own human reality reveals itself to his own eyes as a manifestation of violence. Moreover, no sooner has he lifted a finger than society mobilizes its police forces; they change the worker's setting, they *get* his violence ready for him, they make sure that he pushes it to the extreme. His discontent *must* turn into a strike, his strike into a riot, the riot into murder. When he has fallen into the trap and starts wondering in amazement how the political demand for his human rights led him to strike and to kill, the repression will begin. And the return to calm will not be a calming but a return to the original violence. The primitive contradiction reappears, but now it is reinforced: the striker has experienced the counter-violence of society, it still acts within him and he reacts to it with two contrary feelings, fear and hatred; at the same time, he has discovered himself and he now knows that violence is the law of his action. Meanwhile, the bourgeoisie contemplates with fear and disgust this sudden explosion, which is, in sum, a boomerang of its oppression; it seems to this very shrewd and civilized class that violence *arises* from the oppressed person and that it is due to his barbarity; for this class, the worker is an unfathomable violence that has *become object.* The worker is not unaware of it, he knows that he frightens the bourgeois and, by a new reaction to the "projective personality" conferred on him, he proudly demands this violence for which he is resented. The purpose of these remarks was to show the ambiguity of the worker's condition: for the worker is answerable to a historic right which doesn't yet exist and may never exist; from the point of view of a future society which will be born thanks to his efforts, his violence is a positive humanism;* seen in our present society, it is in part a right (to strike) and in part a crime. In fact, humanism and violence are the two indissoluble aspects of his effort to go beyond the condition of an oppressed being.

The slippery customers have kindly dispositions and violence horrifies them: no wonder, considering that they're bourgeois. The trouble is that they have a marked proclivity for the working class. To solve the difficulty, they have invented the myth of the workers' affliction: violence made its appearance in the world with the Third International. A strange perversion: for, after all, the evidence is that workers' violence is the very substance and the strength of the C.P.; the C.P. has channelized and is nourished by that violence; and if the leaders are understood by the workers it's because they speak the language of violence to them. To be sure, with the Party this violence loses its characteristic of *immediate* eruption: it is "mediated," conscious, it determines itself by its representation of itself; the C.P. is will *made manifest,* hypostatized. No matter: even if there is a certain disparity between the manifestation of violence and the original violence from which it emanates, the working class nonetheless *recognizes itself* in the test of strength which the C.P. institutes in its name.

What have I sought to prove? That the May 28th demonstration was clever, effective, praiseworthy? Not at all. I merely wish to show that it falls within the framework of popular demonstrations. "Why wasn't the Communist Party dissolved?" you said. "We would have established a 'true Left' in its place, affable, courteous, smooth and full of subtle reservations; it would fight capitalism while being just to people; it would, without rejecting violence, use it only as a last resort and, while knowing how to stir up the generous enthusiasm of the proletarians, would protect

* Not a means of achieving humanism. Not even a necessary condition. But the humanism itself, insofar as it asserts itself against "reification."

them, whenever necessary, from their excesses." An admirable program: only, if someone were to deliver this Left to you with the wave of a magic wand (for I can't imagine how you could get it otherwise), I wouldn't give it a week; you would find some of its members in the Socialist group in the National Assembly or on the editorial staff of *Franc-Tireur,* while the others would be out in the streets demonstrating against Ridgway.

"Your reasoning," you will say, "is very fine. Only it must have a weak spot since on May 28th the working class didn't turn out and the mass demonstration was held without the masses." And the slippery customers laugh. All right, let's go back and see.

II. THE JUNE 4TH STRIKE

On May 28th and June 4th the Communist Party organized two demonstrations. What did it expect from them? What was their true significance? If they really were failures, what made them fail? What meaning must be given to this double defeat? What will its consequence be? And, if they prove injurious to the working class, to the entire French nation, and to peace, are there ways to remedy the matter? It is this tangle of questions that I shall try to unravel.

What could the Communist Party expect from May 28th? When the police are out in numbers, what can a crowd manifest except its *passion,* in every sense of the word? Since the official power prohibits marches, how could one march at all without taking power? It's been done: strong indignation has often sent Parisians into the streets; they have marched and sometimes seized a building en route; the February Revolution put the government back in the hands of a fear-crazed bourgeoisie. Today precautions are taken to prevent chance occurrences: political life has become so serious that a party can no longer allow itself to be carried to power in spite of itself. In 1952, a street demonstration can, *at the outside,* give the signal for an insurrection—on condition that it be agreed upon in advance—but not set it off unexpectedly. Always halfway between riot and ceremony, between martyrdom and defiance, these interrupted processions invoke violence, but only to submit to it. They constitute failure-behavior, gestures intended to be ineffective and whose ineffectiveness *bears witness*. The masses are shown their potentially immense powers and their temporary impotence: by giving them a rest from the painstaking work of *organization,* these explosive festivities make them see the need for organization; in short, this is the "street theatre" that Artaud wanted: the role of the Parisian population is usually played by the Parisian population itself, which takes on the job of evoking for its own benefit its glorious destiny and above all its lost spontaneity: everything is done so that these "players" can pretend to be the very ancient crowd which rolled and pitched down our boulevards from the beginning to the end of the last century. And, in fact—it is the same crowd except that the demonstrators are called out, lined up, led and forbidden even to touch store-windows or take anything en route, even the Bastille.

A banned demonstration will inevitably be a failure: but this doesn't mean that it has to start out that way. Now the organizers foresaw a bitter defeat and by no means a symbolic one: they knew the masses wouldn't turn out. *They knew it*: for the last two years, from the dailies to the periodicals, from the great organs of the Right to the news-sheets of the workers' opposition, the entire press has been pointing out and commenting on the "discouragement of the workers"; and do you imagine that the Political Bureau would be the only one not to have noticed it? Just flip through Jacques Duclos' notebook: nothing is said clearly, of course; but you will see the word "explain" recur a hundred times: *explain* to the Marseilles dockers . . . *explain* to the workers . . . we haven't *explained* enough—you will sense the growing concern and the growing desire "to intensify the battle" against a certain wavering in the workers' views. Notice how they always come back to the same worries, the same themes: those people are perfectly aware of their difficulties. If this is so, you will say, why did they choose this moment to invite the Parisians to a political show of force? My reply is: because they were *forced* to. When a procession has been announced a long time ahead, a festival committee has trouble cancelling it even if the weather turns bad. The demonstration against Ridgway had been announced months beforehand: specifically, right after the demonstration against Eisenhower. By protesting against the latter, the Party had tacitly pledged itself to protest against all his successors. A mass party cannot stop at sounding out public opinion: it must amplify and make specific the uncertain trends within it, must bring them fully to light; it must, finally, beam them back to the public: and what better resonator than the masses themselves? The Party will get them to play their desires out objectively, to put themselves wholly into the acts which go beyond them and carry them even further; if the Parisian population is against the Atlantic Pact, it must become conscious of this hostility: and only a violent and hazardous action can make the population conscious. The Parisians aren't too zealous at the moment? All the more reason to decide on a popular show of force. Like every *real* relationship, the connection between a political party and the masses that it can gather is ambiguous: on the one hand, it is guided by them; on the other, it "organizes" them and attempts their "education"; and since it isn't a matter of changing them but of helping them to become what they are, the Party is at once their *expression* and their *example.* When it addresses them in its manifestos, it uses the imperative, then the future, then the present indicative to designate this same reality, the movement which is both a fact and a value: "French workers will be able to remember . . . the toiling masses do not allow themselves to be taken in by this crude maneuver. . . . Workers, demand that they liberate . . . ," etc. What the Party represents in their eyes is their aspirations, their inclinations, their collective will, but *brought to a red heat,* that is to say, to the highest level of *efficacy.* Sometimes they follow the Party and sometimes they even carry it along, but it can also happen that they remain behind. It doesn't matter: if the Party is assured of speaking in their name, if it judges that only an accident prevents them from following it, it will forge ahead: it acts for them and in their name. The masses are action and passion at one and the same time: they will ultimately change the world, but, for the moment, the world is crushing them. Their pressure can at times be irresistible, but cold, hunger, police repression can momentarily get the better of them: the Party is *pure action*; it must advance or disappear; it is the strength of the workers who are at the end of their strength and the hope of those who are without hope. Giving up the May 28th demonstration would have meant "taking a step backward": the Party couldn't take the workers' fatigue into consideration without running the risk of increasing it and thereby making them incline toward resignation. Perhaps, in the Political Bureau, they understood from this moment on that they would soon have to change tactics: but, in any case, that could be only *after* the demonstration. The masses will not come to know their weariness: they will testify through intermediaries; their lagging will be covered up by the violence of the brawls, their action will be shown to them *such as it should have been.* Teams of specialists will be assigned to carry out gestures of violence before them—and it is their own violence which they will see alive and detached from them; in their homes they will witness the battle of demonstrators against cops, a facile symbol of the class struggle.

In sum, what did the Party want when it sent its militants to assault the Place de la République? To seize power? To kidnap Ridgway? To cause the ministry's downfall? Not at all: it simply wanted to make a point. What did it risk? If things had taken their usual course, the bourgeois press would have dispassionately commented on the events and everything would have returned quickly to normal.

Mr. Pinay didn't see it that way. Did he believe in a plot then? Nonsense! He was following the example of those great Prime Ministers who upset the nation without reason so as to give themselves the easy glory of having reassured it. To launch the Loan, the government resorted to a classical tactic: it diverted the competitor's propaganda to its own advantage. Notice how it enlivens the debate, how it lends color to the polemics by banning Vailland's play for no reason. This climate of violence was created by some mysterious individuals who beat up the actors in a fist fight, American-style. People instantly whispered that the Prime Minister had given in to pressure from the American Embassy: excellent publicity; the future clientele of the Loan likes to rediscover the finger of God in the details: if the United States deigned to defend us in such minor circumstances against our unpardonable tolerance, what won't it do in major ones? The excitement was dying down when the Ridgway visit furnished the theme for the second publicity campaign. First, André Stil was arrested. The really clever thing was that the arrest was so clearly arbitrary: the French upper-middle classes detest the republic and distrust fascism, but they are sold on an arbitrariness which they consider aristocratic and which offers them both the image of the anarchy they enjoy and the authority they dream of as obtaining for others. They raised their heads and wondered pensively whether they had gotten hold of that rare bird: an iron-fisted liberal? The day of the demonstration, Mr. Baylot and the government organized panic: the former guaranteed that the masses wouldn't budge, the latter that it was on the track of a conspiracy whose importance it urged us to measure by the number of cops assigned to repress it. The goal of the conspirators? How are we supposed to know, since the vigilance of the ministry has foiled their projects? Fortune smiled on Mr. Pinay. Everything worked to his advantage, even the bloodshed. The police, as we know, fired in the air. A bullet ricocheted against the sky and fell back into the crowd: did it strike a Frenchman? No: the finger of God deflected it in time onto an Algerian. You know what they'll make of that: *so* there were some dirty Arabs among the separatists. And what were they doing there? Use the African regiments to bring the Madagascans to heel, that's just fine: native against native. Only an enemy of France would involve Arabs in quarrels between Frenchmen. In short, by nightfall the forces of order had won the match. A tiny match, a tiny victory: only one corpse and two priests beaten black and blue; that has never been enough to launch a loan.

The demonstration ended; people went home irritated, weary, vaguely disappointed. In the working class neighborhoods, the news was already known: another defeat. They kept still, hiding their bitterness and their sadness under sullenness. This was the moment that Mr. Pinay chose to have a Communist leader kidnapped right off the street. We all know the pious legend which the press spread the next day: Duclos was caught red-handed; terrified for an instant, the police agents glimpsed the perhaps incalculable consequences of his arrest; then out of civic duty, out of disinterested love for law and order they decided to apprehend him. It might have made sense, if there had been laws to defend, but the point is there weren't any: a citizen was driving home in his automobile and the circumstances made him *legally* untouchable. It is a strange love for the law that makes it submit to the worst outrages under the pretext that it has just been violated. You don't understand, people whisper to us: it was a case of extreme urgency; legality was shelved because the Republic was in danger. A conspiracy! You can imagine how much Mr. Pinay believes in the conspiracy! Or Mr. Pleven! Or the right-wing press! Just ask them, *what* conspiracy there was, insist on some proof or at least some information: they'll answer you nobly that the Communist Party is a *permanent* conspiracy and that it should have been dissolved the day after the Congress of Tours. No, indeed. The maneuver stinks to high heaven: in direct contrast to Lyautey, the Government used its strength in order to display it. And to whom? Why, to its future clientele, of course.

Looked at without prejudice, the Pinay operation is disconcerting: no one doubts that it is an act of violence and that it will ultimately jeopardize the cause it claims to be saving: the bourgeoisie aims all its propaganda at formal freedoms; if it destroys them with its own hands, what will it claim to be defending? But if one examines in detail the circumstances of the arrest, everything gets confused. One could take it for a scenario written jointly by two authors, one of whom is apparently very clever and one an idiot. If the Government wanted to show its strength, who prevented it from freeing Duclos immediately after the failure of the strike? Was it really necessary that all Europe hear the sound of the slaps dealt by the Bench to ministerial cheeks? Why did they lie about the time of the arrest? About the radio set? Why the nonsense about carrier pigeons? And that venerable gag about conspiracy—it's a hundred and ten years old! The liberal press doesn't seem to have been sensitive to these contradictions: at the time it still mistook Mr. Pinay for Parsifal. But if you don't share this view, you may have the feeling that the decision of the ministers was prompted by some Machiavelli, that they misunderstood it, carried it out badly, and finally found themselves faced with consequences beyond their capabilities. As for the Machiavelli, naturally, I don't guarantee that he exists: in this clever and foolish operation, the foolishness comes from the ministers and the cleverness from somewhere else; perhaps simply from the circumstances.

Mr. Pinay was pursuing his idea; and his idea was the Loan. A few days later, a newspaper carried this heartfelt statement: "The demonstration ends in defeat, and the Loan promises to be a success: which side are good Frenchmen on?" That's clear: good Frenchmen subscribe to loans and don't loaf around in the streets: Mr. Pinay expected his reward to come not from the streets but from the shops, the banks and the National Assembly. What he was preparing with so much persistence was not the dissolution of the C.P. but the dismemberment of the R.P.F. He tried to bring leftist opposition to heel in order to muzzle right-wing opposition more effectively; and if he kept his bothersome captive under lock and key, it was simply in order to blackmail his colleagues: that was clear when he imposed the vote of confidence on the terror-stricken National Assembly: "My job is in your hands. But whoever takes it will have to take my prisoner along with it." That day, Mr. Duclos saved the ministry.

In short, we were given the Red-peril stunt: an old stunt but one that still works. Only Mr. Pinay didn't give it its classical form, and, according to the experts, it was even a heresy to have tried it in these circumstances: for the trick to work, it is usually considered indispensable that *there not be* a Red peril. Take the Americans: what an innate sense of propaganda and what an admirable understanding of emotions they must have had in order to perfect the somewhat crude process which they got from Europe! And do you believe that they could have fashioned the marvelous propaganda instrument known as *anticommunism* out of it if there were

Communists in the United States? If you meet C.P. militants every day, or even every month, how can you believe they eat children? And then, you can economize on the personnel involved: if *no* one *is* a "Stalinist" everyone is under suspicion of being one; the average man plays both roles: he is a denouncer along with everyone else, a victim of denunciation when alone. Of course the victims will never prove their innocence since the prosecution doesn't know what it's charging them with. By applying the operation without discernment, Mr. Pinay ran the risk of finding out at his own expense that *there are* Communists in France.

However, the whole thing took place as if there weren't any. Are we really to believe that a Machiavelli is advising the Government? The explanation is plausible but not necessary. This short-term operation came at its particular time in a battle which has been going on since the Liberation, with the French bourgeoisie managing to win and keep the initiative. Machiavellianism is involved: whatever Mr. Pinay did, his action, borne, served, surrounded, fostered by other less visible and more profound maneuvers, was bound to reflect a borrowed intelligence; at a certain moment in battles, if one of the adversaries has the advantage, everything helps him, even chance. Mr. Pinay foolishly arrested Duclos the very moment when it became clever to arrest him. There is an objective direction to the "coup of May 28" which was not apparent, *perhaps,* to any of its authors but which is now blatantly obvious after the event: it has become the symbol of a strategy that I will try to define in the next chapter.

Considered from this angle, Duclos' arrest is illegal *because it had to be so.* If it were legal, the Party would have a way out: it could protest through its press and through meetings against the *intention* while at the same time declaring its compliance with the formal legality of the *act.* By kidnapping Duclos, the Prime Minister blocked off all the exits: he publicly challenged the Communists, he attacked them *on the failure* of the demonstration, and when they were in full retreat, he forced them to accept a trial of strength at the time and place of his choosing, with the entire world as witnesses. Why not protest? Hold up the Constitution against the Government? That could be done; it was done: Duclos filed a complaint charging abuse of authority. Naturally, respectable tabloids were ironic: "If our laws are made against you, why do you protest them when they are broken? You flout them daily, what right do you have to yell when *we* go beyond them? You're either for or against the Republic, according to your interest of the moment and you appeal to our codes only to tie our hands with rules you don't observe." The argument is meaningless, and we will take the opportunity to come back to the relation between the C.P. and democracy. But even if the C.P. had no other goal than to destroy democracy, it is still the bourgeoisie itself that postulated the universality of the law against the particularisms of the *Ancien Régime*: why would the Communists abstain from accusing the adversary in the name of its own principles? Then you're defending Maurras? Not at all: Maurras was a bourgeois who drew all his resources from bourgeois society; he had the culture and the affluence which give a real content to formal freedoms; he betrayed his class for the sake of a small bourgeois minority. The Communists speak on behalf of the proletariat, who participate in the economic life of the country but not in its social life: if the worker happens to derive some advantage from bourgeois laws, this doesn't make them *his* laws: for they favor the people who exploit him. Nevertheless, the Party could not be satisfied with a legal action, for the government, in violating the law, sought out the masses on their own terrain—illegality. By publicly insulting their Party, it challenged them: "This is what I'm doing with your chief: and if you don't like it, lump it." The masses had to answer the challenge *on this terrain*: in the case of Henri Martin, the Party can find the reason for the prosecution absurd and the sentence iniquitous; but it doesn't dispute the right to arrest and punish a soldier or a sailor caught distributing leaflets: it will limit itself then to demanding through its press, through meetings or petitions, a review of the trial. Inversely, if a government with fascist tendencies arrests the representatives of a bourgeois party, this party can resort to legal action: for it will want to prove that democratic laws are sufficient to protect us from dictatorship. But if violence is done to a party of violence, the only response is violence.

In our societies, the Government and the assemblies derive their power from institutions at least as much as from the will of the people, first of all because the institutions define the voter, next and above all, because the power, although it may no longer satisfy the wishes of the majority, can remain legitimate on the sole condition that it be guaranteed by the law. After the municipal elections of 1947, a government half disowned by the country was able to remain in power, wait for the resurgence of the Gaullist movement, and concoct an electoral law which assured the return of the same majority to the future Assembly.

The C.P. enjoys an authority which resembles that of a government; but since it doesn't have *institutions,* its sovereignty comes from the masses themselves. You claim that it owes allegiance to Moscow, that there is no democracy inside the movement. This may be so; nevertheless, if the masses suddenly refused to follow it, it would lose everything; as powerful as it is, it resembles Anteaus, who had strength only when he was touching the earth. The five or six million votes given the Party every four years consecrate its electoral importance without legitimatizing its revolutionary action: the voters don't object to demonstrations or political strikes, but their ballots do not reveal whether they participate in them. The C.P. measures its powers in the streets; the amplitude of the mass demonstrations *legitimatizes* its authority. Here then, confronting the abstract and very reasonable electoral system, is a public delegation of powers; it may be obscure, dangerous, and contestable but it carries us back to the very sources of sovereignty. These plebiscites are like divine creation in Descartes: valid at the moment, they must be ceaselessly renewed; even if the whole of France had gone on strike yesterday, nothing permits us to assert that it will do the same tomorrow. There is no *institution* to extend and prolong the result of these popular expressions of opinion beyond the day they took place: and this is understandable since, by its very violence, the torrent of demonstrators expresses a sort of *constituent* will that revokes the laws in force. The bourgeois has never misunderstood it: his intrigues may reshuffle ministries, but it is the masses who give the *real* power; what he fears and detests in the "populace" is raw sovereignty. But since the relationship between the crowds and their leaders is constantly variable, the bourgeois doesn't hesitate to take the Communists at their word and force them to present themselves in a plebiscite when circumstances are unfavorable to them. If the outcome goes against them, it will be made public. The Communists will point out in vain that this is a temporary lapse: an electoral party can survive its defeats but a revolutionary party is not distinct from the revolutionary élan of its troops. The Prime Minister pays the Communists back in their own coin: they appealed to the bourgeoisie on its own principles; it is in the name of their principles that they are forced to show their hand. The raw sovereignty of the people makes Mr. Pinay chuckle: he knows very well that he doesn't have the majority of the country behind him. But until that fact is made explicit by an electoral law, the majority has only the right to keep quiet. On the other hand, he is equally well aware that a revolutionary party doesn't have the right *to give in.* He kidnapped Mr. Duclos and waited; the challenge would certainly be taken up. As a matter of fact, the Political Bureau saw the trap (and if it hadn't seen it, the resistance and procrastination of the C.G.T. must have enlightened it) but it wanted to step into the trap head down: it is better to leave the militant with the memory of a defeat than with that of a retreat. The order to strike was given, the Government was ready: if the masses budged they would be crushed; but it was a pretty good bet that they wouldn't. For June 4, as for May 28, the forecasts of the Political Bureau and those of the ministry were in perfect agreement.

In short, *nothing* was expected, *nothing* happened, and Mr. Pinay has built his glory on just that. The action of June 4 is historic in that it resembles all others. We read in the newspapers the next day that the streets looked the same as ever, that the subway was running as usual; it was one of those working days which a remarkable act of grace changes, in the eyes of the friends of law and order, into a High Festival.

I was abroad, my relations with the communists were good but certainly not excellent: they were no longer saying that I reduced man to a beast, but they were still accusing me of having spied on the Resistance for the fascist bourgeoisie. In the final analysis, the May 28th demonstration didn't seem opportune to me and I feared new clashes, useless deaths. All the more reason to hear of the failure of the strike with indifference if not relief. Yet the news produced the contrary effect on me: the protestations of the respectable tabloids didn't succeed in covering up France's strange silence, and I had the feeling that they announced a minor defeat for man. I didn't know then that there were many of us who saw things this way. Since then, the bourgeois press has written that we had the jitters. Why not, after all? Hooray for the jitters: it's one of the few words which our newspapers can understand. But the jitters *over what?* The imminent police state? The American take-over? The witch hunt? The threat of war? These are things that I find it very reasonable to worry about. But none of them apply here: we're afraid because the working class has disowned the Communist Party. If that's all, then stop worrying; for we're quite calm. The Party won't disappear so soon, and it is not true that the workers manifested their repudiation: On June 4th *nothing* was manifested and *there wasn't* any working class. If you want to know, that was precisely what frightened us; and I am writing this article in order to try to understand why France is silent.

It seems that France is not silent, that she is shouting her scorn in Mr. Pinay's face; in short, the "alleged" failure of the strike is apparently being challenged by the C.P., and our fears were futile. I ought to rejoice, but I've only changed my cause for worry: at present, it's my deafness which grieves me. I see Mr. Caillois smiling: that's how you wind up when you defend the Communists apart from their principles. Does Sartre think they'll appreciate him for loudly bemoaning a defeat which they don't acknowledge? —No, I don't think so. Who would be so mad as to want to be liked by militants, Communists or not? And why would anyone try? If I took the trouble to, what would it get me? The furtive handclasp of a fellow traveler? A soft-liner's pale smile? Neither sends me. No: you either combat a mass party, you join it or, from outside, you reach an agreement with its representatives on common objectives. So much the better if action determines feelings; bourgeois individualism reduced them to moods; let's get back to liking or detesting the whole man on the basis of his works. True enough the purpose of this article is to declare my agreement with the Communists on precise and limited subjects, reasoning from *my* principles and not from *theirs;* we shall see why. It has happened over and over again, since the Congress of Tours, that "left-wing" men or groups proclaim their *de facto* agreement with the C.P. while at the same time stressing their differences of principle. And if their collaboration seems desirable to the Party, it accepted this alliance *in spite of* those differences. It seems to me today that the situation has changed, both for the Party and for us in such a way that the Party must desire such alliances in part *because of* the differences.

As to the reality of the situation itself, can one say that the Party questions it? Yes and no. It admits that the strike didn't succeed, but its principal concern seems to be to exonerate the working class and, to do so, it is willing to accept all the blame. Haste, poor transmission of orders, lack of cohesion, extravagance of tone: everything it reproaches itself with is well known. Strictly speaking, it's giving the devil his due. The enemy explains the events of June 4th as something essential: the evil nature of the C.P. was bound ultimately to disgust the working class: the C.P. acknowledges the facts but explains them as something non-essential: the working class was as combative as ever; it's simply that certain individuals committed errors and didn't succeed in summoning the workers in time. Here's what Mr. Duclos said at the last meeting of the Central Committee:

> The working class was the determining element of the victory. It overwhelmingly supported our Party against the plotters. But that doesn't mean that this stand has always and everywhere expressed itself by strikes, demonstrations, or petitions. The error of the Government and of its agents was precisely their believing that the lack of a strike or a demonstration

> meant that the working class was indifferent. The workers understood that the anti-Communist plot was the prelude to violent attacks against their conditions and their acquired rights, against democratic freedoms, and against peace. And it is beyond doubt that the action of the working class was destined to undergo some very serious developments if the popular movement had not, with the July 1st release from arrest, struck a first severe blow at the plotters.[7]

On one point, I agree with the C.P.: it is impossible to offer the silence of the masses as a consent to repression. "O.K.," I am answered. "But by the same token, you can't pass it off as disapproval either." I'm not so sure about that: naturally, a negative sign is not easy to decipher. But it is hard to believe that an act of violence against the leader of a workers' party, as a consequence of a demonstration—even an unpopular one—can leave the masses indifferent. The workers live under the constant menace of three scourges called price increases, unemployment, and repression. Whatever the long-range future they dream of and for which they are preparing, their short-range future is always somber: they know the hostility of the ruling classes, they know that the latter are going ahead with schemes whose consequences are for the most part injurious to the proletariat but the workers don't know the details of the maneuvers, and the results overtake them often without their having had an inkling of the causes. In this uncertain penumbra where everything they *go through* turns out to be for the worst as a matter of course, sudden changes are ominous. Do you remember those decisive years when we guessed that Germany was getting ready for war, without our being able to measure its rearmament efforts; do you remember our constant concern and the sinister atmosphere of those days: from time to time Hitler made a gesture, gave a speech, and each time we felt that war was a bit closer. Of course, one can't argue by analogy: but when I, a bourgeois relatively well protected against crises, want to understand the climate of the working class neighborhoods, the oppressive atmosphere, the

[7] *La Nouvelle Critique,* no. 39, September-October, 1952, p. 38.

hopeless future, then I turn to that period of our history. By arresting Duclos, the bourgeois got in touch with the proletariat, and the message was bad news. Short of forgetting the workers' age-old hatred of cops, the difficulties of their daily life, the instability of their budgets, and their old unhealed wounds, how can one deny that they saw in the legal action initiated against the Communist Party an advance warning of new persecutions?

Must this covert uneasiness be likened to a *movement*? Can this mixture of apprehension and resentment be considered an *action*? I don't think so. According to Mr. Duclos, the Government committed the error of underestimating the resistance of the masses. Granted, but if Mr. Pinay couldn't see their anger, then on whom could this useless and silent resistance have any effect? And how can we view that release of July 1st [of Duclos and 140 others] as a popular victory? If I were a Communist, I would show my gratitude to Montesquieu, even more than to the proletariat, for the repressive action of the Prime Minister was slowed down for a few months by the bourgeois principle of the separation of powers. A magistracy, scrupulous and proud of its prerogatives, simply refused to abandon to the executive the independence that constitutes its *raison d'etre* and the portion of sovereignty that is its own. The popular movement is supposed to have galvanized the judges. But where does that idea come from? And if the movement was expressed "by neither strikes, nor demonstrations, nor petitions," how could these bourgeois magistrates have known about it? In point of fact, France was immobile and mute, and it was in the midst of a great silence that the Court made its decision. And, for my money, it is not because it underestimated the popular indignation that the Government is guilty; but because it didn't foresee a decision which was so foreseeable: the magistracy has not obeyed anyone since the Third Republic;* why did people expect it to accept masters, particularly when those masters are named Baylot and Pinay.

Thus it is equally false that the masses put pressure on the min-

* Written in 1952.

isters and that they remained indifferent. The fact is that the masses disapproved and did not show their disapproval; this is what seems suspicious: why didn't their very real dissatisfaction seek to express itself?

"Because their rancor was too strong, because they condemned the Communist policy and because they were given the opportunity to show it." By this clever reversal, the bourgeois press transformed the absence of a reaction into the will not to react. Assuming this is so, *what* are they talking about? About May 28th or June 4th? I am told that the two are identical, that the second defeat is only a confirmation and an aggravation of the first. I am not at all convinced: to my eyes, the two days differ profoundly.

Frankly, I don't give a damn about the May 28th demonstration: whether it was a success or a flop, it was a totally run-of-the-mill affair. And above all, it had a *political* character. The Communist leaders studied the international situation, evaluated the forces confronting each other, and decided that a limited operation would contribute in its feeble way to modifying the relationship of these forces. What they did there, others can seek to do on their own: anyone can politically appraise a political action. And, if I cannot believe (we will see why) that the *working class* demonstrated against the demonstration, I will gladly admit (why not?) that a large number of workers abstained from taking part in it with an animosity that bespoke disavowal: "What good does it do? You'll not get anything that way, etc." There may have been a few among them who wished to show by their absence that they condemned this politics of prestige. For the majority, it was even simpler: and the militants know very well that anti-war demonstrations rarely pay off. The failure of Red Day, in June 1929, offers many analogies—at least superficial ones—to that of May 28th. The same appeal to the masses: "Show that you are determined to prevent the anti-Communist crusade." The same "very noticeable" absence of the working class. There is only one difference: it was Thorez who was arrested. The Party understands the problem rather well: it knows that it should in every case base its political positions on economic demands. It hopes to be able to analyze the local situation, to draw from it general causes, and to show the ties between immediate interests and class interests. But we shall see that this is not always easy: it may happen that a link is missing or that the leaders make mistakes. In that case, the political action appears in the open all alone, and it doesn't always succeed in carrying along the masses. Not because the workers feel that political action doesn't fall within their province, not because they forego the use of their usual weapons to denounce colonialism or imperialism: but very simply because the objective is presented to them in a form that is too abstract and too far off. They fight more enthusiastically when they are shown, for example, that in defending their wages they jeopardize the rearmament policy and, indirectly, the Atlantic Pact. Because they are defending their individual interests? No: because their grasp of events remains direct, because they see the detailed effects of the action, because all their "political education" is based on the idea that world events present themselves, on national and municipal levels, under the aspect of local and concrete changes, whose course can be modified by local and concrete action.

But, in any case, the June 4th strike *was not* political. Or must one call political that fury which stirred up the Italian workers when they learned that an unidentified person had fired at Togliatti? Forestalling strike orders, they rushed into the factories, occupied them, put the bosses under lock and key. There was total agreement among Communists, non-Communists, anti-Communists; it was a tidal wave. For two days the Government thought it would not again control the situation. And what were the objectives (political or otherwise) of this demonstration? To protest? Against whom? A madman? For no one thought—even at the time—that the Government or the right-wing parties were stupid enough to have a Communist leader assassinated at a moment when the C.P. controlled a good third of the country. As to the "pressure" of the masses, on whom could it be exerted, if not on God the Father? Nevertheless the event had a far-reaching effect: in a burst of passion, the working class manifested its existence *by an act* before the nation, before Europe: *before* the attempted assassination, there seemed to be only a scattering of groups which attracted or repelled, juxtaposed, or interpenetrated one another, families, associations, enterprises, parishes, etc. Immediately *after,* the barriers exploded, and the proletariat *showed* itself. It was this and nothing else, it was this violent upsurge that the Communists expected from the French workers. It was no longer a matter of attaining more or less distant objectives by more or less circuitous paths; the working class were attacked on bread-and-butter issues and in their elementary rights; the leaders they had chosen were imprisoned under their very noses and the Political Bureau demanded of them —without hope, as I have said—an immediate and passionate reaction. No one asked them to break the Prime Minister's windows or set fire to the President's house. The leaders hoped that the working class would show itself, that was all. It didn't.

"That proves," retort the anti-Communists, "that the workers want to shake off the yoke of the Party. These mass demonstrations, you said, are barbarian rites and it is in the streets that the proletariat renews its confidence in its leaders. Draw the conclusion then: when the streets are deserted, the chiefs are disowned."

Not so fast. In 1951, the masses displayed undeniable signs of exhaustion, yet five million voters voted for the Communists. Since June 4, by-elections have taken place which do not indicate a notable fall-off from last year's averages; right after the unsuccessful strike the F.O. scored a triumph at Renault over which the fine news sheets made a great fuss. This indisputable gain reflects *at least* some rancor on the part of the workers. But what has rarely been stressed on the Right and what seems to me still more significant is that the C.G.T., less than two weeks after its fiasco, maintained sixty percent of the votes. Thus, a majority of workers in the Renault factories still have confidence in the C.G.T. while at the same time reserving their right to disobey it. There are four or five million voters in the country who vote for the Communist deputies without lifting their little fingers to defend them when their parliamentary immunity is violated. Granted the C.P. is in the process of losing this kind of sovereignty which is born of action; and at first sight, these remarks seem to indicate a crisis for its *revolutionary authority*. But it is also a classical and parliamentary party; since in practice it controls the C.G.T., it is a trade-union organization: under these two aspects, it maintains its prestige; sixty to seventy percent of the workers are willing to have it defend their material interests; twenty-five to thirty percent of the voters are willing to have it represent them in the National Assembly. After that, you tell me that the working class is disowning Duclos: O.K. But it seems clear to me that it cannot disown him without disowning itself. I'll admit anything you like: the workers are tired of Communist tutelage, of the Party bureaucracy, of its obedience to Moscow; they have a thousand complaints, and they get indignant at the C.G.T. every day. So what? They weren't asked to give a pledge of love to the Political Bureau, but to respond to a challenge, to an insult and to a threat. Yesterday, by arresting Duclos, the Government annulled their votes with a stroke of the pen; by arresting Le Léap today, it tore up their union cards. Could they disown Duclos *at such a time*? And why, while they're about it, wouldn't they thank dear Mr. Pinay for having rescued them from a tyrant? Or do you sincerely believe that a proletariat, forged by a hundred and fifty years of struggle and conscious of its traditions and its grandeur, will come to you and declare, with a smile on its face: "I'm not too happy with the leaders I have chosen, that's why I don't mind their being arrested, and, while maintaining my confidence in them on certain points, I don't object to having the law violated a little, if necessary, to get rid of them"? I could expect *Figaro's* commentators to view the working class as a foolish virgin. But you "anti-Stalinist" Marxists, who count on the workers' perspicacity to rescue them from their present leaders, how can you admit that they have calmly opened the door to police repression? You have said and repeated after Marx, after Lenin: the bourgeoisie foisted suffocating laws on itself; the interest of the proletariat is to force it to respect those laws. We must, you said, rise up against all abuses of power. Are you going to add today: except when it's at the expense of the Stalinists? I know: you can permit yourself anything since your attitudes have no effect on the masses; you have signed a non-intervention pact with realities: they go by without bothering you, without weakening or confirming your theories; in return, you have pledged never to interfere with their course. But the reactions of the F.O. and the C.F.T.C. will be considered more alarming. Whether reformist or revolutionary, independent or controlled, all unions have one thing in common: they developed within the framework of bourgeois democracy and they used all the weapons that legality furnishes. If the Government violates the law or changes it, they are all affected: in order that the working class have confidence in its own strength, it must see it in broad daylight; the 1936 strikes, for example, took place in a hall of mirrors. Imagine a sudden return of clandestine existence; partisan action will remain possible, but not mass action: Samson will have been blinded. You say things haven't gone that far? No, of course not; but it wasn't very long ago that we came out of clandestinity and we all have memories which should make us sensitive about the matter of arbitrary arrests. "Granted!" I'm told. "But it's easy for you to talk: you may have been insulted, slandered, but not persecuted. An F.O. militant is the victim of systematic and uninterrupted persecution: he's insulted, he's put in quarantine, his work is sabotaged, from time to time he's beaten up. When people speak to him of the Communists do you imagine that he thinks of separatism, camps, bureaucracy, Titoism? Come now! He thinks: 'What I've had to take from them, the scum. But just wait until things change, and it'll be my turn to give it to them.' It would after all, be too convenient if the C.P. only had to call out 'I give up!' to have all its victims rush to its aid."

Granted: the divisions in the working class must make life impossible for many workers: as to grudges, they exist: it's a fact. But what were they being asked? To forgive everything? To reestablish trade union unity? To hold out their hand to the C.P.? Not at all: they were asked simply to participate in a strike of limited duration and of symbolic significance in order to defend the working class and their own organizations. It was easy for them to make their reservations known and to proclaim for example: "We have not forgotten our dissensions, but we are putting them aside this once; however deep they may be, we will never permit them to go beyond the limits of our class and we thrust aside once and for all the kind assistance of the government and the employers under whatever form it is offered: even if their intervention seemed at first to favor us at the expense of our opponent, we know that it must ultimately injure us all; anyone who practices violence against any representative of the workers practices it against all of us and the unity of the proletariat will be reestablished against him."

Nothing happened. The leaders of the *Force Ouvrière* doubtless would have joined a "spontaneous" and irresistible movement in order not to lose the benefit of it. But, foreseeing the failure of the strike, they hoped that it would be a crucial experience for the masses and that it would reveal to them *in full* their disagreement with the Party. Was this a wise calculation? The strike failed and who stands to profit from it? Our bourgeoisie and its ministers.

An "inspired writer" in *Preuves* accuses me of making a great to-do about nothing: these events are ancient history and I am the only person in France who recalls them. I reply that there are at least two of us who still concern ourselves about them: what continuously brings them back to my mind is the fact that Mr. Pinay proves daily that he won't forget them. A successful strike would have stopped him on the spot: he would no longer be Prime Minister and Le Léap would not be in prison (I won't go so far as to say that it would be the other way around). Instead, the unsuccessful strike taught him "at what point he was going too far." For this single and obvious reason, I say that the June 4th strike was intended to serve not only Communist interests but those of the proletariat and the whole nation. What makes you think that the *proletariat* was reprimanding its Communist leaders? When, to better oust the competitor, a trade union acts as the tacit accomplice of the class enemy, I say that the proletariat is out of it.

"Then, *who* refused to strike?" Well, *individuals,* and a great number of them at that: if you like, the great majority of workers. "And isn't that what's called the proletariat?" No: it's not. After the strike, the non-Communist press published opinions on the state of mind responsible for the failure. Why not refer to them? I believe they are accurate—at least partially—first of all because I have been able to check some of them; secondly because the facts reported remain almost identical throughout the range of the poll: finally, and above all, because they manifestly go against the interests of those who quote them and because they prove just the contrary of what was meant to be proved. None of these reasons would be convincing by itself; but in toto, they are not without cogency. These opinions are striking primarily for what they are lacking. If you seek in them clear and politically motivated refusals, you will be disappointed. In the corner café in petty-bourgeois neighborhoods, any drunk you meet considers himself the electoral body, the nation; he takes a position for or against the Atlantic Pact, he explains what a government "worthy of that title" should have done in Tunisia: his judgments have the force of law, he speaks on behalf of all of us and he demands that everybody agree with him. In the matter under discussion, you will find nothing that resembles this attractive self-confidence of the voter secure in his right. The worker restricts himself to refusing to participate *personally*; he doesn't pass judgment. And far from wishing, like Kant and the drunks of the Fourth Republic, "to raise the principle of his own act to a universal law," he strives to keep it private. Of course, if his comrades treat him like a "scab," in short if they try *first* to show him his historical role, he will defend himself on the terrain which they have chosen, he will try to prove to them that he was politically right and that they ought to have acted as he did. But, on the contrary, if those around him hesitate and if he senses that his abstention could start a mass abstention, he becomes frightened and points out that other attitudes are possible, that his own commits only himself: it is the *individual* aspect of his case that he emphasizes. Is he actually turning his back? What he means, it seems to me, is that he *cannot* obey: "You (who do not have my family responsibilities and are sure of keeping your job, etc.), you're free to do what you want. But I'm not . . ." Decide not to strike? Be unable to decide to strike? He wavers between the two. He doesn't really know whether he wants his example to be followed throughout France or his absence to pass unnoticed; he dreads equally a demonstration which would be carried out without him and a mass abstention which could have serious consequences. Strongest of all is his feeling of powerlessness. Ordinarily, trade-union directives impose themselves as duties, and the functionaries do their utmost to persuade him that these duties can be done: You have to, therefore you can. Today he replies: I don't have to because I can't any more. "You know very well that we won't get anywhere, that we'll lose our wages for nothing." Or else: "The *Force Ouvrière* won't even budge: we'll be alone." Or else: "Go looking for trouble a month before our paid vacations? That wouldn't be very bright." Or else: "I can't because I've got three children, and my wife just had an accident," etc. Which of these arguments has to do with class interests? Behind so many dismal answers, one detects a return to the fatalism that continues to threaten the oppressed, that the ruling classes constantly seek to develop, and that the revolutionaries still fight against. This discouragement is born of isolation and in turn engenders it: by breaking this circle the working class asserted itself, and the somewhat forced optimism of the Communist militants bespeaks their desire to save the cement of the proletariat—hope. Those who say they won't go along because the F.O. refuses to go along—could they make it any clearer that the working class is in pieces? And yet the non-Communist organizations contain at the very most one-fifth of the organized workers. What is a twenty percent opposition within a single body? Almost nothing: soreheads, outsiders: the majority disregards them and declares unanimity. Once these outsiders organize among themselves, everything changes. That proud unanimity which considered itself the working class is now merely a trade union representing the majority. Only yesterday it deemed itself infallible; its decisions were the only possible ones; at each instant the proletariat was only what it could and had to be; "its goal and its historic action were traced for it irrevocably and visibly in the very circumstances of its life;" each of its reactions expressed it totally. Now the decisions of the C.G.T. are *accidents*: Isn't it a proven fact that other and sometimes better ones, are possible? The strike is no longer the voice of the proletariat through the mouths of its leaders: it is *a certain manner* of reacting to the Prime Minister's challenge. In short, the resoluteness of the leaders no longer commits anyone but themselves. They may be *good* leaders but this in itself signifies that they might also be *bad;* although they are not at fault and have not changed, the masses will tend to regard them as benevolent despots who think for them. It is clearly understood that for the moment I am not questioning the "authoritarianism" and the "bureaucracy" for which the C.P. is reproached: I am simply recalling the effects of *any* sort of trade union split. Workers' dissension tends to bring about a certain defection of the masses, who, instead of asserting themselves in a unanimous reaction, are made to choose one of several likely policies. Involved in an action of which their comrades disapprove, the C.G.T. members have the feeling that they are fighting without support; it is no longer only the outcome of the operation that is uncertain; it is the operation itself. Impoverished, conjectural and limited, the action reflects the *opinions* of certain specialists. And if there are specialists in "the general interest," how can anyone be surprised that the worker is inclined to concentrate on his "individual interest" first?

For after all, does anyone believe that the strikers of 1920, of 1936, of 1947 were all bachelors and childless, miraculously insured against unemployment and provided with a savings account passbook? Or, inversely, does anyone believe that today's worker has lost even the memory of working-class interests? Does capitalist exploitation seem more just and more humane to him? Does he accept more willingly colonialism, imperialist wars, and police repression? Will he sacrifice his leaders to get closer to his bosses? Try an experiment: approach one of those who refused to strike, speak to him in an open manner, and discreetly slip into your conversation a few poisoned darts against communist policy: who knows, he may agree with you; but that won't prevent his breaking off the interview flatly after detecting the class enemy behind your smiles. In short, today as always, the workers have the same concerns, the same goals, the same loyalties. Nevertheless, this one risked death in 1942 and yet ten years later wouldn't risk even one morning's wages. What has changed? Causes? Motives? No: their relationship; the system of evaluation. And what produces these changes if not the course of the world, that is to say, day-to-day history? The historical whole determines our powers at any given moment, it prescribes their limits in our field of action and our *real* future; it conditions our attitude toward the possible and the impossible, the real and the imaginary, what is and what should be, time and space. From there on, we in turn determine our relationship with others, that is to say, the meaning of our life and the value of our death: it is within this framework that our *Self* finally makes its appearance, in a practical and variable relation between here and there, now and forever, formerly and tomorrow, this thing and the universe, a continuously revocable decision on the relative importance of what is improperly called "the individual interest" and "the general interest." To contrast the alternatives, in which a collectivity submits to the course of the world or contributes to shaping it, its members take refuge in the immediate present or have access to a future extending well beyond their deaths, clutch the little that they have or risk everything for a cause whose victory they will not live to see, adjust their undertakings to their needs or decide on their needs in terms of the undertaking. It is history which shows some the exits and makes others cool their heels before closed doors. Today, as in 1950, the worker still doesn't own his instruments of labor: hence the basic nature of his demands doesn't change. But the organization of capitalist society has not ceased to evolve nor the situation of the worker to change: you will find, according to the era, that he more or less falls in line with his political action or that he becomes one, more or less, with his working life; his ties to class organizations tighten or loosen, the great goals proposed to him—reforms or revolution, it doesn't much matter which—seem real to him, sometimes even within reach, or else far off and sometimes imaginary. If he loses hope, no speech can give it back to him. But if action takes hold of him, he will believe: action is in and of itself a kind of confidence. And why does it take hold of him? Because it is possible: he *does not decide* to act, he acts, he *is* action, subject to history; he sees the final goal, he touches it: the classless society will be achieved in his lifetime. The immediate reality is the Future; viewed from the far reaches of the future, private interests are abstract shadows; death itself is not frightening: it is a very personal event which must happen to him in the midst of that Future which he possesses jointly with everyone else.

Several times, action has ended in a disaster: then the workers, who were the collective subject of history, again become individually its objects. The worker changes his skin, he sees the world with different eyes: the things that were obvious yesterday have been extinguished, new ones light up, nearby, everyday, disagreeable things: Why struggle? You won't change anything. If you hope to win, if you have nothing more to lose, you'll fight. But if there remains something to lose—even a miserable wage—and if you give up all hope of winning, you keep quiet. Those who risked their lives without giving it a second thought now fear hunger; they say: "We don't want to starve to death." When Koestler, already dismissed by infinity, had not yet chosen to be a zero, he told us the story of the Spanish shepherd who fought *in order to learn to read:* risking your life for education is perfectly reasonable; on the condition, however, that you have a chance of winning. When all is lost, when the victors have decided to develop illiteracy and to base their power on ignorance, hunger becomes their accomplice: as long as a chance remains, you eat if you can, you eat in order to fight; in order to fight, you put up with not eating; when everything is over, you eat to live and you live to eat. But needs can engender a will to union, hunger does not always nor even most often collaborate with the powers that be: for hunger to serve them, one more turn of the screw is needed; hunger will be reduced to simple stomach pangs if the future is carefully blocked off: the future is born of action and turns back on it in order to give it a meaning; reduced to the immediate present the worker no longer understands his history: he was making it. He looks upon it now as if he had always submitted to it and sees in it no more than one single uprising, always resumed, always crushed.

Unite? With whom? After defeat, he is given over to that strange recurrent isolation which no one wants and everyone suffers as the backlash of other people's isolation: "I'd certainly go along, but the others won't." When the worker is reduced to his worn-out body, to the gloomy daily awareness of his exhaustion, death seems to him all the more absurd the more his life loses meaning; death inspires in him a horror all the stronger the more tired he is of living: the bosses have nothing to fear—neither revolt nor a man power shortage—when the worker has no other reason to live than the fear of dying. If he wants to turn away from himself and look outside, they are lying in wait; everything is prepared to reflect his powerlessness to him: in a crowd kept under surveillance, he walks along anti-riot boulevards;* the fake landscape of factories and city outskirts must present the image of a harsh and inhuman system; he is surrounded by an opaque setting of resignation. Common sense, a cool calculation of the chances—everything tells him to let go, to give up the struggle against enemies who have weapons, troops, money, machines, and science. His lot has not become better nor his masters fairer: they are the stronger, that's all. His defeat doesn't put him in the wrong: it simply proves that the world is bad. Of course, *there were* other hopes, another truth: suddenly workers saw bank notes turn into dead leaves and troops refuse to fire on a crowd. But these truths were alive and concrete only in the struggle: it was action which brought them to light; when action becomes impossible, only abstract memories remain. There is a special obvious fact for the conquered: it is that man is an error.

By all *the evidence,* the June setback can be explained by discouragement: the respectable newspapers tried to show us the proletariat rising in protest against its leaders and we had, on the contrary, the feeling of witnessing its internal collapse. By refusing to appreciate the political implications of the strike, the worker voluntarily placed himself *this side of* his class interests; he increased

* A reference to the radical city planning of Paris: the boulevards were laid in such a way as to allow the speediest possible movement of troops and cavalry. Trans.

his isolation by the reasons he invoked to justify himself; he broke the collective ties, he lost contact with his leaders: the strike failed to take place, not because it was condemned by a unanimous outburst but because it aroused millions of aversions that sought to remain individual. The collective goals, the values, the ideals were not affected; but they retreated, they moved beyond reach. The workers refused to fight because they were sure of defeat: they had lost confidence in the power of the working class; they felt that it lacked a grip on events and that history moved without it. War? They're against it of course: "But if the Americans want to go to war, the French worker can't prevent them." Political action? Of course, it would be right if the worker could make his opinion count: "But what have we attained in the last five years? We've demonstrated a hundred times against the war in Indochina, against the Atlantic Pact, against the rearmament of Germany: and what has come of it? We don't succeed in making our economic demands come to anything: prices go up and, in spite of our efforts, wages never catch up with them." Revolution? Michel Collinet claims that the new generation doesn't know the meaning of the word. This is scarcely believable—and particularly for his readers, since he strongly stresses, on the other hand, the copiousness of Communist propaganda. What seems truer is that the attitude of the French workers has changed profoundly in the course of this half-century. Before the First World War, many workers thought they were reaching the goal: they *would see* the "general strike." The war and the policy of the Socialist leaders disconcerted the masses, but the historic October days gave them back their confidence: the Third International was constituted in an apocalyptic climate: the Revolution would begin in Germany and spread over all of Europe. The worker of 1952 is told over and over again with an insistence which is almost suspect, that he will see the coming of socialism: "It is not only our children who will enjoy socialism but we ourselves."[8] But he doesn't really believe it any more: he

[8] Lecoeur's speech on the XIX Congress of the C.P. of the Soviet Union, October 29, 1952.

knows that the dictatorship of the proletariat is not just around the corner. Has he gone over to reformism? Not at all. Industrial equipment is beginning to age, and the employers remain Malthusian; our industry is being towed away, rearmament and colonial wars are ruining our national economy;* a fillip would suffice to make the machine, which has been patched up a hundred times, fall to pieces: in these conditions—and if it were only to improve his *immediate* situation—how could the worker put his trust in a slow, measured, progressive action, in compromises? If he wants to achieve the least reform in anything—from foreign policy to economic conceptions—he has to overturn everything: for it is all held together with loose string. He knows it, he learns it daily: will it be called revolutionary, this conviction—however obscure—that one must go from the whole to the parts and from structural changes to detailed reforms? Perhaps not: the conviction exalts people in action but discourages them during breakdowns; in any case, it is radical. Furthermore, the French proletariat has some very special grounds for rancor: once in its history, just once, it trusted in its employers and the latter, naturally, betrayed it. It was at the moment when they were trying to acclimatize the "second industrial revolution" in France: they disarmed union resistance by promising to employ new techniques to increase production. The semiskilled workers accepted additional overwork in the hope of raising their standard of living. Who knows? If the promise had been kept, one might have seen a neo-reformism arise and prosper. Harassment at the factory and well-being at home: in the U.S.A., this regime of hot and cold showers is the best auxiliary of the employers. The French employers as a group preferred to reduce their expenses and maintain prices: to make order prevail, they put their trust in the good old methods, that is to say, in bullets. Today, the group wears with a brooding insolence, as a dunce wears his dunce cap, as a cuckold his horns, the title of "the most backward group of employers in the world," a title bestowed

* Written in 1952.

upon it by the Americans. As to the worker, his work is as hard as that of his American comrade, but his real wages are lower than they were in 1938, and barely higher than in 1920. An ambiguous situation: he wears himself out on the job but he *sees* the oppression. It is not a matter for him only of surplus value, of surplus labor, etc., notions that are difficult and that don't always make sense to him: but he also knows that in other capitalist societies, in Scandinavia, in the U.S.A., the working conditions inflicted correspond to a buying power greater than his: so he is twice robbed. That's why it is better not to talk to him of the collaboration of classes, of their understanding, of the solidarity of Capital and Labor. Duclos quite definitely expressed the opinion of his working-class electorate when he said of such a bond that it would be "that of the traitors and the betrayed." Moreover this "rationalization" [of industry. Trans.], by augmenting the number of nonskilled workers and by liquidating the last internal structures of the proletariat,* crams the masses together, removing them from the influence of the workers' "elite" and making of them a relatively amorphous and perfectly homogeneous substance. It is a very sure way of pushing them to radicalism: they are no longer governed by a relatively moderate "aristocracy," from now on they tout their own point of view, that is to say, the requirements and the demands of the *least favored,* those which are least compatible with the maintenance of our social regime.

For all these reasons—and for others as well—the French worker maintains a rather exceptional intransigence. Perhaps he doesn't know what Revolution is: but what can you call this irreconcilable violence, this contempt for opportunism, this Jacobin tradition, this catastrophism which puts its hope in a violent upheaval rather than in indefinite progressive steps? For my part, I see in it the principal characteristics of a revolutionary *attitude.*

But, precisely what is an attitude? An action begun tentatively

* For example, these myriad solar systems of unskilled workers gravitating around a skilled worker.

and not followed through. If it is not expressed through acts, if it is not integrated into collective *praxis,* if it is not registered in things, what remains of it? Nothing: a negative disposition. Today the future is blocked off by a bloody wall. The worker remains faithful to his beliefs and his traditions: but he is a revolutionary without a Revolution. He does not claim that the latter is never to take place or that it is a myth, as the "general strike" was for Sorel, neither does he make of it a *value* or a *virtue*. But he doesn't manage to see in it the necessary outcome of "prehistory," much less the *reality* of the proletariat. In his eyes it is a partly accidental event, which must occur at a date that is uncertain but posterior to his death. Others who will start again from scratch will carry it out: the worker of 1952 no longer even has the feeling of preparing the way for them. There are, from time to time, short-circuits in history; everything stops and nothing anyone does has any consequence so long as the current is not reestablished: the worker of 1952 must have been born during a breakdown. If he still happens to say to himself, looking at children: "They'll see it—I won't," it is above all a way of thinking of his death—like the shopkeeper who muses: "We won't go to the moon but our children will." In the great moments of the workers' history, the Revolution was neither a future event nor an object of faith, it was the movement of the proletariat, the daily *practice* of each and every worker; not the apocalyptic conclusion of an adventure, but the simple power to make history; not *a* future moment but, for these men exiled in an unlivable present, the sudden discovery of a future. The Revolution was a task, the "infinite task" of the proletariat; it was the justification of individual existences and the universal dimension of all private behavior; in short, a constant liaison between the individual and the class and between the particular and the general. Each episode of the struggle had both tactical and strategic significance and corresponded to a double system of references: through and beyond the immediate objective, one saw the distant objective. For today's worker, it is the tie between these two significances that is broken: he can still defend his interest, demand and obtain an increase in wages, but he establishes no relationship between this small, everyday victory and the destiny of the proletariat. He doesn't grasp the "revolutionary thrust" of his demands: quite the contrary, he feels that he has lost the initiative and that he is defending himself step by step against reaction. Inversely, whether or not he obeys *political* orders, whether or not he strikes against the Vietnam war or against the Atlantic Pact, these demonstrations have a sort of unreality in his eyes. Peace in Indochina will serve the interests of the proletariat, he is sure of it; perhaps he even perceives a tie between world peace and the coming of socialism. But his actions seem vitiated by inefficacy: he has lost his hold on history and therefore can't change the course.

I have said that there were no general reasons among those which he invoked before the June 4th strike to justify his refusal to take part in it. That is not entirely true. From time to time, a declaration is pointed out which can pass for a general assessment of a situation: the worker admits that he is fed up. But with what? With the Communist Party? With the C.G.T.? With Moscow? No: with politics. And it is not the politics *of the C.P.* which disgust him, but all kinds of politics. Today one hears workers saying: "Politics, that's for the birds," or wives who say to their husbands: "You'd do better not to bother with politics: what good does it do?" What good does it do, *since you will change nothing?* It is not even *political activity in general* that they blame: in other countries or at other times or for other men it may be suitable: for the French workers of 1952 it is forbidden: "Politics isn't for children." For the moment, you will hear such reflections only from women—and from a few men. Never mind: it is a sign. First of all because the June strike, rather than being a maneuver, was to be a demonstration of solidarity: the working class was to rally around its threatened leaders. The day when workers label "political" everything which goes beyond the limits of their immediate interest will mark the end of the proletariat. At times when the working class is aware of its own power, it never thinks of setting limits to its action; quite the contrary, the most narrow directive becomes radical of itself, and the local action recapitulates the movement of the whole. But when one limits oneself to defending wages from day to day, one leaves the initiative to the employer, one stays on the defensive, one gives up hope of winning so as not to risk losing. And by failing to act at the same time on all the factors of social life, one may prevent the lowering of nominal wages, but not the rise of prices. That is why the true, the only limit which the worker recognizes for his acts is their efficacy: if today he shuts himself up in his personal interest, it is because he is prevented from getting out of it, and if he *will no longer* "play" the political game, it is not in order to obey a theoretical conception of trade unionism: it is simply because he *can no longer* play it. That the bourgeoisie should triumph is normal; but I address myself once again to all those who claim to be Marxists and anti-communists at the same time and who rejoice today because the working class "is in the process of detaching itself from the C.P." I remind them of these words of Marx which they have read, reread and commented on a hundred times: "The proletariat can act as a class only by shaping itself into a distinct political party," and I ask them to come to their own conclusions: whatever they think of the "Stalinists," even if they think the masses are mistaken or deluded, what maintained their cohesion, what assured the efficacy of their action, if not the C.P. itself? The "proletariat shaped into a distinct political party"—what is it in France today if not the totality of the workers organized by the C.P.? If the working class wants to detach itself from the Party, it has only one means at its disposal: to crumble into dust.

It was in order to hide this disquieting truth from the masses that Mr. Robinet, soon followed by the entire press, celebrated the *victory of the proletariat*. An admirable precaution: by buying *Paris Presse* or *France-Soir* on June 5, the worker learned *the opinion of the working class*: it had decided that the strike was contrary to its class interests and it had repudiated its leaders. Disconcerted, the worker put down his newspaper and wondered if he was thinking all that on June 5: he remembered, however, that he had not *really* rejected the strike; nor had he passed judgment on the policy of the C.P. He had simply preferred his own interests because he could not recognize and prefer the interests of his class; he had gone home uncertain, neither very proud nor very happy. And now these ruminations, multiplied, underwent a metamorphosis and became the sacred verdict of the proletariat. A curious virtue of statistics: the abstention of the Picardy and Provençal workers revealed to him the significance of his own little isolated defection. He had simply thought he was slipping away; objectively, he was taking part in a plebiscite. He considered with astonishment this opinion which he had just discovered and which was, at the same time, his and everyone else's; perhaps he wondered what attitude to take vis-à-vis "a party which the working class repudiates." But no: he wouldn't go along with the press. He began to suspect that it wanted him to believe the moon is made of green cheese and to mistake the unorganized mass of non-strikers for that organized collective which the proletariat is supposed to be.

This time we are touching the heart of the problem: if the class is to repudiate the Party, it must be able to remake its unity outside of and against it. Is this possible? Depending on the answer, the C.P. will or will not be replaceable; its authority will either be legitimate or it will be usurped. The facts have not permitted the detection in the June 4th affair of the presence of a collective reality. But there is more: not only have we not *seen* the class set itself against the Party, we can show that such an opposition is not even conceivable. No one believes any longer in the proletariat fetish, a metaphysical entity from which the workers might alienate themselves. There are men, animals and objects. And men are real and individual beings who are part of historical wholes and are comparable neither to atoms nor to the cells of an organism. United? Separated? Both. There is no separation that is not a mode of presence, nor is there any liaison so intimate that it does not carry with it a secret absence. If the class exists, it will be something of a new proximity of each to all, something of a mode of presence which is achieved through and against the separative forces: it will create *unity* of the workers. The sophism of the anti-communist is that he has simultaneous recourse to two contradictory procedures: to deprive the Communists of credit for having unified the masses, he begins by making the class a sort of passive unity; then, to set the Party up against them, he endows it with a mysterious spontaneity. I therefore think it necessary to recall a few truths which were once known by all and which now seem to have been forgotten. One can well imagine that I have no ambition to make or remake a theory of the proletariat: I wish only to show that class unity cannot be passively received or spontaneously produced.

It Cannot Come of Itself

The unity of the workers cannot be mechanically engendered by identity of interests or conditions.

As for interests, it is obvious: their identity engenders competition and conflicts. As for condition, this is another matter. Since I am not constructing theories, I have taken this word to designate, quite roughly, the mode of work and of remuneration, the standard of living, the social relationships. In everyday practice these criteria suffice: I can *place* a newcomer if I am told what he earns and what he does; is this enough to establish his class?

The sociologist thinks so. He wants only facts; he doesn't, however, accept them all; the June 1848 days, the Commune, the Decazeville strike were facts: he won't take them into account. Some people were killed? So what? Does one prove the existence of a class by dying for it? If the proletariat exists, the scholar must consider it from the outside with a total scientific objectivity and like an inert object. If you can demonstrate that certain objective factors determine the condition of manual laborers, if this condition is the same for all and if each one reacts to it by similar behavior, you will have established the reality of the proletariat. Same factors, same situations, same reactions: that defines a class.

After that, of course, some will prove that there are classes ("whereas we have established by rigorous methods the specific characteristics of the working class, we acknowledge for it the dignity of a real object"), and others that there are no classes ("whereas a rigorous inquiry has not allowed the establishing of objective characteristics which are peculiar to it, we conclude that the so-called working class is an illusion"). I give the decision to neither: their courteous jousting hides a profound complicity: one group claims that the proletariat is a *real thing,* the other that it is an *imaginary thing;* both agree to "thingify" [*réifier*] it. And the more underhanded method is that which loudly proclaims the existence of the working class in order to reduce it thereafter to that of a sack of potatoes. Let's take the better of the two: they tackled the problem without preconceived ideas and had recourse to statistics to determine experimentally the class characteristics. Even outside the activities imposed by production, in the domains where he seems to enjoy a relative independence, we will note that the proletarian distinguishes himself from other men by his behavior. His condition gives him a nature, that is to say a "primary habit:" in Marxist terms, production produces the producer. For example, the comparative study of budgets brings to light certain specific constants of workers' consumption. In extending their research to language, to imitation, to sexuality, etc., the investigators will finally establish beyond doubt—something completely obvious. Let them now bring these constants closer to certain social constants; let them establish functional relationships between the latter and the former. Let them go further still: let them pass from statics to dynamics and bring to light the impact of changing social processes on the behavior patterns of the proletariat. Will they finally have discovered the class? They say so, but I think rather that they will have transformed the proletariat into a zoölogical species. If one treats the members of a social group as passive and interchangeable products of universal factors and if one begins by setting aside all the influences which these individuals might exercise on each other, what can one hope to find in the final analysis except the species, this isolated, endlessly repeated hopelessness; we thought we were dealing with sociologists; our mistake: they were entomologists. I've known some entomologists too. One, especially, who was devoted to crayfish. He neglected the singularities which interest only the crayfish themselves, as well as the relationships of crayfish to crayfish. Thus he established without difficulty the absolute identity of all the representatives of the species. After which, he constructed ingenious apparatuses by which to study the action of alternating currents on the psychic characteristics of the eternal crayfish. How can one be surprised, since he had reduced his eighteen thousand items to eighteen thousand reproductions of a single model?

We'll let it go when it's a matter of crayfish: we will be less indulgent toward those who apply the same methods to men in slavery and who replace the soldiers of a fighting unit by inert products of objective factors. I begin to suspect that our sociologists have bamboozled us: for each notion, they have substituted an ersatz-concept which resembles it, and which proves exactly the opposite of what the notion claims to demonstrate. In the name of objectivity, they have set aside all proof of working-class *praxis;* in its place, they produce false events which crumble to dust when they are touched, and the deceptive unity of their averages covers up the infinite dispersion of the incidents which they add up. The worker consumes a lot of meat! And of a mediocre quality! So what? In Vitry and Saint-Denis, I'm willing to concede that the same cheap cuts appear each day on the dinner tables, but you cannot make me take these thousand meals for a collective event: you are only adding up isolated reactions which may have their cause in a common objective process, but which scatter in the dust of the industrial outskirts like a thousand drops from the same cloud. You claim you are showing us human facts and you slip physical facts in their place. Deprived of culture, you say, exiled from the refined core of society, kept in a state of dependence on nature by fatigue and gross needs, the manual laborer tends to prefer quantity to quality. Well, what have you done? You have defined some men by privation and by the mechanical action of need;

one might say that you were giving us a recipe for making them.

Will it be said that the analysis isn't serious? That it enumerates for us a plurality of unrelated causes, that it does not link the worker to the system of production? That is true. But the point is not to change the factors, but the bias. Here is a definition by Bucharin which I came across in Mr. Goldmann's book:[9] "A social class is a collectivity of persons who play the same role in production and who sustain the same relations of production with other persons participating in the process of production." This time the accent is on production, but what have we gained by it? In a word, the definition is stupid and not very Marxist: it is, in effect, by the *similitude* of persons that Bucharin seeks to define the class: they play the *same role,* they have the *same relations* with other persons. Is calling them a "collectivity" enough for them to constitute a class? But this collectivity is either a sum, which takes us back to the species, or it is a *totality,* in which case the generative principle would have to be given in the definition itself. Marx said that production produces the producer; but even if one made of the productive process a single and monstrous cause which produced a hundred thousand incarnations of the worker's essence, the unity of the operation could not guarantee the synthetic unity of the products. If the proletariat is only the inert dregs of industrialization, it will break down into a dust of identical particles. The living unity of the process of capitalism can brand the workers it creates: by being refracted in an inert, non-cohesive milieu, it multiplies and becomes the formal identity of diversity: a moon cannot unite the waves; it is the dispersion of the waves that scatters moons over all the sea. In short, I would have distrusted Bucharin: his definition is mechanistic like those of Messrs. Sorokin, Gurvitch and Halbwachs.

All these scholars promised to show us the unity of a class, and they showed us the identity of the items in a collection. Now, unity and identity are contrary principles: the first establishes

---

[9] L.Goodman: *Sciences humaines et Philosophie.*

concrete ties among persons, and the second, abstract ties among cases. Thus, in claiming to reconstruct the proletariat, their method destroyed all possibility of any real liaison among its various members: to remain unchanged, the identity of essence requires the absolute separation of existences. If the worker in Lens and the one in Amiens could know each other; if each, in making himself, made the other; in short, if they participated in the same struggle, each, in his living reality, would depend on the other, and they would resemble each other less and less the more closely they were united; it is by community of action and not in isolation that each would become a person, and the sociologist would no longer have either the means or the pretext by which to study individual behaviors separately, since they would all relate to the collective undertaking and would be defined by it.* Inversely, if the sociologist substituted identity of condition for unity of class it was in order to persuade us that collective action is an impossible dream. If the workers are *made* before uniting, union will no longer be able to *make them;* external factors have given them a *nature;* from then on, whatever their human relations, those relations will slide over them without leaving a mark. A proletarian wrote about the proletarian in these very pages [in *Les Temps Modernes.* Trans.] last month: "He is recognizable amid a thousand other people. Everything about him is characteristic: his language, walk, gestures, his unobtrusive silhouette, his way of eating, of drinking, of amusing himself, of loving, or hating." There's a confirmation of your statistics. Just one reservation to make: the worker described to us is completely without hope. That's what I wanted to get at: your sociology is applicable to the worker only if misery has reduced him to despair. It is his resignation that your sociology reflects back to him, his passivity, his surrender: and that is also what Mr. Robinet, a sociologist without knowing it, sought to reflect back to the proletariat. The victorious class he called up with his trumpet was a sum of lost hopes and isola-

* What makes things even more suspect is that the sociology of primitives is *never* liable to these criticisms. There they study true *significant wholes.*

tions; what he presented to us as a collective reaction was an average of discouragements; and what was *identical* among all these exhausted men was the will not to unite. Mr. Robinet gave the working class the right to vote so that it could publicly declare that it didn't exist.

In point of fact, what did it cost *Figaro* to acknowledge in the workers this kind of passive cohesion engendered by identity of condition: the bourgeois press long ago established that there is no *given* unity. Inertia is the absence of ties, hence indefinite divisibility: it is necessary to count, draw the lines, carry over endlessly the connections among disparate elements which are going to break up; in short, unity is only the wrong side of a unifying act. Take a closer look at this "class" which Mr. Robinet congratulates: it is disintegrating. What do you find in its place: molecular swirls, a multiplicity of infinitesimal reactions which reinforce or cancel each other out, producing as a result a force more physical than human. It is the mass. The mass, that is to say precisely the class denied. Since the effects which the mass produces always have their cause outside of them in a swarm of Lilliputian behaviors, the mass is *exteriority*. It cannot have needs, feelings, will or behavior: for the individuals, by making individual decisions, have neither foreseen nor willed the public result of their hundred thousand private wills. It is a fragment of nature which remains within our societies. Of course it only knows how to destroy: to build, it would have to have, if not the unity of a person, at least that of an organization or an enterprise. Finally, it is composed of irresponsible elements: strictly speaking, the workers don't know what they are doing, since their individual acts tend to swell away from them, add themselves to actions the workers have no knowledge of, and come back to them finally in the form of senseless storms. Revolutionary days of action? They're only stampedes: the beasts are chased from their holes by hunger or by fear; they roam the city, breaking, burning, pillaging, and then go back home. Class hatred? How could this molecular disorder love or hate? It is simply that its mechanical state and its perpetual disintegration tend to make us see an enemy of man in what is only the mechanical nature within anti-physic.

They want us to take the workers' reaction to the June 4th strike as a class verdict. But, deep down, Mr. Robinet is convinced that it is a matter of mass panic. Doesn't it have all the characteristics? The overall results were neither foreseen nor desired by the individuals; the results have a negative character; they bespeak no collective intention; they did not have the effect of bringing the workers closer together but, quite the contrary, of increasing their isolation and the distances which separate them. Does this mean that the class does not exist? It's certainly what they'd like to make us believe. But we know that the worker's world is not a dance of atoms: even on June 4, on many points à propos of other objectives, the workers engaged in common actions. What we learned is that the mass manifests an extreme state of isolation and abandonment, into which the individual worker may never have fallen, but which he approaches each time he breaks discipline and escapes his organizations. The simple objective condition of producer defines the concrete man—his needs, his vital problems, the orientation of his thought, the nature of his relationships with others: it does not determine his belonging to a class. If the tie of solidarity were broken, the worker would remain a producer, a manual laborer, a wage earner, but he would no longer be quite a proletarian, that is to say an active member of the proletariat. Classes don't just happen to exist, they are made.

Who makes them? Not I, says the bourgeois. And it is true. Under the *Ancien Régime,* the division into orders was maintained by the aristocracy and by the monarch; classes were official institutions with statutes. Nothing could be clearer: the privileged preserve a hierarchy which favors them and the oppressed want to blow up the walls which imprison them. But today, by a prodigious reversal, it is the privileged who repudiate classes and the oppressed who appeal to them. The bourgeoisie has never thought of imposing a class statute on the workers: quite the contrary, its jurists quickly erased from the codes and constitutions all that could *in principle* resemble an inequality. "The true classless society," says the liberal, "is capitalist society." And I believe that the bourgeois ideal would be a classless and oppressive society—that is to say, simply a society in which the oppressed would accept oppression. The goal of the operation which the bourgeoisie has been pursuing for two hundred years, with infinite resources, is to prevent the worker from becoming a proletarian by taking away from him the means of being a man: they will maintain individuals in an isolated state, and the laboring crowds in a state of fluidity, so true is it that oppression tends to become its own proof and to make the oppressed precisely what they would have to be to legitimize it: the bourgeoisie has to be accused of engaging, against the proletariat, in a permanent attempt at "massification." Inversely, it is against this attempt that the class makes and remakes itself continuously: its movement, action, and its degree of integration is measured by the intensity of the struggle which it wages against the bourgeois manoeuver. The class, a *real* unity of crowds and historical masses, manifests itself by an operation that can be located in time and referred to an intention. The class is never separable from the concrete will which animates it nor from the ends it pursues. The proletariat forms itself by its day-to-day action. It exists only by acting. It is action. If it ceases to act, it decomposes.

I am not saying anything new: you will find this in Marx. He strongly stressed the fact that an identity of needs sets individuals against each other: "The organization of the proletarians into class . . . is at every moment broken . . . by the competition of the workers among themselves." What enables the workers to overcome their antagonisms is the struggle against the employers: "The proletariat goes through different phases of development; its struggle against the bourgeoisie begins with its very existence. In the beginning, the struggle is undertaken by individual workers . . . in this phase, the workers form a mass scattered all over the country and broken up by competition . . ." Why can Marx, in this text, speak indiscriminately of proletariat and of "mass . . . broken up, scattered" to designate the same object? It is because he already finds in the workers a transcending of the situation which is made for them, a combativeness which must *necessarily* produce their union. The worker makes a proletarian of himself to the very extent that he refuses his state. For those whom want, exhaustion, circumstances dispose toward resignation, Marx has very harsh words: they are "brutes," "subhumans." But he doesn't blame or condemn them: he passes a factual judgment on them. The worker *is* a subhuman when he simply accepts being what he is—that is to say, when he identifies himself with this pure product of production. This subhuman will become a man only by "becoming conscious of his subhumanity." His human reality is thus not *in what he is* but *in his refusal to be such,* that is to say in his "revolt against retrogression." He can, without a doubt, try to escape his condition by his own means, to pass over the line, to integrate himself into the bourgeoisie; he will then be a deserter. It is the existence of these deserters which brings Marx to specify that the revolt must contain a principle of union: the worker who would be a proletarian is he who wishes to bring about a change for all his fellows workers as much as for himself. It is only then that his "real task will be to revolutionize the conditions of his existence." From there on, the phases of the struggle merge with the periods of unification. The proletariat "is kept in motion by the consequences of its acts." It is movement which holds together the separated elements; the class is a system in motion: if it stopped, the individuals would revert to their inertia and to their isolation. This movement, directed, intentional and practical, requires an *organization.* It is for this reason that Marx could speak of "an organization into class," a formula which carries us quite far from Bucharin's definition; a class *organizes itself.* Not to enjoy itself, but to attain concrete objectives. The definition which Marx gives of communism can be applied equally well to the proletariat: "It is not a stable state, an ideal to which reality will have to adapt itself . . . (it is) the *real* movement which abolishes the present state of things." One can understand, beginning here, why Marx suddenly defines the class by its *praxis*: "The proletariat will be revolutionary or it *will not exist*;"* and why, finally, he refuses to distinguish within

* My emphasis.

action, the totality of the agents and the apparatus which brings them together: "The proletariat can act *as a class* only by constituting itself into a distinct political party." Of course, the system of production is for a class the necessary condition of its ability to exist. It is the total historical evolution, the development of capital and the role of the worker in bourgeois society which will prevent the proletariat from being an arbitrary grouping of individuals; but this condition is not *sufficient*: *praxis* is necessary. It matters little that this *praxis* is or is not engendered *dialectically* out of the proletarian condition: the nature of dialectic is that its moments transcend and yet retain within themselves prior moments. In accomplishing his real task, the worker *makes manifest* the proletariat and makes himself a proletarian: it is striking that Marx, when he sketches out a sort of phenomenological description of the fighting worker, finds in him *entirely new* characteristics which arise precisely from the struggle: the proletarians "make of their revolutionary activity the greatest joy of their lives." The economist would be greatly mistaken if he believed that the worker calculates the cost of the strike: "(this would be tantamount to ignoring the fact that) the workers are generous at heart . . ." That means that they place their human reality much more in collective *praxis* than in the satisfaction of their personal needs. "When the communist workers meet together, their initial goal is doctrine, propaganda, etc. But they thereby simultaneously appropriate a new need, the need for society, and what seems a means has become an end." In passing from the mass to the class, the worker has shed his old skin: if the pressure of circumstances, defeat or exhaustion brings him back to the consideration of his interests, he falls outside the class and becomes again what he was made. The working class, you say, demonstrated its disapproval of the C.P. Of what class are you speaking? Of this proletariat which Marx has just defined, with its cadres, its apparatus, its organizations, its party? It would have been necessary for it to *have asserted its unity* against the Communists, to have demonstrated *as a class* through the repudiation it inflicted on the C.P. But where would it have found the leaders, the tracts, the directives; where would it have gotten this discipline and this force which characterizes a fighting class? Can you imagine the power which would have been necessary to clandestine organizations to carry out such a task successfully and to turn all the workers from Lille to Menton against their leaders? To carry "the masses" to a collective repudiation of the C.P. would have required nothing less than the Communist Party itself.*

The Unity of the Workers Does Not Come About Spontaneously

"Of course. If this repudiation had been provoked, we would have been less pleased about it. What use do we have for inspired demonstrations? We don't want to give new tyrants to the masses, we want to give them back their freedom: in our eyes the June 4th reaction is important only because it was *spontaneous.*"

Rumor has it that the anti-communist has hit the bull's eye: since Rousseau's tears, spontaneity has benefited from a favorable prejudice: the first impulse is the good one; one always comes back to the first impression. With what childlike pride we display our most secret truth to the light of everyone's day: "Yes, it's me, it's really like me, it's really me, I'm like that." In this mixture of nature and freedom, freedom submits to nature: one invents oneself as one is. Breaking with custom and rule, adapting to circumstances without being determined by them, the spontaneous élan is a beginning, a real find, but one which reflects our individual essence. This amounts to subordinating doing to being, action to passion, the visible to the invisible. The man of "first impulses" escapes the harsh necessity of continuously unifying what he thinks, what he feels and what he does: the unity of his person is already there, it blooms like a rose in the dark; it is the secret convergence that historians will discover in his acts. Instead of making himself, he plucks himself and smells himself. Enough: the subject has

* In November-December 1947, at the time of the referendum concerning the general strike, there was some resistance. But it was effective only in the enterprises where a non-C.G.T. organization existed (Christian trade unions, etc.).

inspired a very considerable literature; it may be consulted not without some distaste, but fruitfully nevertheless.

What is new—well, not *very* new: in fact a century old—is that spontaneity is being used for political ends. That happened all by itself: social facts were treated as things, then they began to be treated as people: and the masses become "first impulsers"! Good, just, authentic, their spontaneity moves everyone to pity and its verdict is without appeal, like that of dogs and children. Any government that would oppose it would be very foolish and very mean. Why, in Tunisia, to go no further, if it were proven that the population *spontaneously* wished our departure, you can be sure that we wouldn't stay there a minute longer. But the sad truth is that the disturbances were *provoked.* Let's be reasonable: organization stifles the free élan of the heart, *therefore, true* spontaneity can not stand being organized. *Therefore* a riot *cannot* be spontaneous: necessarily, since there can be no riot without a leader. You ask what *is* spontaneous? Let's see! free consent to oppression. Don't think, moreover, that the mass parties reason differently: what they prefer, in this line of ideas, is directed spontaneity. In demonstrations which are prepared and conducted without surprises, they willingly recognize the impetuosity of a mountain stream; but what they detest is the unexpected, and all these stupid tidal waves which wash over the leaders and drown them: those are fomented by the adversary. Still, today we can't read the press of July 1936 without mirth: since they were still celebrating the victory of the Popular Front, the masses took it into their heads to occupy the factories. People looked at each other and they wondered: Who's pulling the strings? Why of course, said the bosses, it's the Communists. A Communist worker told Simone Weil: it's the bosses. People spoke also of Hitler and the Fifth Column. For *Le Temps* the culprit was Thorez; for Thorez it was Trotsky. But no one, at the time, would have attributed the movement to the spontaneity of the masses: what an idea! A movement that arises *of itself,* and *does not have* any leaders? There's more there than meets the eye.

June 4th, on the contrary, is perfectly reassuring: the masses didn't react at all. That's great! Here's some excellent spontaneity that's very apathetic. The anti-communist press exulted: "Eloquent silence: the people have spoken." It will do no good to object that the collective will cannot be reduced to the sum of individual spontaneities. Ninety-eight percent abstentions, doesn't that tell you anything? You don't sense the quality of this silence and that it is a heart-rending cry, the most desperate, perhaps, of all those which human ears have not heard? There is a stiffening, a hardening of the workers' conscience. Where does it lodge, this erectile conscience? In the unconscious, of course; it's there that it erects itself turgid and at first invisible, only to be dispersed afterwards in thousands of rejections.

To make a class without leaving your office, the recipe is simple: take the mass—which is pure number—and pass it off as the crowd —which is a rudimentary organism; make the crowd into a person, for example a poor woman who has "the Word;" all you will have to do is decipher her message. And if she were to keep quiet? Never fear: there are ways to make her speak. Why, in the case at hand she rather seems to want to keep quiet: among the workers who refused to strike, none had the *avowed* intention of disapproving of the C.P. Never mind that: the anti-communist Left reminds us of one of Marx's ideas: It matters little what a proletarian thinks he is doing, what counts is what he is forced to do. It goes without saying that one can give this formula a purely objectivist sense—and that is what even Marx seems to have done: the ideas which we form about our acts modify neither their internal logic nor their objective structure, nor their historical consequences. But this is a dangerous interpretation: it would lead to the conclusion that on June 4 certain objective factors kept the workers in a *state of dispersion,* increased their "massification." If one were to consider only the acts and the contents of conscience, what would have become of the revolutionary élan of the proletariat? And where would its combativeness have gone? Has one ever seen a proletariat without combativeness? And didn't Marx say that it would be revolutionary or it would not exist at all? Now, *it exists, it has to exist,* otherwise the anti-communist Marxists would lose their hope and their *raison d'être.* Therefore, there *must* exist in the proletariat an élan, duped, misled, warped by the wicked. Can no trace of it be found? That's because it is not directly perceptible to our senses. It will suffice to drag Marx's formula towards psychoanalysis: the conscious is a lie, lies are the reasons it gives itself for acting: the analysis of acts and of their subjective significance directs one to the profound spontaneity which is their source. If you don't admit the existence of this spontaneity, you will simply conclude that the workers' abstention, their hesitations, their uncertainties express their objective state of exhaustion. But, if you begin by thinking that the proletarian *must be,* at all times and in all places, a revolutionary, and if you illuminate his attitude by his historical mission, *then* the discouragement and inertia which he has displayed *can be* only the superficial and deceptive outward appearance of a profound élan. Since he is *necessarily* active, his passivity is the form of action which he chose because it could be adapted to the circumstances. In terms of spontaneity, abstention becomes censure. For an anti-Stalinist Marxist, the revolutionary *praxis* of the masses could not be confused with the maneuvers that they execute under the direction of the C.P. And since they do nothing but conduct these maneuvers, their *true praxis* is manifested by what they don't do. We have seen that freedom can get mixed up with nature: likewise, here, objective and subjective intermingle and finally a strange reality emerges which is at the same time the objective and elusive unity of the masses, insofar as one infers it from their dispersion, and their subjective and invisible élan insofar as one deduces it from their temporary immobility. This ambivalent concept is proposed to us thereafter under the name of *class.* Everything goes on as if they were calling class the subjective spontaneity of the masses insofar as it is perceived from outside their objective unity. Since spontaneity is situated behind individual consciousnesses, objective unity will lodge behind their dispersion. Naturally, the experiment continues imperturbably to show us the same cloud of particles. No matter: the intelligible character, the choice prior to experience, the absolute transmuted into a multitude, the plurality's unity of might and right, the principle of fire circulating through inert matter, it is the class which produces men and not men who produce the class. The goal is attained.

For that was the goal. Some time ago, with the candor that hatred sometimes bestows, Mr. Laurat wrote:[10] "By isolating (the Communist leaders) from honest people, by cutting them off from the mass of the nation and from the working class, one would soon have reduced them to impotence." And the other anti-communists smiled bitterly: "To cut off is easily said: give us the knife." Now, it just so happens that as a result of small jolts, honest people are leaving the Party: its hold over souls came to it from their acquiescence, and a sign of the cross suffices to send it back to hell.

Perfect. But let's be very careful not to demonstrate by the absurd the necessity for the C.P. Just imagine this: the working class is possessed, it is exorcised; the instant its devil flies out, the proletariat opens its eyes and breaks into a thousand pieces. Can you see us *without a proletariat*? If the truth must be told, this eventuality is not likely to terrify the right wing of anti-communism, which goes around repeating that the worker is a fool who believes he is a proletarian; but the left wing can't bear even the thought of it: with the disappearance of his *Belle Dame sans merci,* the non-Stalinist Marxist loses everything, and first of all the honor of being faithful without hope. It is for his personal use that this eclectic notion was perfected: the *élan*-class. If you look at the world through such glasses, you will see that class everywhere, even if the proletariat has been shattered. And since it's a matter of refusing to give the Party credit for achieving the unity of workers' action, the magic principle of this unification will be situated somewhere between the objective organization of production and the subjectivity of the producer, like individual spontaneity between being and doing, like the Freudian *libido* between the body and pure

[10] Laurat: *Du Komintern au Kominform.*

consciousness. Strong in its elasticity, this rubber proletariat can stretch itself without snapping or pile itself up without caving in: it stretches out and gets thinner, flows out through the open spaces of its cage and reassembles outside or else it compresses itself, takes off, rolls between the bars of the apparatus and goes bouncing away in the midst of its true friends.

This nonsense charms socialist optimism as the mountebankery of "natural goodness" charmed bourgeois optimism: one more reason for distrusting it: optimism and pessimism are the two sides of the same mystification. When the suicide rate rises do we deplore a hardening of "the national will to suicide?" And when it lowers, must we congratulate ourselves on a bracing of the national instinct to live? Don't tell me that the class exists and that the nation is only an abstraction, since that is exactly what would have to be proved. For you depend on the identity of the class (that is to say on the identity of conditions) to prove its spontaneity and on its spontaneity to establish its unity. But let's leave that, let's admit that the abstentions of June 4th bespeak a collective repudiation and see where that leads us.

I open a Trotskyist newspaper that comments on the recent events.[11] According to one of its editors, Mr. Germain, the origin of the workers' discontent goes back to 1944: from the Liberation to the end of 1945, the masses had several opportunities to take power and they were compelled to let their chance pass; thus the leaders of the C.P. did "violence to the instinct and the revolutionary dynamism of millions of militants." Did de Gaulle crush the working class? Not at all, answers Mr. Germain, who recalls the "complete paralysis" of the bourgeois class at the time of the Liberation. Besides, it was not a question of establishing the dictatorship of the proletariat. It was necessary to sound the "people's power of expression . . . to create and develop the seedlings of a new power, seedlings that the masses had, moreover, constituted themselves (committees of liberation, factory committees, etc.)." The Political Bureau of the French C.P. missed its chance because Stalin

[11] *La Vérité des travailleurs,* October 1952.

sacrificed the workers of Europe to his desire to collaborate with American capitalism.*

This explanation is as good as another. Let us note, nevertheless, that there is nothing specifically Marxist in it. To tell the truth, Trotskyism, in spite of itself, suffers the fate common to all oppositions: the party in power is realistic since it asserts and claims to prove that the actual is the only possible. There is only one policy to follow: mine. The member of the opposition declares that there is at least *one other* and that it just happens to be the better, which forces him, in spite of everything, to take an attitude more or less tinged with idealism: there are possibles which don't reach realization; the *real* course of events ceases to be the measure of man since that which is not is truer, more effective and more consonant with general interests than that which is. The systematic analysis of the facts ends up in the nonexistent (what has not taken place) and, finally, the explanation of history is continuously referred to missed opportunities which exist only because they are *thought*. This is precisely the case here. When Monsieur Duclos writes: "The Communist Party . . . is conscious of never having let any historical possibility escape . . . if the path followed . . . had been different, the fascist de Gaulle would have had a pretext for crushing the working class with American aid . . ."[12] Mr. Germain has an easy time making fun of him: *a pretext*? What's that? "For a Marxist, social classes do not act according to 'pretexts,' but according to their interests and to the relationships of force which permit them to attain those interests." Nevertheless, Duclos is more faithful than Germain to the spirit of Marxism: Marx is certainly far from denying the existence of the *possible* but he means by that the stages of future action, such as they appear to us in the course

* A classical reproach: at the end of World War I, the minority reproached the majority in the C.G.T. with having sacrificed the interests of the working class to those of the nation. Greffuelhe writes: "The bourgeoisie reckoned with the obligation of making heavy sacrifices to the proletariat. . . . But it quickly pulled itself together, it triumphs" (February 1920), and Monmousseau, in April 1920: "The working class is simmering . . . But take care! let's not abandon unity: the Nation is in peril . . ."

[12] Nantiat speech, September 28.

of its preparation. Leaders and militants must be able to say to themselves, looking back on the past: "We did all that was possible (that is to say, our action extended as far as the circumstances permitted)—nothing was possible save what we did (events showed that the solutions which we set aside were impracticable)." This attitude leads to an identification of reality and action. Everything which is real is *praxis,* everything which is *praxis* is real. Such are, without any doubt, the principles which *also* inspire Trotskyism. But Mr. Germain, in his capacity as a member of the opposition, aims at establishing truths which will contradict those principles: 1. the masses in France had the immediate possibility of taking power: this possibility was the most consonant with their interests, the best adapted to the circumstances, the one which was the result of the relationship of forces in play, the shortest path to World Revolution, in brief, the one which summed up in itself the most *reality* and the most *efficacy*; however, it is the one which did not materialize; 2. *If* the masses had seized power, the bourgeoisie *would not have* budged. Mr. Germain's attitude is somewhere between that of the militant who analyzes the present situation with a view to the decision to be taken, and that of the theoretician who determines the significance of past events. It is true that the former has the right to draw up the inventory of possibilities: but his analysis is subject to the pressure of the moment, clarified by the events, modified by "the historical process," constantly corrected by experience and, finally, it is tested in *praxis* itself. The theoretician can claim to provide us with an indubitable truth on the condition that he confine himself to what is, and does not concern himself with what *might have* been.* Mr. Germain bases his opinion on a dead reality; he cannot claim certitude when he tries to establish the possible consequences of what did not happen. As for the goal of his research, not having really existed, it will be the abstract object of an idea; in a word, it will *be* because it is thought. Thus, one abandons the properly Marxist scheme for a probabilistic

* I am speaking of the Marxist historian and not of the bourgeois historian whose eclectic conceptions accommodate themselves simultaneously to the contingent and the necessary, to freedom and determinism.

idealism, the inductions of which are based most often on simple extrapolations. And besides, what is to be understood by a word as ambiguous as "the possible?" The working class *could* have conquered: O.K.! But under *what conditions?* The relation of forces were favorable to it, its interests impelled it toward taking power, but its leaders prevented it from doing so. Granted: but *could they* not do so? What made them what they are? Their obedience to the Politburo? But you have been denouncing it for years. According to you, it is precisely this relationship to Moscow that characterizes the French C.P. Could it change its fundamental structure in 1944? And what does that mean? I know that you discern—I am not saying that you are wrong—a left-wing current in the Party and that you support the amusing theory of a C.P. that is revolutionary in spite of itself: but how would the Left have imposed itself right after the Liberation, when everything was expected from the U.S.S.R., when the bourgeoisie seemed reduced to impotence, when many people still believed in American pacifism, if it is true, as you say, that the leadership of the Party succeeds even today, while in full retreat, in imposing silence on the dissatisfactions of the base? What about the policy of the U.S.S.R. then? Will you say that it is to blame? Perhaps: but at what moment would it have been possible to change it? Doesn't it reflect a determinate society, with its economic and political structures, its social strata and its internal conflicts? Will it be necessary to go all the way back to the death of Lenin? There are those who go that far: apparently the match was played and lost about 1923-1924: in the autumn of 1924, after the defeat of the German proletariat, Stalin spoke for the first time of "socialism in a single country." That day the angels wept. One would think we had returned to original sin and to Leibniz's discussions with the great Arnauld on predestination: Stalin becomes the little father Adam of the atomic era. The theory is admissible: one can admit that historical circumstances combine sometimes; but they very rarely do so in such a manner as to permit an effective human action which determines the historical orientation. If you miss the boat, you have to wait around for twenty years, perhaps half a century, until it comes back; Trotskyism would then be an art of waiting. But what then becomes of the "possibility" of 1944? The chips were down. And if a few enthusiasts could believe that they were going to lead the working class to victory, it was because they had seen the details of the situation without considering its totality.

Others—and Mr. Germain is perhaps one of these—claim the contrary: that even if this were a counter-revolutionary period, we could exercise a continuous influence on the course of the world provided we remained ready to exploit all its contradictions. They have on their side agreement from Marx and Engels who admitted the contingency of detail* and from Lenin who refused to apply to the study of day-to-day history the principles and methods which he used to decipher the greater wholes of universal history. They are permitted to believe that the obscurities and vacillations of minor history will disappear from the observation of the future historian. Perhaps one day we will have a better view of the place and role of present events; perhaps we will then perceive that they were the *only ones possible*. But so long as history is not finished, so long as we see the particular from a particular perspective, we cannot explain the detail of a policy by going back without intervening steps to general considerations. If the universe is a dialectical process whose every local movement has its reason in the movement of the whole, the Trotskyists will be able to understand Stalin's policy, but how will they manage to condemn it? It will have been at all times and in all circumstances what it had to be and what it could be, nothing more nor less. Perhaps we will come to understand that the cards were dealt in such a way as to render socialism impossible *from the very beginning*. Or, on the contrary, as Merleau-Ponty says: "The path which seems to us to be circuitous will perhaps appear, in the fullness of time and when

* That is to say a strict but circumstantial determination of the particular fact. It matters little that these particular facts are eliminated later and that the course of history—imperceptibly retarded or deviated—regains its overall direction. One must still explain the particular by the particular; you have the right to replace the fact in universal history only if you have entirely deciphered its particularity.

total history has been revealed, as the only one possible and *a fortiori* as the shortest there was." In any case, the French C.P. is not involved. There are not nor can there be *non-realized possibles* except at the level of this vacillating history where events come always behind or ahead of the appointed time, remain partially undecipherable; where a conflict, however deep its causes, can, for lack of an occasioning cause, remain buried for a long time, like a delayed bomb. In the case envisaged, the conflict is there. It is the class struggle; the relationship of forces defined: in 1944, the working class had the concrete opportunity to take power. What was lacking? The occasioning cause: a different orientation of Communist policy.

But there we are: the Marxist member of the opposition is astride two theses. To demonstrate to the "Stalinists" their errors or their lies he intends to be irrefutable. He will therefore utilize the methods and views of broad dialectical history. On the other hand, in order to establish that a different action remained possible in this or that circumstance, he has recourse to probabilistic inductions. When Duclos refuses to "furnish a pretext" for repression, Mr. Germain is amused: a pretext! "Since when have the fascists waited for pretexts to strike at the workers' movement?" In sum, the C.P. has the naïveté to believe that it was *possible* for de Gaulle to act differently than he did. And that this action was not *carried out* for lack of an occasion! "Once given the relationship of forces," replies Mr. Germain, "one always finds an appropriate 'pretext'." Note how the level of debate is lifted: de Gaulle shrinks visibly and loses his particular features; first of all he becomes the fascist—and the fascist is nothing other than the full use of the powers at his disposal in favor of the interests he serves. Then he melts into his class and it is the bourgeoisie itself which we are gazing at. Why doesn't the bourgeoisie strike at the workers' movement? Because it doesn't have the power to do so. Each force tends, of itself, to go to the very end of its effect, taking into account the other forces which are in play on the same point: the event, a resultant of diverse forces, is always all that it can be. As to the factors of local history, they have vanished: the origin and character of the team in power, the real structure of the bourgeoisie in 1944, the special interests, the prejudices, the beliefs, the ideologies, the necessity of day-to-day politics—all are eliminated. De Gaulle is considered a fascist in 1952: *therefore* he was one in 1944. Is it possible that the general who was certainly not very favorable towards the Republic but who had promised to reestablish it, could get bogged down at the time in personal contradictions? That does not affect the course of things. Could the bourgeoisie, right after a ruinous occupation, still find it less costly to temporize and still feel repugnance towards violence while holding itself ready to resort to it? No importance whatsoever. Since the bourgeois class did what it did, the fact is it could do nothing else. Fine.

I apply these principles to the working class: I didn't know that it would have taken power, but I'm told—and I believe it—that it was in its interest to take it and that the relationships of force were favorable to it: Then it must have taken power without anyone's realizing it. Not at all! says Mr. Germain. It *could* have taken it but its leaders prevented it from doing so. Well! And what leaders they are! "Those leaders of the French C.P. who value what we call bureaucratic conformism, who are, in other words, ready to go to the right or the left in terms of the needs of the Kremlin's diplomacy, and who are ready to sacrifice the fundamental interests of the masses to those needs." Those wicked men! But *why* are they like that? The fascist, I understood a while back, was the pure expression of his class and its anonymous instrument. Soviet "bureaucracy," I see also, when I read Trotsky or *Vérité,* expresses the interests of certain social strata and is conditioned by the very society from which it emanates. And I even find this remark in *The Revolution Betrayed*: "The present Soviet society cannot do without the State and even—in a certain measure—without its bureaucracy. And it is not the wretched remains of the past but the powerful tendencies of the present that create this situation." That's what reassures me completely about the Politburo. The personality or the individual desires of its members matter little. It's the U.S.S.R. who, through them and by them, provides herself with the apparatus which she needs at present.* But from what does the bureaucracy of the French C.P. arise? It doesn't come from the masses, since you accuse the Political Bureau of "sacrificing their fundamental interests, of doing violence to their revolutionary instincts." Nor out of the structure of our society since it is a bourgeois society and the C.P. doesn't play the role of a governmental party in it. Nor is it the result of the relationship of forces since, according to you, the relationship was favorable to action. And as to its submission (*inféodation*) to the U.S.S.R., there are two possibilities: either you show that this submission is necessary today for a revolutionary party—then every "possible" disappears and with your own hands you tie the lot of the proletarians to that of the Soviet Republics; or you will say, like Bourdet, that it is *possible* to escape this domination: in this case, individual errors, lack of understanding of the situation, character defects (conformism, cowardice, etc.) will explain the inertia of the C.P. The man you quote as your authority wrote: "A revolution cannot be commanded; it is only possible to give political expression to its internal forces."[13] And yet you admit that the working class, in full *élan* and in a revolutionary situation, could be checked by the individual action of its leaders. In short, you reject any occasioning causes for the bourgeoisie but you concede them to the proletariat. And for only one reason: guilt is *necessarily occasional*: it got along for better or worse with the fatality of the ancients; with the necessity of the moderns, it is clearly compelled to disappear: and so now you need a culprit.†

From this compromise between necessity and contingency, be-

---

* Mr. Germain doesn't claim—let's be fair—that it *had* to take power: "That would have been a risky act." He says that the working class had the necessary force and élan to seize it. But then, if he had been its leader, after having led it along this path, *in the name of what* would he have checked it?

[13] *La Révolution permanente,* p. 317.

† The incredible Mr. Monnerot has his ready-made explanation: it was *selection* (by the Russian bureaucracy, of course) which created in France "a type of man who has the characteristics of the prudent civil servant, the wily parliamentary politician, the good-natured democratic leader and the professional agitator of the masses." Naturally he is the leader of the C.P. Isn't that charming?

tween rigor and indefiniteness, between what is and what ought to be was born your conception of spontaneity: "the revolutionary instinct" which you acknowledge in the masses has only one function: to engrave in the absolute *what might have been.* And you would even accept the fact that an inflexible law has governed the course of events since October 1917, perhaps ever since the first original sin, if one conceded to you that, among so many vicissitudes, the revolutionary instinct has remained unshakable. It must remain deep in peoples' hearts, an eternal availability which circumstances veil but which can neither destroy nor create; for it is the profound reality of the proletariat, the sentence that capitalism passes on itself, in short the merciless exigency that expresses itself objectively by a pressure exercised on the Party and its leaders and that has no object other than the Permanent Revolution. By endowing the proletariat with a revolutionary spontaneity, you contaminate it with your opposition. You have considered, as a matter of fact, that the political action of the C.P. was neither correct nor appropriate, that one could have and should have conducted another. But in looking around, you discovered only relationships of forces, interests, acts; in short, being and facts; never any ought-to-be. And to begin with, who sets the ends to be pursued? By yourselves, you are in no position to reproach the C.P. for having abandoned revolutionary objectives. Condemnation must be made in the name of the masses; but what proof do you have that you speak in their name, you who have no access to them? Just this, that far from wanting to make them happy in spite of themselves, you limit yourself to deciphering the messages from their revolutionary instinct. If this instinct exists, it will be the exigency which defines the goals and the means of attaining them: objectively, as a matter of fact, it reveals itself as exigency only in manifesting itself as *praxis.* The masses have a spontaneous power to create and to organize. The effect of this is a hastening of the advent of the proletariat: it is thus that in 1944 they produced by themselves the committees of liberation and the factory committees: these first steps defined the path, the C.P. had only to continue the movement. And since these spontaneous steps showed the direction to be taken, you can condemn the leaders who didn't take it: the popular instinct *makes manifest* what should have been done, what, with different leaders, would have been done. Spontaneity engenders possibles: it is the masses, with their intransigence, their combativeness, the sharpness of their demands, who create the *possibility* of taking power; the impossibility comes from the leaders. But they are nothing; it seems that they can be changed on the spot; the masses are *everything*; so go ahead and try to change them. Their spontaneity has the inexorability of dialectics, since it is production which produces the producer; at the same time, their spontaneity is free since it expresses the essence-in-movement of the proletariat. For the second time in history, it signifies—in the face of the original sin we have all inherited—nature sustained by Grace. And it must be acknowledged that this Grace saves you Trotskyists; without it you'd be off to a bad start: what would happen if the "dynamism" of the masses depended on external factors? Suppose it regulated itself by the state of forces, the degree of the combatants' exhaustion, the memory of prior struggles, the solutions reviewed, the policy of the leaders.* Suppose the spontaneous action of the masses, instead of having the future in view, were reduced to being only a rebound of the past; suppose their exigency, instead of being a measure of their strength, had the insubstantiality of a dream; suppose it were dependent on their fatigue, on a false hope: we could then bid farewell to humble collective prophetism, to spontaneity. You could still oppose Marx to Stalin; you would no longer summon the proletariat to the bar of justice to bear witness against its leaders: the policy of the leaders and the mood of the masses would both, in this hypothesis, be functions of the external circumstances; ultimately one reacts on the other, they modify each other, adapt to each other and, finally, equilibrium is established, a reciprocal accommodation, the *possibles* go up in smoke: like leaders, like

* The C.P. replies quite correctly that the masses were permeated by powerful nationalist currents aroused and oriented by the myth "de Gaulle, chief of the Resistance" and that it was necessary first of all to undertake a powerful work of demystification.

mass; like mass, like leaders. The destiny of the proletariat? Perhaps Marxist methodology will permit you to *foresee* it; not to make it: you will be augurs. Anyway, you no longer count. "But," you will say, "this conception isn't dialectical." Why not? In any case, it's Engels': "History is accomplished in such a way that the final result flows from the conflicts of multiple individual wills, each one determined by a given quantity of particular conditions: there are, then, innumerable forces which intersect, an infinite group of parallelograms and the resultant, the historical fact, can be considered the product of a force which operates, on the whole, unconsciously and without will. What each one wills is in fact thwarted by the others, and what results from it is something which nobody willed." In this perspective, the "unconscious and involuntary force" is a convenient fiction; as for spontaneity, there isn't any.

You address yourself today to the C.P. and you hand down the order to propose unity of action to the Socialist leaders. This political advice is—for the *present* moment—both entirely reasonable and entirely absurd. Reasonable, because it is certain that if it were followed, France and Europe would be changed; war would be further away. Absurd, because you well know that the C.P. will take no step (Lecoeur's speech testifies to the temporary triumph of those who seek to drive the Party into isolation); even if the C.P. wanted to, the Socialists would refuse flatly. But, you say, the failure of this attempt would open the eyes of the S.F.I.O. militants: you obviously don't know them if you underestimate their resentment of the C.P.: they will not leave their party, they will congratulate their leaders for having frustrated the manoeuver. If it were simply a matter of considering what will really take place, your advice could pass for a pious desire without importance or foundation. But you insist to the contrary that: this "common front . . . is neither utopian nor venturesome." Why? "Because there are millions of workers, of civil servants, of artisans, of shopkeepers and small farmers who want things to change."*

* It's true: they want things to change but you underestimate the ravages which anti-communism has wrought in their ranks.

In a word, it is in the will of the masses that Trotskyist reasoning finds its objective guarantee. "For a Marxist" every true idea must be practical since truth is action; the Trotskyist idea would remain a purely lifeless abstraction, an idealistic, unforeseen event (since it doesn't produce effects by itself, since it points to a path which it knows will not be followed) if the masses, through their action and their demands, did not take on the responsibility for giving these pure subjective concepts a beginning of realization. Not that the idea acts on them: there is preestablished harmony; the Trotskyist decides that his speech is the verbal expression of the collective spontaneity. He is on one side, the proletariat on the other: never do they speak to each other, but between the intellectual system of the former and the *élan* which carries the latter beyond his wretched condition, a profound and tacit agreement is established virtually over the head of the militant Communist who contents himself with really speaking to the workers and definitively directing their movement. The vital and unobservable impetuosity of the masses is the guaranty for an ineffective diagnosis; or, if one prefers, Trotskyism bases the abstract rationalism of a member of the opposition on a pragmatic irrationalism. It goes without saying, of course, that the spontaneous aspirations of the laboring masses are there only to be violated. We come back to the scheme described earlier: spontaneity is the name given the secret censure which a group inflicts on the leaders it has chosen for itself, the silent complicity of a society integrated with the members of the opposition which it has exiled.

Let us come back to June 4th: is it the workers' spontaneity which repudiated the C.P.? I very much doubt it. First of all, neither Marx nor Lenin believed in the permanence of a "revolutionary instinct" in the masses. Whereas Trotsky* insists on their "profound conservatism" which seems to him "a factor of social stability." In order to "free the unhappy from the constraints of the

* Who, all the same, set the example for you and reconstructed the Russian Revolution to show the spontaneous movement of the masses as an essential factor of history. But his conception remains much richer and more complex than yours.

conservative mind and to lead the masses to insurrection" exceptional circumstances are necessary. In this case, their feeling is at first purely negative: the leaders have plans, programs: but the masses feel quite simply "that they can no longer bear the *Ancien Régime.*" Dragged along by the event, it is only then that they get their *revolutionary experience* by "actively orienting themselves through the method of successive approximations" and always more to the left. When their *élan* breaks on "objective obstacles," the ebb begins, which leads to reaction: "The great defeats are discouraging for a long time. The groups lose their power over the mass. In the latter's consciousness ill-digested prejudices and superstitions rise to the surface again. The newcomers from the countryside, an ignorant mass, thin out the workers ranks during this time." In a word, the masses are revolutionary when the conditions for the Revolution are ripe; their *élan* and their powers must be evaluated according to the concrete possibilities of the situation, instead of establishing these possibilities according to the force of the revolutionary "dynamism." In particular, if their supposed "instinct" is the result of circumstances, its violence doesn't prove that it must be obeyed. It is Trotsky again who writes: "The masses intervene in events not following the instructions of doctrinaires but according to the laws of their own political development. The Bolshevik leadership . . . clearly saw that it was necessary to give the bulk of the reserves time to draw their own conclusions from the adventure. . . . But the advanced strata were rushing into the streets . . . [Now] independently of thc will of the masses, the experience could be transformed into a decisive battle and, subsequently, into a decisive defeat. In face of such a situation, the Party reserved the right to remain on the sidelines . . . this party of the masses had, certainly, in order to help them, to follow the masses onto the terrain where they had placed themselves, but without sharing, in any way, their illusions." Trotsky himself claims for the party the right to evaluate the popular "dynamism" in the light of the general situation; he doesn't hesitate, in certain cases, to call the grounds for this sudden outburst "illusions"—and Mr. Germain, a Trotskyist, censures the C.P. for not having trusted the instinct of the people. He will say that the situation was different. Granted: but if we refuse to believe in the infallibility of the masses, what remains? Two doctrinal conceptions—that of the Italian C.P. and that of the French C.P.—two ways of reasoning and two "scientific" interpretations of the situation.

Let's admit that the repudiation of June 4th variously represented as a document and as an opinion, is a fact and is hidden beneath the fatigue and the discouragement of the workers. Does that get us any further? *What was repudiated?* The unfortunate initiative of May 28th? The policy of the French C.P. since 1948? Since 1944? Since the Congress of Tours? The bureaucracy? The Allegiance to Moscow? The Soviet policy? And why not Marxism itself? Who is to decide? You say that everything is connected: even if the censure were expressly directed at only one detail, the logic of the linkage is such that everything becomes suspect. But this is not true: we are dealing with local and day-to-day history, opaque, in part contingent, and the connection between the terms is not so tight that we cannot vary some of them within certain limits without modifying all the others. I read, the other day, that the proletariat is tired of the interference of the Soviet leaders in its internal affairs: it is not that it directly condemns this interference: in point of fact, the proletarian doesn't sense it and couldn't care less about it. But, and this is tantamount to repudiating the interference, the proletariat can no longer endure the "bureaucratism" of the C.P., which is the obvious consequence of that interference. But I remain sceptical: to convince me, it would have been necessary to show me that one cannot fight this bureaucracy without having first of all broken with the U.S.S.R.; thereafter and inversely, that today a revolutionary party which is not tied to the U.S.S.R. does not risk being bureaucratized by the circumstances of the struggle. Lacking these precisions, I do not know how to limit the scope of this alleged censure. I certainly see that the C.P. admits it made an error, and I also see that it localizes it in the moments which immediately preceded the strike: the fact is it wants to extricate itself the best it can. I see members of the bourgeoisie persuaded that the masses passed sentence on Marx: that's because these bourgeois are anti-Marxists.

Hence I don't know the grounds for the sentence; but as if that weren't enough, I no longer even know who the judge is. For I conceive of two kinds of censure: that which a revolutionary class imposes *in the name of the revolution* on the leaders who seek to stop it; that which a defeated, broken, resigned class imposes *in the name of the ideology of the victorious class* on the revolutionaries who seek to drag it along into new ventures. In the first case, it is the subject of history which condemns a traitor, and the condemnation is inscribed in the history which it is making. In the second, it is a class that senses itself becoming a mass again, that rediscovers, with its old chains, "its ill-digested prejudices and superstitions," and uses them to condemn its own glory. With which of these two judges am I dealing? The Trotskyists assert that it is with the revolutionary:

"The French working class . . . was sacrificed. . . . In spite of all justifications, this criminal error is today obvious to everyone. On the next occasion, no worker will commit it again."

How can one believe them, short of having confidence in the irrepressible spontaneity of the worker. And then, speaking frankly, I find the reactions of this revolutionary a bit thin: his class has been sacrificed, he knows it, and, for sole retaliation, he sulks about an untimely strike? Good eyes are needed to find his *dynamism,* better ones still to discover mass pressure in the June 4th events.

For the respectable newspapers, on the contrary, there are no more revolutionaries. Were there ever any? History has quite simply just carried out the requisite discrimination: it has put the villains on its left and the heroes on its right. The abstentionism of the worker must be attributed to his *wisdom;* that is to say, to the penetrating force of good principles: he is fed up with this useless violence, he asks only to work in peace, he already finds life difficult and feels that he doesn't need to waste money on stupidities. In short, it is the bourgeoisie itself which is repudiating the Party through him; I leave it you to decide whether or not the bosses are happy: their good friend the worker is finally cured; it seems that the scandalous rent in the fabric of our modern societies has been definitively stopped. Classes? That was a nightmare: if, as is logical, the title of bourgeois is granted to every individual who belongs to bourgeois society, there will no longer be anything but bourgeois in the West, some desperate and the others not too discontented.

If it were so, one can guess that the French C.P. would be profoundly hit by the disaffection of the masses. But the wherefores of their repudiation would leave it cold.

The anti-communist was waiting for me at the corner: "Then the masses can't judge the Party apparatus?" I answered that when they are set in motion they sometimes push their leaders ahead of them.* He went on: "But *the rest of the time,* they can't judge them?" Ah! Socrates, I see where you are leading me. Well then, I admit it: they judge their leaders when their leaders follow them, but not when they don't follow their leaders. Socrates triumphs: "You are indebted to the bourgeoisie for your freedom to write, and you use it to deny freedom of thought to the people." The verdict is handed down: scorn for the people, the temperament of a sophist, the shameful taste for autocratic forms of power; carried away by servility, I grant the C.P. much more than it ever asked: it claims to be guided by the opinion of the masses, it doesn't care whether or not its absolute hold on them is justified; it hides it.

When I am criticized, I push masochism to the point of wishing that it at least be for good reasons. So I will explain why those of the anti-communist are bad ones.

First of all, I don't concern myself with what would be desirable nor with the ideal relationships which the Party-in-itself (*Parti-en-soi*) sustains with the Eternal Proletariat; I seek to understand what is happening in France, today, before our very eyes. Good friends have been kind enough to point out to me the existence of Anglo-saxon and Scandinavian trade unions: these organisms, "proper in

* Remember, for example, the strike in May 1947, at the Régie Renault; the leaders of the C.G.T. metalworkers union were booed by the workers whose action supporting their demands the leaders sought to check. The C.P. immediately understood the lesson.

all respects," are supposed to be better adapted than our C.G.T. to the advanced forms of capitalism.* Perhaps: but what does that prove? That one must regret not being Swedish? I come back to my country, which does not have the reputation of being among the most "advanced" bourgeois democracies. The French employers are the laughing stock of the world: to push your argument to the very end, we would see that one has the class struggle one deserves.

In France, both then and today, since one must be precise, the conditions imposed on him forbid the worker the use of the formal rights he has been granted. You know it, you who arranged that he could not make use of them within the framework of our institutions: why do you get indignant when he renounces mirages and becomes militant? You who cry "scandal!" when you hear that a union election was conducted by a show of hands, you who fixed up the law to reduce a good third of the electoral corps to silence. You accused the C.P. of alternately defending and attacking democratic liberties according to its interests of the moment, but do you do anything different? When it comes to criti-

---

* Moreover what do these isolated examples signify? Has anyone established that the prosperity of the "advanced" countries is not based on the misery of the others? Are these paradises the image of what we will become, or the beneficiaries of the present inequality? You want to make me accept quietly the first hypothesis, but you don't prove it; were it true, besides, there would be no occasion for rejoicing: if the American trade unions had taken cognizance of their political duties, they would try to check the race towards war instead of sending spies and propagandists to the French. If history is one day to give to the American Government the title of "war criminal" which until now that government has been content to award to others and which it seems to want to claim for its own, it is to be feared that the American workers, taken in by their "advanced" unions, will be its involuntary accomplices, as the German proletariat—duped or crushed—was the accomplice of the emperor in 1914, and of the Nazis in 1939.

But may I remind you—one courtesy deserves another—that all humanity lives in a state of undernourishment? If it were—by chance—necessary that the worker of India or Europe die mouth open in order that American business maintain its high payroll, the *truth* of our present situation would not be the Ford or Kaiser factories but the starvation which ravages the world. And in this case the truth of *praxis* is not the well-behaved reformism of workers well-nourished, but made brutes by exhausting work and by constant propaganda: it would be revolutionary activity.

cizing the Communists, you demand full freedom for the worker; you deprive him of it when he decides to criticize you.

That is not all: a close look reveals that our liberties were conceived by the bourgeoisie for the bourgeoisie and the worker could never enjoy them short of becoming a bourgeois himself. Our liberties make sense only in a regime of private property and they are precautions that the owner of goods takes against the arbitrary action of the group. This presupposes that the group exists *already.* In point of fact, the bourgeoisie has been amusing us for two hundred years with its propaganda for "rugged individualism" which it calls "social atomism"; but its purpose is to confuse the poor classes: for the bourgeoisie forms by itself alone a strongly integrated collectivity which exploits them. Are we supposed to be born free and solitary? Are we supposed to form the community by binding ourselves with a contract? Are we supposed to give up our freedom in order to have it returned to us a hundredfold without entirely renouncing our natal solitude? But just look at us: solitary? When does one sigh for solitude except in company? Free? Yes: free to engage in certain very concrete activities which generally have their source in our economic power or in our social functions. The industrialist who can fire a fourth of his personnel without explanation is free; free the general who can decide on a murderous offensive; free the judge who can choose leniency or severity. *True* bourgeois freedom, positive freedom, is a power of man over man. Society makes the decision before our birth: it defines in advance our capacities and our obligations; in short, it places us. It *ties* us to others: in sum, the most insignificant of our gestures and the most unobtrusive trait of our characters are in fact synthetic acts which, in particular circumstances, affect the unity of the bourgeois class: each of our behavior patterns manifests our belonging to such and such a family or professional group; each contributes to integrating us in it further.*

---

* Such an industrialist, you say, is authoritarian. But what is authority? A character trait? No, or at least, not immediately. It is first of all a concrete right: he owns a factory, puts a hundred workers to work and *can,* in the name of the work contract, demand certain behavior from them. The ex-

What becomes of these unfortunate negative rights which bourgeois democracy claims to make such a big issue of? If they hardly enrich us, they don't risk making us poorer. They simply represent the safeguard of our concrete powers; they establish an imperceptible distance between each of us and the collectivity, they prevent us from dying of suffocation. But one certainly knows that bourgeois reality falls outside them: our industrialist does not think of defining himself by the rights which he shares with everyone else, but by the authority which he alone exercises. *Habeas corpus?* He hardly is concerned about it: no one would think of arresting him; his true freedom sails the high seas: it is the machine he has just bought in the U.S.A. Politics? He may well amuse himself by voting for the Radicals, abandoning them for the M.R.P., coming back to them: he won't change his person. His person is his factory, his family, his plans. The political tie in our societies is—in calm periods—the loosest and the most fragile one: it breaks at the least jolt. There is nothing surprising if we freely criticize the parties: to criticize is to stand back, to put oneself outside the group or the system, to consider them as *objects*; now even though we be members of a political grouping, we are never *inside*. But what about your boss, your director, the head of your office? Have you ever criticized him to his face and publicly? Of course not, because you belong to the enterprise, you are integrated in it: if you are fired, you lose at once your means of livelihood, your powers, and the purpose of your life. One expresses oneself freely on politics because it seems to be reduced to a purely formal activity; the liberal government resembles, on the surface, the principle of identity: it allows each one to be what he is and to have what he has. But as soon

ercise of this right is an action: he commands, he "runs" the enterprise. The repeated action becomes a competency: "He's the man we need: he has an iron fist." Finally, all is caught up in an oath which he swears to himself: "I will be boss." All that comes down to assuming for his own account and to making exist *in act* the abstract relationship between Capital and Labor, that is to say the exploitation of man by man. His authority is not lodged in a compartment of his brain, it is outside, in things, he does nothing but interiorize it.

as it's a matter of a job, of a *praxis,* of any synthetic activity which an integrated group pursues, you can say goodbye to freedom of thought. Now bourgeois politics is *also* a synthetic action, a class action; in times of crisis, when the bourgeoisie is threatened by the people, this politics reveals its true face: the "powwows" of the deputies had no other goal than to amuse the public, and their so-called divisions masked the existence of a *single party,* a class party, as authoritarian and tough as the C.P., whose organs are the police, the administration and the army, and whose function is to crush the resistance of the poor. At those times, the bourgeois will not stop until he has thrown his freedom of thought down the drain. What would he do with it? It is the moment to forget divisions; he is lost if he doesn't think as everybody else does. Criticize? He's not that crazy: criticism is likely to disunite, to hinder governmental action. He abandons his rights to a mop-up team which in return guarantees him his true powers and his possessions.

But for the worker, politics cannot be a luxury activity: it is his sole defense and his only means of integrating himself into a community. The bourgeois is basically integrated; solitude is the game he plays; the worker is basically solitary; politics is his need. The former is a man who supports a party to exercise his right as a citizen, the latter a "subhuman" who joins a party in order to become a man. The bourgeois glimpses in flashes the *reality* of politics, that is to say, the class struggle; the worker's primary experience is the class struggle, he is the object of it and he sometimes has an inkling that he could direct the action in his turn. For the bourgeois, outside of politics there is all of life; for the worker there is nothing outside of it; nothing except that "workers' sadness" which Navel said one overcomes only by action. Sadness, that is to say, isolation. Let's not conclude, however, that this isolation is *natural*: in order to persuade us of it the bourgeois have perfected their "social atomism." But it will suffice, in order to understand the sense of all this philosophy, to refer to the grounds of the Le Chapelier law on the "alleged common interests" of the workers. No: the isolation of the worker doesn't come from nature; it is *produced;* work, fatigue, misery, the tender care of the bourgeoisie have, if I may say so, arranged for the workers an artificial "state of nature"; the so-called *mass.* I will detail the processes of massification later; what counts here is that they are all aimed at imposing isolation—not the total disappearance of social relations but their mechanization. In this operation, democratic rights have an essential role: for an integrated bourgeoisie, we have seen that they offer only advantages; for the man alone, continuously exposed to the forces of disintegration, formal freedoms are chains. Look at the free contract, the keystone of the mechanism: how happily it combines the threat of death and the freedom to work; the worker is a man who signs freely under penalty of death. In this amalgam of necessity and autonomy, necessity prevents the wage earner from arguing about his price, freedom makes him responsible for the price imposed on him. By what right can he complain: after all, he could have refused. In a general way, the free contract forces the worker to accept responsibility for the destiny which is made for him; he consents to his lot, he goes one better: was it the boss who came to look for him? wasn't it he who asked for the job? Didn't he accept supplementary tasks, doesn't he try to improve the output of his production? Doesn't he voluntarily increase the risks of sickness or accident? And isn't it he who, quite criminally, lowered his demands in order to steal his neighbor's place? After that, who would dare to speak of solidarity: it is the law of the jungle. Class struggle? Oh no: the struggle for life. In short, it is he who did everything, who is guilty of everything, he who asks for misery, solitude and forced labor. Before the contract, he was only a victim; after the signing he is an accomplice. In vain, moreover, does he throw himself into chains: no one owes him anything. Once the work is done and paid for, the two contractants become free again; they didn't know each other before, they no longer recognize each other the next day. Let the Wall Street market fall; one small jolt will suffice to shake loose the personnel. The free contract transforms the worker into a detachable particle. When the British Parliament, towards the middle of the nineteenth century, took it into its head to pass the first workers' laws, there was only one cry: Protect the women and children if you insist, but *not the men*! They are adult, reasonable, free: they can defend themselves *all alone*. Those are the words which count: all alone. The freedom of the worker is his isolation; no one can intervene in his favor without the risk of enslaving him, and the government will all the better assure freedom to work the more it endeavors to protect the workers against all protection, even that of their own trade unions.

The right to vote is the last straw: the worker finds in these mechanical summations called elections no trace of the solidarity he is seeking. It is a matter of voting *in isolation,* for a program which he did not draw up and which he found out about in isolation: and the greatest number of isolations wins, in the name of the majority. But the winning idea does not unite at all: it is the same in each and in all; *identity* of opinion does not bring people together. Will he let himself be persuaded that all politics is reduced to this parlor game? Under the pretext of giving him access to culture, the bourgeoisie will infect him with individualism: with freedom of thought and expression, it will encourage him to sample probabilism, tolerance, scepticism and objectivism: all opinions are respectable, all are equal; why choose one rather than the other? He is led astray. Democratic freedoms sanction massification and give the worker a juridical mass status. *De facto* separation becomes *de jure* isolation.*

Freedom to criticize, to doubt, to vote, to die of hunger: you think that is what he is seeking? He really would be crazy! Should he plunge into isolation when he would like nothing so much as integration? Should he separate himself from his

* Later, *integrated into the class,* he will demand these same freedoms to conduct his class action. But it is at the very moment when the bourgeoisie seeks to suppress them. And if he demands them, moreover, it is for the militant he has become, for the member of the workers' Party, not for the isolated man he was.

comrades and stand back in order to criticize their acts, when he would like only to unite himself to them in confidence? And what would he do with a scepticism that confuses ideas and threatens to blast the meanings of the universe *just when* daily reality is absurd and he is ardently wishing life and death to have meaning. Doubt and uncertainty: these seem to be intellectual virtues. But he must struggle to change his condition, and these virtues of the mind can only paralyze action: ask him to question the cause he serves or to die for it, but not both at the same time. An action of some importance requires unity of direction; and he, precisely, needs to believe that there is a truth. Since he cannot work it out alone, he must be able to trust his class leaders profoundly enough to believe he is getting the truth from them. In short, at the first opportunity he will chuck these freedoms which strangle him: not that he does not want the power and autonomy of the working class; but he places this autonomy, this power, in the community; he doesn't think of exercising it except as a proletarian.

Meanwhile, what can he do? Nothing: he can't even conceive of this fighting community in which he would take his place. Crushed by the bourgeois forces, overwhelmed by his feeling of impotence and exhaustion, where would he find the germ of that spontaneity which you were demanding of him a little earlier? Action can catch him up, turn him upside down, change his universe, but where will the action arise? It is not a question for him of passing progressively from less to more, it is by an internal revolution that one becomes revolutionary; he will become *a different man* only by a sort of transformation. And he cannot have a presentiment of the sudden appearance of another universe and of another *self* as the subject of history so long as he remains crushed on his rock: how could passivity imagine activity? To be a bourgeois is not difficult; it is enough to pick the right parents; afterwards one lets nature take its course. On the other hand, nothing is less easy than to be a *proletarian*: one asserts oneself only by a thankless and difficult action, by going beyond fatigue and hunger, by dying to be reborn. In order for action to be possible at any moment, *praxis* must exist within the masses themselves as a call, an example and also, very simply, as a sort of *figuration* of what can be done. In short, there is needed an organization which is the pure and simple incarnation of *praxis*. Very well, you will say, why not the trade union? I will tell you why in the third part of this essay. But for the moment, trade union or not, what counts is that, by the very necessity of the situation, the organism which does the conceiving, the executing, the assembling and which distributes the tasks—whether it be a revolutionary trade union or a party or both—can be conceived of only as an *authority*. It is anything but the delightful product of workers' spontaneity: it imposes itself on each *individual* as an imperative. It is a question of an *Order* which makes order reign and which gives orders. Magnanimity, enthusiasm will come later, if they come. But first of all the Party represents for each one the most austere ethic: it is a matter of entering a new life by casting off one's present personality. Tired out, the worker is ordered to tire himself out even more; powerless, he is ordered to throw himself head-on against a stone wall. As long as he is still on the outside, *praxis,* that is to say access to the class, is presented to him in the form of a duty. But if it were necessary to legitimize the existence of an imperious and always *too* demanding organ, I will take as grounds its necessity rather than its origin: were it spontaneous, its authority would not be the firmer for that. What proves that initial impulses are the best? Whereas the Party, wherever it comes from, derives its legitimacy from the fact that it responds first of all to a need. Without it, there is no unity, no action, no class. Naturally, the great majority of workers don't join it: can one be militant after ten hours of work in a factory? But they give birth to the class when they all obey the orders of the leaders. In exchange for observing discipline, they have the right not to be bothered by "powwows." Two trade union federations, two or three workers' parties: each is weakened by the others; when a man is outside, what voice has he? He remains outside. You claim that the masses *do not demand* a single Party? You are right: the masses demand nothing at all, for they are only dispersion. It is the Party which demands of the masses that they come together into a class under its direction. And the slogan "a single party" was not launched by the French C.P., not even by Lenin; but—outside of Marxism even—by Blanquists such as Vaillant; in 1899, the First National Congress of socialist movements proposed as its goal to achieve "the political and economic Organization of the Proletariat into a class party for the Conquest of Power."

If the class is neither the sum of the exploited nor the Bergsonian *élan* which raises them up, from where can you expect it to come if not from the work which men do on themselves? The unity of the proletariat lies in its relationship with the other classes of society, in short, it is its *struggle*. But this struggle, inversely, has meaning only through unity; each worker, through and beyond his class, defends himself against the entire society that is crushing him; and reciprocally, it is by this struggle that the class makes itself. The unity of the working class is thus its historical and mobile relationship with the collectivity, insofar as this relationship is achieved by a synthetic act of unification which, by necessity, is distinguished from the mass as pure action is distinguished from passion. Even if it were only a question of transforming opposition and competition into a community of interests, it is certainly necessary, short of supposing that all the workers will receive grace at the same time, that a linking principle act simultaneously in several places and guarantee to each the sincerity of all. That doesn't mean, of course, that the militant doesn't emerge from the mass: but when he does, he distinguishes himself from it. In this respect only: the man of the mass is still weighed down by his individual interests; he must be wrenched away from them. The linking organism must be pure action; if it carries with it the least seed of division, if it still conserves in it any passivity—sluggishness, self-interest, divergent opinions—who then will unify the unifying apparatus? Ideally, it would be pure linking, the relation which surges up wherever two workers are together.* In a word, the Party *is* the very movement which unites the workers by carrying them along towards the taking of power. How then can you expect the working class to repudiate the C.P.? It is true that the C.P. is nothing outside of the class; but let it disappear and the working class falls back into dust particles.

Is it to be understood that the worker is passive? Quite the contrary. He transforms himself into action when he enters the class, and can assert his freedom only in action. But this freedom is a concrete and positive power: the power to invent, to go further, to take the initiative, to propose solutions. It is only by *outrunning* the situation and catching up with the movement that this freedom can enrich him. Freedom of criticism, on the other hand, makes not only the cell leader or the union representative frown: everyone is afraid of it *in others;* it recalls the earlier isolation, the discords. Let us understand, in any case, that criticisms, even if they were tolerated, could not emanate from any spontaneity or from some revolutionary "instinct": the worker, transformed by the organization into a moving force, finds his practical reality beginning with his metamorphosis; whatever he thinks or does, it begins with his *transformation*; and the latter, in its turn, takes place in the actual framework of the Party's policy. His freedom, which is simply his power to transcend the given situation—in short, to act—manifests itself then within this given reality which is the organization; he forms his opinions on the problems which the Party submits to him and does so within the context of the principles which the Party gives to him. In short, he doesn't judge the Party in the name of a policy whose principles are engraved in his unconscious, produced by his spontaneous reaction or by the contradiction of bourgeois society. Trained, molded, raised above himself by the Party, his freedom is only the power to transcend each particular situation by acts, within the very body of the organization and towards the common goal.

* "Ideally." In point of fact, there are seeds of division in the Party as everywhere else and the exhausting struggle which it conducts continuously against "factional" activity is known. We will return to this whole analysis.

In a word, the Party is his freedom. Today, a worker in France can express and fulfill himself only in a class action directed by the C.P.; he is molded by the arguments of the C.P., by its ideology and its principles; if he tried to turn them against the Communist policy, they would of themselves proceed to justify it. If a serious error is committed or a defeat sustained, he does not have the tools by which to understand the meaning, nor the presentiment to guess at it; he simply lets go, his effort is broken, he falls back into the field of bourgeois attraction; the class goes to pieces. But when he has fallen back, it is to rediscover, under the agency of hostile forces, his despair, his ignorance and his feeling of powerlessness. The Party has regrouped far away from him. It is inaccessible, like an imperative which one does not judge, but simply finds *too hard,* inhuman, in the sense that one could say that Kant's ethic is inhuman. Which amounts to declaring that all class action has become impossible.

"In sum," says the anti-communist, "we said that the working class repudiated the Party; *you* say that it has reduced the workers to despair. We don't feel like pursuing these idle discussions any further and we say you are granting us all we asked."

I grant nothing. I note, like everybody else, the discouragement of the masses; but I still do not know whether the policy of the C.P. bears the responsibility for it. And then, between our two interpretations, I see a chasm; if you have found only a verbal difference, it is because you don't give a damn about the working class. Imagine a proletariat, clear-eyed, completely fresh, which would repudiate the C.P. and immediately form a new party (you know, that famous very French Communist Party which would distinguish itself from the French Communist Party by its independence, and which would manifest its national character by reviving true internationalism.) If such a proletariat existed, one would have to deal with its wishes: who else could decide? If the proletariat returned to the natural stage of atomism, but were still seething and always ready to regroup, to take up the struggle again, you could, in a pinch, hope to palm off your trash on it, and even offer it a substitute Party. But you know very well that the working class is collapsing, that it is taking the measure of its powerlessness, and that it risks turning its millions of defenseless men over to the steam hammers of the bourgeoisie; you know that in the coming months everything will conspire to increase the isolation and the resignation, the distances between men, to make the proletariat an archipelago. When the workers have touched the bottom of bitterness and disgust, do you really believe that you will be able to sell them your clap-trap? I have already told you: if they lose confidence in the C.P., they will distrust all politics, they will distrust their class; the universe will be bourgeois. And if you hope that they will climb up the slope again, you must know that only the C.P. can help them do so; if they rediscover their unity, it will be in order to gather around the C.P.; if they realize their combativeness, it will be in order to obey Party orders. Already people are whispering: "You're crazy! To desire an independent Left and in league with the Party! Do you want it to regain its influence on the masses? Keep discreetly out of it; let the disintegration go on; one day the Party will blow up." Things aren't at that point, fortunately: but even if they were at the worst possible point and you were the irreconcilable adversary of the Party, I cannot help considering contemptible those who are awaiting Communist discomfiture from the worker's despair. I am told that the worker will pull himself together, that I fail to recognize the intestinal fortitude of the French proletariat; it is said, God save the mark, to have a psychological profile, to be known for its hibernations followed by sudden awakenings. Just look at 1848, 1870, 1936, 1948. I am looking: but rather than violent acts of an explosive temperament, I discover in these battles the action of precise factors; and in the "sleep" which followed, I see the effect of defeat and Terror; the workers' strength was annihilated each time and it took long years for it to reconstitute itself. If we believed you, there would be little need to worry. In twenty years, in fifty years, we would see a fine, brand-new proletariat reappear. In short, one would cultivate patience: after all, life is not so bad and anticommunism pays off.

Good. We will wait. Twenty years, if necessary. Unless in six months the Third World War breaks out. In which case we run the risk that there will be no one at the rendezvous: not you, nor I, nor the liberated proletariat, nor France.

III. THE CAUSES

I have shown that the discouragement of the workers could not be considered even implicitly as a condemnation of Communist policy. The reason for it, then, remains to be found. That is the goal I assign to myself today.*

One can duck the question in two ways, both of which proceed from the same sophism. The anti-communist "of the Left" will not even hear mention of the workers' lassitude: he shows us a proletariat of steel plunged to the hilt in the decaying bourgeois carcass. The anti-communist "of the Right" shows us the bourgeoisie in the guise of a young giant who is carrying a dying proletariat in his arms. In both cases, it is a matter of quietly ignoring everything that might resemble a reciprocal conditioning; in short, of denying the class struggle.

The anti-communist "of the Left" knows the French bourgeois from close up; he willingly admits that their national characteristics have been produced by circumstances. On the other hand, he simply denies the existence of the French proletariat: only the proletariat-in-itself exists, manifesting itself simultaneously within all capitalist nations. How could this proletariat be tired out? And

* Will people say that this discouragement is a passing matter? I willingly concede it. Will they want to add that the August 1953 strikes presage an awakening of the working class? I am less sure of it. These strikes of the civil servants are remarkable for their breadth, and what gave them their extreme importance is that they were the occasion for a rapprochement *at the base* among the strikers. But they did not affect large-scale private industry—or almost did not; and then the leaders of the C.F.T.C. and F.O. finally torpedoed them to avoid being forced to achieve unity of action with the C.G.T. I ask that you be patient and that you not accuse me of pessimism or of stopping at negative conclusions. It is not my intention to ascertain a state of impotence: I am undertaking to prove that *only* a Popular Front can give back its vigor to the workers' movement.

what relationship ought this hypothetical product of capitalism-in-itself to have with our so regrettably empirical bourgeoisie? The latter was formed little by little through the agency of accidental (hence negligible) factors. (Let us cite, for example, the Revolution of 1789.) Determined exclusively by the contradictions of capitalism, the history of the former is limited to reflecting the successive transformations of large-scale industry. Our bourgeoisie becomes frightened and plucks up its courage, makes mistakes and repairs its errors, directs its affairs poorly or well; the proletariat never loses a battle nor wins one, never makes errors and never discloses any particular truth. Irresistible, incompressible, everlasting, it matures. Relentlessly. It is the most terrible enemy of capitalism-in-itself. One doesn't see what harm it could do to the French bourgeoisie: this proletariat will never encounter it.

This conception would relieve one of making a historical explanation—and perhaps any explanation—if its partisans had not also taken it into their heads to denounce the crimes of the C.P. Without the C.P., the French proletariat would not have an empirical history: the Party lodged itself in the working class like a grain of sand in Cromwell's bladder. What is it then? A disease of the proletariat-in-itself? You will be informed that the proletariat-in-itself doesn't have a disease: it can neither slow down nor accelerate the movement-in-itself which animates it. Its misfortunes come to it from a very historical failing of its leaders. If Stalin's heart had been tenderer, the face of the world might have been changed. And do not ask how it happens that the empirical militants of the C.P. can throw the wheels of the hypothetical proletariat out of gear: for having begun by eliminating history, the anti-communist is constrained to reintroduce it at the end in its most absurd form, as a series of accidents, in order to account for the distance which separates reality from his calculations.

For my part, I maintain that the development of capital, taken in its generality, accounts for the aspects common to all worker's movements. But these in-principle considerations will never of themselves explain the particular traits of the class struggle in

France or England between two given dates. A concrete fact is the singular expression of universal relations; but it can be explained in its singularity only by singular reasons: to try to deduce it from an absolute but empty knowledge or from a formal principle of development is a waste of time and trouble. In truth, there are dialectics and they reside in facts; it is for us to discover them there, not put them there. I have spoken of discouragement: if one wants to prove that I am mistaken, one must establish by evidence that the workers have kept their "combativeness." And even if one established it, this preserved courage would remain a specific emotion and would call for a specific explanation, just like discouragement. The French proletariat is a historical reality whose singularity was made manifest in recent years by a certain attitude: I do not go looking for the key to this attitude in the universal movement of societies, but in the movement of French society; that is to say, in the history of France.

The anti-communists "of the Right" arrive at the same conclusions by the opposite reasoning. To the workers of flesh and blood, they oppose eternal France, you know, a France of splendid upheavals, a France which a providential man always saves at the last moment; trim, lively, and alert, always busy, always running, this France resembles the Madelon of the song. Knights and captains of industry, merchants, bureaucrats and country folk—everyone sings, everyone works, everyone participates in the bustle. There is only one dead weight: the proletariat. France looks around, worried: "Who then prevents my workers from following me?" And whom do you expect it to be if not the Communist Party? Since it contemplates our destruction, don't be surprised at the fact that it has undertaken to stupefy the French worker. The latter, of course, is not entirely a dupe: he rediscovers in flashes the common sense of his fathers and understands that his interests are one with the employers' interests: at heart he would ask only to work to take out his fair share of the national income. But the Communists have befuddled him: if they fail to set him against his good masters, they retain enough strength to keep him from joining them. Divided between the distrust that the C.P. inspires in him and that which his boss inspires in him, he freezes in a kind of tetanus. How far wouldn't we go, to what couldn't we aspire, if the filterable virus of Stalinism had not infected our proletariat!

Dear slippery friends, are we to believe France is immortal? How long do you think you can hide from us the fact that she is dying? The sickness which paralyzes the proletariat began by hitting the entire society. You who are talking, are you so alive? Your tail still quivers when you hear the word "communism" but your body is flaccid and limp; it is getting colder every day. And the others? All the others? Where are our great hopes, our great ambitions, our great undertakings? The peasant scratches the soil with his hands, the industrialist wallows, the banks are moulting into savings institutions. We live poorly, very poorly: the salaries of half the population of France do not exceed the subsistence minimum; the youth suffocate or become expatriates, saying that there is no longer anything to do in France. And the government? Does it govern? Maintaining discord by lies, rigging the electoral law, imprisoning opponents, forbidding their sons to enter the best graduate schools, establishing over our divisions the sly and hypocritical dictatorship of weakness, putting off indefinitely the vote on social laws, making promises to the State workers and civil servants and then refusing to keep them, crushing the country under the weight of an absurd tax system—can all this pass for a domestic policy? Kidnapping the Madagascan chiefs in planes in order to drop them from the sky onto the roofs of their villages, showering the Vietnamese with napalm and sacking Vietnam, impaling Tunisians on bottles, firing point blank on the Moroccan workers—can this pass for a colonial policy? Sinking billions in a war which is already lost, which we pursue for lack of the courage to end it, and which spreads from one ministry to another like the clap; horse trading French sovereignty, accepting the domination of the United States over half the world and German hegemony in Europe, can that pass for a foreign policy? Are they statesmen, these weak-nerved Catholics who faint at the rostrum, roll under banquet tables, and think they are Richelieu because they have blood on their hands? These socialists who fire on striking miners? These great patriots who traffic in dollars? These ignorant and puffed-up lackeys, always ready to lick boots or to show their asses, so long as the price is right? If they remain in power, it's because no one in bourgeois France cares about politics any more. Remember, in 1952, the newspapers were shouting victory because at the elections only five million non-voters were counted. You speak of apathy when the workers hold aloof from a demonstration: what will you say when the voters hold aloof from the voting booths? In today's France, the working class is the only one with a doctrine at its disposal, it is the only one whose "particularism" is in full harmony with the interests of the nation; a great party represents it and it is the only one whose program includes the safeguarding of democratic institutions, the reestablishment of national sovereignty and the defense of peace; the only one which preoccupies itself with economic rebirth and the increase of buying power; the only one that *lives,* that swarms with life while the others swarm with maggots. And you ask by what miracle the workers follow most of its assignments? I pose the opposite question, and I ask what prevents them from always following them. There can be no doubt about the answer: if the proletariat gives signs of exhaustion, it is because it is affected by the anemia of the nation. In order to struggle against the French sickness—this sickness that is eating away at all of us—it is not enough to line up alongside the working class: the disease must be known by its causes. Leaving eternal France at grips with the proletariat-in-itself, I am undertaking to explain events rigorously defined in time and space by the peculiar structure of our economy, and the latter in turn by certain events of our local history.

We live poorly because we produce too little and at prices too high. You ask who is responsible? It's the German who declared two ruinous wars on us; the Russian who, from Moscow, slows down reconstruction; those who have resigned from the birth rate, who, by refusing to be born, deprive us of future customers; the backward peasants who won't make up their minds to consume; the subsoil, finally, which betrayed France by giving way under her feet. In short, everyone is guilty except the ruling class.

That is just what bothers me: too many traitors. So many

causes so poorly tied together is called an embarrassment of circumstances. Is France dying by chance? We will come back to the Muscovite and the worker at our leisure. But as for the two World Wars, how can one imagine that they are responsible for our stagnation? From 1913 to 1929, in spite of fifty-two months of devastation, French production increased by thirty percent; after which it has remained stationary until today; that is to say, for a quarter of a century: in the same period* England was increasing its production by half. And then what? We are told that we have been marking time since 1929: whatever the ills that overwhelm us, wouldn't it be absurd to seek the reason for them in a disaster occurring ten years after their first manifestations? At the origin of so continuous a deterioration, there must be a structural fault, a defect.

The subsoil then? Let's leave that to the spelunkers and the cavernicoles. Blame the coal, blame the oil, blame the nonferrous metals for hiding abroad like vulgar capital, when our merits gave them the duty of burying themselves under our feet: you will not be any further ahead for it. Has nature betrayed us? That's too bad; only it betrays all of Europe at the same time, and look: equally betrayed, the Belgians, the Swiss, the Scandinavians live better than we. As for the British, at the end of World War I they had a fine occasion to cry "traitor!" While their backs were turned, their ungrateful clientele left them flat: it bought American coal, Japanese cotton, German steel. If England had had to do then what we are doing today, she would have let herself fall on the dungheap to attend her own ruin, prophesying the while but without lifting a finger to stave it off. England had all the excuses: her glorious old industry seemed the bone structure of the nation; can one change one's bones? England broke them: since the ancient foundations of her industrial preponderance had been undermined, she decided to change in order to remain the same, and to maintain her equilibrium by upsetting her production. Within twenty years, she has transformed her anatomy and her physiology, She has

* To be exact, from 1939 to 1952.

reversed her population currents, reclassified and redistributed her manpower, abandoned her mine pits and mining cities, and has oriented herself deliberately towards the manufacture of highly specialized products. Is our problem so different? For us also, it has been a question of getting around a difficulty which couldn't be attacked head on and of intensifying production by a reorganization of our economy. But an inspired propaganda persuades us that our constitution is immutable in order to prevent us from modifying it: France has soft bones, Pott's disease; let her stay in bed: at the least effort of the patient, the vertebrae would break. In short, we are supposed to believe that the moon is made of green cheese and mistake Nature for Destiny. Don't believe any of it: Nature shuffles the cards and deals; each gets his hand from her, but not directions on how to play the game: Nature asks the questions, but doesn't know the answers; she orients the economy without governing it. Better yet: the economy makes Nature quite as much as Nature makes the economy. Industrialization can take many forms and the scarcity of natural resources does not exclude them all *a priori*: it was known from the beginning that France, unlike Victorian England, could not even attempt to make her entire production dependent on extractive industries: was she forbidden to favor her manufacturing industry? Couldn't she specialize, develop together and one by the other the importation of raw materials and the exportation of finished products? The problem was declared insoluble very quickly, but what can be known about it since, until recent years, they were careful not to state it? We can acquit the mineral kingdom: it is men who have made the French economy, who make it each day. Our present decline, just like our former grandeur, is a human adventure, and we are both its victims and its artisans.

Suppose the burden of responsibility is put on the back of the consumer? The narrowness of our internal market would keep production this side of a certain threshold beyond which the flow of products could no longer be assured. Great idea! Its principal merit is to bring us back to the human kingdom. And then the peasant consumes little, that's a fact: at least, in the southern half of the country. Only here's the problem: short of believing in eternal France and in the unchangeability of the French "character," I don't see that one can seriously offer the shrinking of our markets as a primary cause. Are we supposed to be nationally tightfisted? You're joking. If the farmers don't fulfill their "social duty as buyers" isn't it more likely that it's because they live on the products of their land? What forces them to do so? Damn it, the constant diminution of their buying power. Do you want to know where this progressive impoverishment comes from? From the fact that working the fields no longer pays, quite simply. Thus we are sent back from consumption to production. Will you say that it is their fault and that they stick stubbornly to their old routines instead of buying tractors? It's true. But in societies as in feedback machines, the conditionings are reciprocal. In stagnation of consumption, one must see an effect as much as a cause, or rather a cause which is at the same time the effect of its own effects. Let us reason clockwise: few tractors are bought; therefore few are produced; and, since the markets are too small to amortize the expenses of retooling, the agricultural machine factories have no interest in modernizing. Conclusion: tractors are expensive because the peasants hold back from mechanization. The reasoning is precise and, moreover, marvelously suited to encouraging inertia: if you choose the farmer right off as an independent variable, you deprive yourself, by hypothesis, of any means of acting on him. Let us salute in passing this fine example of reactionary pessimism: greed and habit are in the peasant nature; *therefore* our economy will not change.

Now, let's reason counter-clockwise: so long as the index of industrial prices remains higher than the index of agricultural prices, the small rural farmers will not have the means to modernize their farms; they hold aloof from mechanization, because mechanization holds off from them, and their habits will not be overcome until machines are put within their reach. This second conclusion, as legitimate as the first, has the additional advantage of being *practical*: it opens the exit which the other had shut. But isn't the peasant himself bothered by the strangling of the agricultural market? Yes, of course. But we find again, on this new ground, the same circularity of effects and causes. Clockwise: the harvest cannot be absorbed; therefore, France produces too much wheat. Counter-clockwise: the French are underfed; therefore, France doesn't produce enough wheat. Since it is necessary to turn, let us turn. But from where do we start? Is there primacy of supply or primacy of demand? That depends on what one understands by "consumer." Are our producers thinking of yesterday's customer or tomorrow's? And who are these irritating buyers who run from their duty: the rich who are stingy or the poor who can't pay? In the last century, the manufacturer boasted of creating needs in order to satisfy them: "In a competitive system," he said, "production is increased in order to reduce costs. The narrowness of markets is only a temporary accident: a market is either conquered or invented. Since there are forty million Frenchmen, we have forty million customers. True, most of them are consumers unbeknownst to themselves. That need be no obstacle, we'll discover them as buyers. If necessary, we will seek them out in their homes and no matter how little they can pay, we will ask them still less." In short, according to the manufacturer, production depended on machinery and conditioned consumption; demand varied as a function of supply. And it was on the continued enrichment of the nation that capitalism based its sole justification, the great myth of progress. In other countries, the movement of the competitive economy was to find its logical outcome in mass production which aims at a mass clientele and for which, in theory, the market is inseparable from the entire nation.*

Good. But what are they telling us today? In the France of 1954, would demand condition supply? This was true at the time of the crusades: a stratified society whose economy was dominated by agriculture furnished a fixed and customary clientele to artisans, who worked according to inherited recipes. Do they mean that we have come back to that? And could it be that our em-

* It is true that mass production creates its own limit: maximum production does not coincide with maximum profit; competition disappears in the face of ententes. But that Malthusianism, as harmful as it is, has nothing to do with ours.

ployers no longer believe in progress? In that case, how do they manage to justify their privileges in their own eyes? Each year, for the last twenty-five years, they have been deploring the fact that consumption remains stationary. A fine excuse: we live on what there is. Even if we should all die of starvation, how could we eat more, since we are not given more to eat. It is true: the children will not leave the slums that their fathers lived in. But where would they go, since people refuse to build? Neither destiny nor human nature is responsible for the constriction of the market; and production, whatever one says about it, has not ceased to regulate consumption. But here, production, instead of pushing consumption, slows it down. Everyone has heard of those night clubs where champagne costs a fortune because the management seeks to "select its clientele." France has come to resemble such night clubs. It is the elite who consume, and prices are quite deliberately set to exclude the rabble; housing is refused to the shelterless, food to the starving, shoes to the barefooted. The time is near when on the windows of bakeries will be posted the notice: "To buy bread, proper dress is required." That's what seems clear: even if consumption, half-strangled, turns on production to strangle it in turn, it is production which moved first; in it resides the constitutional vice of our economy.

This vice is obvious, provided one looks for it where it is: it is called dispersion. In the United States, as early as 1930, manufacturing plants employing more than 260 wage earners represented four percent of all enterprises and absorbed more than half of the man power. In France, in 1953, the plants which provide employment to more than 100 wage earners absorb only forty-six percent of the man power and represent only one one-hundredth of French industry. Around a few giants, the micro-organisms multiply rapidly: in Paris, for metalworking alone, 18,000 enterprises have 400,000 workers. In commerce the dispersion is accentuated: the establishments which employ more than 100 wage earners possess twelve percent of the personnel and represent one tenth percent of the total. These facts are known to everyone; people conclude from them that France is a museum piece contemporary with the Moral Order and gas-lighting: this piece of machinery with innumerable wheels apparently survives through a caprice of history and apparently continues to obey the laws of the last century. Which convinces some people that we will experience the fate of Athens, and others that God is French. They are all mistaken. Our economy is of its time and the nineteenth century would not have been capable of producing it; to give it its wrinkles and its little old-fashioned air, nothing less is necessary than the powerful means at our disposal today. Of course, at first glance, the 500,000 odd French enterprises with their eight to ten million wage earners evoke the fine days of liberalism; but it is only an illusion. Much more than by its dispersion, the liberal economy was defined by the competitive system that leads normally to concentration. In order to preserve the archaic dispersion of our stores and factories, competition had then to be suppressed: minor businesses can exist only if large-scale industry and high commerce refuse to absorb them. In short, the big have agreed to sell as dear as the small. Thereupon, the small are prohibited from being competitive: a truce *sine die* is imposed on them, and peaceful cohabitation. From Dunkirk to Menton, prices are controlled by more or less clandestine associations which gather a multitude of two-bit tradesmen and of shopkeepers around a few large concerns. To drive its tiny rivals to ruin, the big employers would only need to push production a little. They are careful not to do so and, if they agree sometimes to refurbish their equipment, it is not in order to produce more and to sell more cheaply but to increase their profits by reducing costs.

But whatever care they take to spare their neighbors, they have done nothing if they don't effectively protect them against crises: at the least puff they will be blown away. They will feed them a mouthful at a time—at the consumer's expense: at Lyon there is no doubt that the *Fabrique* could noticeably reduce its costs by entrusting the work of weaving and spinning to its own workshops: it prefers to have it done by dispersed enterprises which live on it alone. That is still not enough: the State must participate in this charity, multiply the tax reductions and bonuses, strengthen customs control. The State, that is to say the taxpayer and, to get to the point, all of France. The principal function of the tax system is to redistribute revenues: but this redistribution, in France, profits the enterprises which the normal play of competition would have eliminated. The Frenchman pays taxes in order to be able to buy his national products at high prices. As for the money which is left over—admitting that there is any left after these various deductions—a special providence keeps watch over it. Like Claudel's angel who tirelessly turns the young Prouheze away from young Rodrigue in order to put her back in the bed of an old man, the angel of Malthusianism does not tire of deflecting the flow of new investments towards the most decrepit enterprises. Just try to finance a new company in the making: they will make you repent your stubborness: "What are you trying to do? Cooperate in the development of productive forces? Who asked you to? Is production going to be developed at the very moment when large-scale industry does not dare stir for fear of crushing small-scale industry? Fortunately, capital goods are very expensive: this is normal, since they are produced at great cost. It's better to patch up the old machines: they were around when we were born and can still be of use." If you insist upon going ahead, the banks will get into the act: take your savings to them and they will give them to the State, which will swallow them up in the Public Debt. In short, people are not content with stealing the money of the poor, they sterilize that of the rich. From there on, everything is in order: outdated equipment, high costs of production; industrial prices rise rapidly, the agricultural customers desert the market. The farmers, in turn, using decrepit instruments, produce at great expense, and the rise of agricultural prices deprives agriculture of urban customers. Look at this splendid circle and see how the effects reinforce the causes: a branch of industry restricts its productive activity, it deprives certain enterprises of their habitual outlets and thus provokes the shrinking of the market; the affected enterprises will in turn restrict themselves in order to survive, which will cause new pullbacks; this revolving depression will finally come back to its point of departure, giving rise to new restrictions on the part of the manufacturing concerns which were its origin. Thus consumption adapts to production and production, in return, adjusts to consumption. The motor turns over; only one problem: it slows down with each turn and will finally stop.

When a social system is the object of so many cares and calls for so many sacrifices, can one maintain that it is the product of chance? The heavy mechanism would have broken down long ago if someone had not kept close watch over it; the cumbersome multiplicity of its wheels would have been simplified through use without the interference of an invisible hand. In other words, the "directed" dispersion of our enterprises presupposes the unity of an intention and the unity of a policy, hence the secret unification of our economy. In France, as in the United States, large-scale industry controls all the sectors of national life. The difference is that the Americans killed off their little employers, while we keep ours in chains. They live, but just barely, and their docility has been assured by persuading them that they were already dead and that they would crumble to dust if their permits to live were not extended periodically. For this reason our economic regime presents a certain resemblance to feudalism. Against competition, which daily grows more severe, against the ferocity of the barons, an increasingly dense crowd of two-bit tradesmen and shopkeepers sought protection. They finally offered their property to the big employers who gave it back to them immediately in the form of vassal-type fiefdoms and not without having, in passing, stamped them with their seal. At present, they have no more than the usufruct of their stores and factories. Or would you call them proprietors—these unfortunate vavasors who work hard, cover their expenses with difficulty and are their own wage earners? What can they do? Expand? Renew their equipment? Rationalize their enterprises? Produce or sell more? Nothing at all. However, these reprieved dead cover up for the great lords of industry: in exchange for a protection which keeps them from sinking into the proletariat, they are obliged to render services of a very particular nature: their function is to save the appearances of competitive capitalism by hiding the monopolies. Is our economy an anachronism? Say rather that it is aberrant: This system, artificially created and maintained by the efforts of our big capital, aims at the integration of productive forces: but it substitutes for technical concentration the concealed centralization of the directing organs.

It is difficult to understand why our great feudal lords are bent on ruining France. Note that they have a ready-made answer: "It is," they say, "in order to limit the damage. Let's grant that the *Fabrique* has committed the error of opening weaving workshops: come the crisis, it would have difficulty in closing them. It will be easy, on the contrary, for the *Fabrique* to drop the suppliers: the small employers are the future oblates of an elastic defense." These remarks do not enlighten us. Is it possible to admit more ingenuously that they are throwing themselves into the water for fear of rain? In case of really rough times, the encirclement preserves a certain freedom of maneuver for large outfits but, if circumstances are favorable, it prohibits them from profiting by them. If, tomorrow, demand increases, the small enterprises will be incapable of satisfying it: and it is to them that big industry has tied its fate. On a steep slope, the prudent automobile driver puts his motor in low gear. Likewise, our sagacious producers, fearing that production will bolt, put brakes on it with its own machines. For them, the future is heavy with menace and never with promise: there will be crises and then more crises and then catastrophes and then the deluge; they make themselves very small in order to offer less surface to disaster. Increase the national income? You know they don't give a damn about it: as for their own income, they think less of augmenting it than of preventing it from decreasing; they have chosen the worst policy. We know how Marxism explains overproduction and periodical crises: in a competitive regime, invested profits become increased means of production and the consumption of the wage earners declines. Could our great capitalists have read *Das Kapital?* In order to avoid crises, they have strangled competition, organized underproduction and reinvested their profits abroad.

Thus they have made us a depressive economy by their terror of depression.

The operation owes its success to the cooperation of the small employers. They mask from the consumer the Malthusianism of the higher-ups. Forced to pay their wage earners very poorly and to sell their products at high cost, they must either fold or determine prices and wages. If the Government decided to regulate the market, a bureaucrat's stroke of the pen could condemn 500,000 enterprises. Besides, these two-bit tradesmen have powerful lungs: let a minister dare to tax them, and they scream blue murder; let their personnel demand a wage increase, they will prove, figures in hand, that they do not have the means to grant it. And that is not entirely untrue, since they are always on the brink of bankruptcy. They alone are seen, they alone are heard; it would seem that the sole business of the nation is to be concerned about them: these frantic, dying men give us daily proof that nothing can be changed in France without bringing everything down. Meanwhile, sheltered behind them, the big employer proceeds with the scientific organization of his factories: if he wanted to push his machines to full capacity, prices would cave in on the spot: but he finds greater advantage in assuring himself a profit without risks by augmenting to the furthest extreme the gap between his costs and market prices.* Since that necessitates maintaining an important fraction of French industry at its lowest potential, he solemnly recognizes for the small proprietors their nominal ownership of their enterprises, i.e., he perpetuates their powerlessness and the frittering away of our resources. In return, the two-bit tradesmen will perform their function, which is to produce little at great cost: this unjustified surplus profit has the character of an annuity paid to big industry by small industry.

Thus our bourgeoisie is becoming bourgeois: it prefers comfort and stability to the indefinite growth of profits; our great feudal lords are quite simply *rentiers*. Nevertheless, this conservatism

* It even happens that large-scale industry agrees to pay slightly higher wages than small industry. It's a matter of showing its good will to the wage earners and making the two-bit tradesmen realize its power.

must be explained. Is it possible that our distrust of the future boils down to a fear of future crises? Naturally, our evolution must be seen within the European framework: the period of expansion has ended. Europe is losing its markets one after the other, everywhere one notes the tendency to exchange profit for dividends. But why has this general retraction been accentuated to such a point in France? How explain this Malthusian mania that we seem to be dying of? I think that our history will furnish the answer.

History advances in disguise: when it takes off its mask, it marks the actors and the witnesses for all time. We have never recovered from the two "moments of truth" which France experienced in the nineteenth century, and our bourgeoisie is playing a losing game today because it saw its own true face in 1848 and in 1871.

Under the July Monarchy, the French population was composed of bourgeois and animals. The king was bourgeois and the bourgeois was king; the bourgeois was man and man was bourgeois. The animal was an animal; they harnessed him to machines. Often enough, hunger drove him through the streets: they calmed him down by setting dogs loose on him. And then, one day, everything changed—that was in June of 1848. The government had heard rumors and had glued its nose to the windowpane: instead of ordinary livestock, it saw an army; the proletariat was bursting into official history and waging its first pitched battle. What a shock: these beasts fought like men; everyone was struck by the obvious logic of their maneuvers. In short, the "haves" discovered man confronting them in a species that was still foreign to them. This was the origin of their great fear: since the Other claimed to be man, all Humankind became Other and the Bourgeois recognized himself in the eyes of the Other as other than Man. If the wretches belonged to the human species, the bourgeois was distinguished from them only by the violence he inflicted on them. Suddenly, the bourgeois was defining himself by his refusals: in arrogating the right to prescribe limits to his species, he had set his own limits; if the excluded were to make themselves the measure of man, the bourgeois would perceive his humanity in others as an enemy force. Rarely has the question been better posed: submen had infiltrated mankind, they had to be dislodged from it. How? By hanging the ringleaders? That could not suffice: the bourgeoisie had lost its calm certitudes and would not regain them short of finding itself all alone in the world. And then, if the massacre had begun, it would have been dangerous not to carry it through to the very end: the massacrers would be acquitted only if they had taken care to get rid of all the witnesses. In a word, the working class had to be exterminated. The affair looked promising: mad with rage and shame, the bourgeoisie, stripped naked, wanted to put out the eyes of all the proletariat; the National Guard made it a point to shoot the wounded. Unfortunately, the repression was stopped prematurely. The elite was dismayed: ten million dead would have cleared it; 1,500 shot transformed it into a pack of murderers. When everything was over, the elite so strongly feared to see itself and to be seen that it abandoned its political rights to a mop-up team who in return guaranteed it its ownership rights. Atrocious crimes which clearly showed their bestiality were attributed to the dead; the survivors were kept in their animal condition. All the "haves" had developed a hatred for Paris: to make it healthier, it was cut into pieces; the hike in rents finished off the job by forcing the poor back outside the walls. The workers disappeared from official history. Nevertheless, they continued to live, piled up on the shadowy beaches which encircle the cities. From time to time their eyes glittered; then quickly, the heap was fired into. It was not enough to have deprived them of speech: the bourgeoisie tried to take away their memories. In vain; the workers jealously guarded their memories, preventing the bourgeoisie from freeing itself of its own: it did not for an instant forget its terror, nor the horrible visions it had had, nor the blood with which it had covered itself. This was quite clear at the fall of the Empire, when the representatives of the bourgeoisie, letting their jitters and their resentment burst out, refused to meet in Paris. The insurrection exasperted the bourgeoisie without surprising them; they were expecting it. One minute wiped out a twenty-year interlude. People returned to the fundamental question: they or we? In the eyes of their prisoners—those fixed eyes which pretty Versailles ladies practiced putting out with the tips of their parasols—the sons discovered the intolerable truth which had enraged the fathers; they resumed the interrupted carnage: by 20,000 shot and 13,000 imprisoned, of whom 3,000 died in jail, the French bourgeoisie let the world know that it had improved its techniques of extermination.

It had cause to regret it: in spite of its performance, it had started the error of 1848 all over again and, for the second time its arm had stopped too soon. Having failed to annihilate the opponent, it had won only a battle and risked losing the war of attrition. Meanwhile, Europe looked on with amazement: when it came to exploitation, foreign employers could have given us a handicap. Only—was this cleverness or clemency?—they had, in general, spared themselves recourse to weapons. Never would the English capitalists have agreed to kill the worker with their own hands; they were satisfied with bestializing him and, for the rest, they let natural laws "operate freely;" they left to God the bother of eliminating surplus workers. The British capitalists did not forgive France for revealing the nature of capitalism and changing the class struggle into civil war. Under their scorn, our bourgeoisie felt quite alone: it would have boasted willingly of having carried out in twenty-five years the two prettiest massacres in contemporary history, but the German and British puritans treated the French bourgeoisie like a black sheep. When it cried out to them: "Let us make common cause," they backed away, holding their noses. To top all the misfortune, the French bourgeoisie had to live from day to day cheek by jowl with the victims: and the victims were curiously emancipating themselves thanks to the good offices of the Cavaignacs and the Galliffets. Fifty years earlier, the workers had begged the employer to look down on their misery, certain that it would suffice for him to see their misfortunes to want to cure them; in 1848, they still believed Lamartine when he spoke to them of "the tragic misunderstanding which separates the classes." After 1871, they understood; so much the worse for the bourgeois. Elsewhere the masters succeeded in remaining invisible, in effacing themselves before what they call "the hard necessities of the liberal economy." For this reason, the worker does not really hate them—can one hate abstractions except with an abstract hatred? And besides, even if he should hate them, his hatred would carry with it his own transcendence: he knows that they consider him a beast that aspires to humanity and that must be continuously held back, but he considers them men who don't know themselves or who insist on not knowing themselves. Whatever the violence of the Revolution he hopes for, he has never proposed exterminating his class enemies: the liquidation of the bourgeoisie is to free the bourgeois from his ignorance and from the bourgeois abstraction in order to restore to him his humanity. It is not the man he detests in the bourgeois, it is the idea of suppression, the negation of man: as long as the struggle is carried out on economic terrain, the worker's hatred stays within the realm of generality.*

In 1848 and in 1871, the French bourgeoisie came out of the clouds; its arm was seen to strike. Of course capitalism, like all oppression, maintains itself by violence. But it did not require *that* violence or *that* ferocity of repression. In 1848, the insurrection of misery did not really endanger the employers. In 1871, negotiations had been initiated, a conciliation remained possible: the men of Versailles rejected everything; they were the first to pass to the attack because they wanted to kill. In a word, they played the zealot. Our bourgeoisie let itself get characterized by the insolence and cruelty of its officers, by the timorous cruelty of its politicians, by the hardness of the owners and manufacturers, by the abject terror which it showed at first, then, after victory, the ignoble jubilation of its respectable press and its respectable women; its acts have sculptured its face: it incarnates them. The workers' hatred immediately becomes incarnate in turn: its object is no longer the capitalist abstraction; the workers detest the man in the French bourgeois, the man of flesh and blood, who was made real by his historical undertaking. For all the workers of the

* He may hate certain employers famous for their harshness, but this is the *accidental* and subjective aspect of the class struggle.

world, the bourgeois is the product of capital; for our workers he is also the son of his works, a killer—and he will remain so for a long time. The young working-class generation grew up in the stifling silence of the Second Empire, it witnessed, powerless, the slayings of the Commune. When it finished its apprenticeship, the class struggle had been transported onto economic terrain. But these newcomers will never forget what they saw: when they want to anticipate the reactions of their bosses, they will remember Thiers, Galliffet and Schneider and on the basis of ineffaceable memories they will judge the boss capable of anything; they will expect to see the beginning social conflict degenerate into civil war at any moment, or rather civil war seems to them the *truth* of the class struggle; these young men are going to be irreconcilable enemies of the bourgeois: because they have learned, at a price, that each class pursues the death of the other, and above all because *wrong was done them.* Everywhere else, the working class is starved; in France alone, it has been bled. The proletarian of 1886 sold his labor power to the men who killed his father or his older brother; hence his attitude towards them, a very special mixture of twice-fired hatred, of cold hardness, of scorn, of fear and of explosive violence. Everywhere else, the workers' leaders more or less openly renounce revolutionary action in order to exploit thoroughly the advantages of universal suffrage: the laboring classes will have their representation in parliament. This means choosing integration: one accepts *the fact* of capitalism and one defends the interests of the national community in order to obtain as counterpart the improvement of social laws. Reassured, the employers develop their enterprises; people will not worry about the concentration of labor when they have the good fortune to possess an integrated proletariat. Social democracy served as hostage and intermediary; its very ambiguity* enabled it to assure the permanent linking of Capital and Labor; by simply existing, it prevented the workers' secession. When the oppressed choose

* The Socialist deputies are bourgeois and rooted in the people; they see in the bourgeois state an organ of oppression and yet they participate in public affairs.

oppressors to express their grievances, all is in order, communication is established, national unity is preserved; and then, since they use language, language can be used to mystify them. It is when the oppressed are silent that they frighten people.

In France they were silent; the proletariat had seceded. After 1871, this class that had been decimated and wronged cut itself off from the nation and formed a society within society. What did universal suffrage matter to it! This class believed it had learned at its own cost that electoral friends are most often class enemies. After all, universal suffrage gave power to the butcherers of the proletariat. The state—be it democratic or not—is "the concentration of employers, carried to the highest power." For this single reason, even if it had a chance to influence the debates, the proletariat could not agree to take part in public affairs. Send representatives to the Chamber of Deputies? Who could represent the proletariat which despises both the Right and the Left; in its eyes, all politicians are bourgeois: does anyone believe that a bourgeois, whatever his label, can defend the interests of the workers against those of the other bourgeois? France, at the end of the nineteenth century, was the only country where social democracy was deprived of a working-class base. The worker did vote, it is true, but listlessly, to satisfy his conscience, without making a tie between his functions as a voter and his activity in support of his demands. He fulfilled the former as a non-integrated individual, as an abstract citizen lost in the abstract crowd of other citizens; he supported the second as an *organic* member of a closed community. As a result, the working class, walled up in its savage isolation, now relies only on itself: it rejects Millerandism and condemns social laws when the members of parliament take the initiative to get them passed. Its leaders lose no chance to assert the autonomy of the workers' movement nor to point out the antagonism between the unions and the Party. The S.F.I.O. multiplies its advances in vain; people merely accuse it of "violating union independence." In the face of these "powwows" and these "routines," the proletariat, without any other experience than *its own,* blazes its own trail; it keeps the struggle on the only ground it can call its own: that of labor. Revolutionary syndicalism is the proletariat itself, exalted by its isolation and proud of its abandonment: betrayed by the peasants, twice betrayed by the petty bourgeois, it decides to draw everything—even its ethical values—from its own resources. The workers are living a very special moment of their history: the moment of separation. In 1871, the national community threw them out: they accepted their exile and turned the negative into the positive; what is sometimes called trade union imperialism or working class totalitarianism is only the admirable about-face of a caste of pariahs: they wished only to be *something;* they are condemned to be *nothing,* so they will demand to be *everything.**

Our bourgeois were dirtying their drawers from terror. Since the proletariat repudiated its self-styled defenders, all bridges were burned, a no-man's land peopled by corpses separated the workers from the employers. The bourgeoisie could no longer even resort to considering this silent crowd a herd of animals: since they had held the regular troops in check, the proletarians were men. Not entirely, however: if the bourgeoisie did not want them to become judges, it was quite necessary that they remain animals. A combination of man and ant, the proletarian appeared at once transparent and opaque: he put intelligence, energy and courage at the service of a mysterious animal nature and of incomprehensible instincts. The employers became fascinated by this obscure mass and discovered in it only the reflection of their own violence. They were not mistaken either: the secret of the working class is that it regards the French bourgeoisie as a gang of criminals. By seeking to challenge their silent judges, our elite confirmed their sentence:

---

* That the proletariat is the carrier of human values is not to be doubted: what it demands *for itself* it must necessarily claim *for all.* That it is the *only* carrier of these values is still admissible. But Sorel must be reproached for having confused *the fact* that the working class is the only one faithful to the humane with *the idea* that this class would be the carrier of a *unique* and actually incommunicable message. This is transforming the radical humanism of the proletarian into a *particularism*; it is stopping the proletariat *at what it is* today and refusing to take its movement into consideration. This factor of Sorelian totalitarianism resembles that of *négritude* for the colonized black.

these good people, having prolonged the massacres for a long time after the victory, could not invoke self-defense: so they had to prove that their victims deserved death by nature. They went to work on it: the proletarian, they said, is neither man nor beast. If he were a man, we would have respected him; if he were a beast, we would have caged him up without hurting him. But he is a human beast, that is to say a beast that attacks man with human means; or, if you prefer, a man whom irresistible forces drag along always towards the worst; he is sufficiently free for one to have the right to punish him, sufficiently slave by nature for one to be able to despair of his redemption; in short, you have to keep your eye on him and be ready to slaughter him at a moment's notice. Thus, in order to cleanse itself of a crime, the bourgeoisie gave itself the right to repeat the crime at will. Perhaps it should have pleaded with some appearance of reason that rage and fear had driven it insane and that it was only guilty on occasion. But no: it has insisted on justifying its offense; by justifying it, the bourgeoisie changed and became criminal by vocation.

As for the young employer who, around 1890, assured the succession of the generations, it seemed at first that he could be reproached for nothing: he was, doubtless, a murderer's son, but he was too young to have taken part in the summary executions, and the blood spilled by the parents could not be allowed to fall back on the heads of the children. So he had the choice and could, at will, repudiate his father or become obdurate. He chose, as we know, obduracy. The fact is he was brought up in hatred: he was taught to detest the victim so that he might not judge the executioners. He took everything, credits and debits, the factory and the parental crimes. Then he was forced to go one better: "On entering the factory," he said, "I found hatred and I hadn't done anything to provoke it. What do they reproach me for? We young employers haven't killed anyone yet; as far as I know, none of the young workers has as yet been killed." The proof is given: since the young bourgeois has not yet slit the worker's throat, the worker's hatred is unjustified, it is an *a priori,* the fundamental relation between the worker and his boss; the proletarian is hateful by nature;

the bourgeois is the innocent object of his detestation. The poor bourgeois! Whatever he does, it will always be the *other* who began it. I tell you, the workers seek our death! Today this argument is still the delight of the reactionary columnists: it is more than sixty years old and there's not a wrinkle in it.

From 1890 on, there wasn't a small employer who didn't identify with bourgeois society. Why was a raise demanded of him? Because they wanted to destroy the national community. Why did a trade union congress question capitalism? Because they wanted to slit his throat and rape his daughters. Thanks to this conjuring trick, the bourgeoisie, at the end of the last century, granted itself a supplementary right which could be called the right of perpetual self-defense. This select class uses as a pretext the blood it spilled in order to imagine that it is in a state of siege, beleaguered by the human beast, and that each of its members, from the cradle to the grave, is in permanent danger of death. In a word, the children of Versailles detest the French workers wholeheartedly, just as the German barons, thirty years after the peasants' war, still hated the sons and grandsons of the serfs whom their fathers had tortured. Killers will kill. A third generation of massacrers enters the race course, finds in it the dust of its elders and the track of their virtues. These younger massacrers do what they can to give the class struggle a slight appearance of vendetta; they show their hatred so that the workers will make their own apparent. Thus, each enmity is reinforced by the other; they try to maintain social tension at the extreme in such a way that the least incident can set off riot and bloody repression.* The weapons are polished up and

* The social and ideological causes of anarchism are fairly well-known; to them must be added, as far as France is concerned, an historical factor: the bloody days of 1871. Anarchist terrorism draws its psychological justification from prior massacres. An economic situation is enough to give rise to a strike movement but, to engender a murder, another murder is necessary or, in any case, special and longstanding circumstances. That is why the Ravachols have something in common with Robin Hoods and dispensers of justice: they kill those who have killed. One can say that each of them has generous and ideological motives ("Society" is this or that, Capital engenders this or that situation) and a very concrete impulsion to revenge the victims of the men of Versailles. It will be noted that Italian anarchism

the justifications are right at hand: these fine young people are getting ready for "tomorrows that sing." One can well wonder what miracle saved the proletariat from a new Saint Bartholomew's Day.

What miracle? Why quite simply the "second industrial revolution": it originates in the United States, and arrives in Europe and France. Our great bourgeoisie is on the threshold of twenty-five years of plenty which will double our cast-iron production and triple our steel production. There is good cause for rejoicing, naturally, but not without some reservations: the trouble with capitalism is that it engenders its own gravediggers; and it just so happened that the gravediggers began to multiply rapidly. Not only does the working class grow continuously from the rural influx but, on top of it, it is the working class—in the urban centers—which is having the most children. The statistics of 1906 reveal the frightening truth: for 100 white-collar workers, 299 offspring; for 100 employers 358; for 100 workers 395. And it must be added that the neo-Malthusian propaganda of the anarcho-syndicalists penetrated the "upper strata" of the proletariat: it is the unskilled workers who are the most prolific. As early as 1869, Leroy-Beaulieu gloomily noted: "The workers on the bottom rungs, those who have the crudest and and most poorly paid jobs, continue to have large families, due to lack of understanding their own interest or because of the impossibility of continence." The result: the working class represents twenty-eight percent of the population at the beginning of the Second Empire and thirty-five percent at the beginning of the twentieth century. If a name had to be given to the miracle which safeguards the proletariat, I would call it the multiplication of gravediggers. The employers get frightened: the traditional physiognomy of France is changing; in 1850, one Frenchman out of seven lived in a city of 5,000 inhabitants or more; in 1900,

---

came close on the heels of the massacre of the Milanese workers and manifested itself as a *vendetta* by the death sentence and execution of Umberto I. This phenomenon does not have an analogy in Germany and England because the class struggle, as pitiless as it has been, has in general remained on economic ground.

one Frenchman out of seven lived in a city of more than 100,000 inhabitants. It was the "country people" who aided the men of Versailles in 1871, in their great work of purification; supported by the countryside, the bourgeoisie was sure of crushing the working-class minority at the least outburst: after all a soldier is a peasant. But what would happen if the relationship were reversed? Whose turn would it be to massacre? Hatred is very contagious. Whether or not they were born in the working class, the new arrivals appropriated its memory and assumed the sufferings of the *Fédérés*. During this time, of course, Paris was purified: people lived there in a bourgeois manner, people voted well there, people tolerated only the nicer poor. But when the people of Passy raised their heads, it seemed to these bourgeois that their favorite obsession had materialized: an enormous crowd was massed at the gates of the city and grew larger and larger; the capital was in a state of siege. Our gentlemen mounted the fortifications: there was the proletariat as far as eye could see, the proletariat without end, covering the countryside and trampling down the harvests. Meanwhile, from the four corners of France, the poor wretches were setting out to join the army of gravediggers. The men of Versailles had assassinated only a handful of persons; their children suddenly discovered that these dead had innumerable descendants. This must be stopped.

How? People were already talking of integrating the working class: more easily said than done; integration means paternalism and the 1871 fusillades shattered paternalism. In the North, the Company integrated with all its might: but that was because it was operating in isolation. In these locked and bolted departments which no one entered and no one left, the question of population never arose, everything was under control; the inhabitants changed trades almost without changing residence; they left their villages only to settle in the workers' housing development nearby. There they found cadres and customs, a feudal hierarchy in which their places were already marked out. In a word, the company manufactured proletarians by imposing controlled levies on the native population. But on the outskirts of Paris, of Lyon? How could capitalism *direct* the metamorphosis of the peasant into a worker? Factories rose up ceaselessly from the land and others closed their doors; ceaselessly, the requirements of the market forced a modification in the techniques of production. These upheavals have been expressed by a permanent instability of jobs; the workers no longer have any geographical link with their place of work. In Levallois-Perret, in Charenton, the active population explodes and scatters every evening; another replaces it which returns from all over. Should one run after these semi-nomads? Where can one look for them? Competition pits itself against paternalism: the former continuously recasts the physiognomy of the working-class suburbs; as a result, these heaps of men have been perpetually stirred up by pendular movements which mechanically accomplish the transformation of the rural people into proletarians. Well then? Decentralize? Break up this enormous mass in which the least rumor is amplified to the point of becoming thunder? This dream is not new, and the employers indulged in it well before the French Revolution, when they entrusted work to the peasants outside the walls in order to escape the regulations of the guilds. Deconcentrate, decentralize, decongest: substitute for the great uncontrollable mass "little masses" spread throughout the country and therefore easier to keep well in hand! Unfortunately, the moment was not propitious; and to achieve an understanding, a master plan would have been necessary: it was again competition which interfered by sowing discord among the employers.

Well? How could capitalists prevent the terrifying rise of the proletariat? They cannot, after all, fire into the heap. The policy of extermination suits periods of unemployment. In 1848, it was the obvious thing to do; they were right to bump off men who were costly without bringing anything in. Anyway, the liberal economy—that admirable machine—would have taken on the responsibility of reestablishing equilibrium by itself; it had only been given a mere push, and no one could find fault with the good faith of those who shoot the workers to prevent them from dying of hunger. But in times of prosperity these very reasons forbid fettering the free development of economic forces. Whatever the growth of the working-class population, man power supply remains lower than demand. To fire on a man when he is worth so much is wasteful. From time to time, government can take the liberty, as it did at Fourmies, of a local rectification of the working-class forces. But even then it must act with prudence: if the working class should get angry, millions would be lost. Taine and Renan advise having recourse to the gentle forces of social Malthusianism, its effects being sufficiently slow to pass by unnoticed at first. Since—as Leroy-Beaulieu showed—the unskilled worker doesn't know his true interests (which evidently demand that he die as soon as possible and without descendants), one could try to open his eyes for him. Our Government should assign itself two tasks: to root the peasant to the soil and to facilitate the continence of the poor. A campaign of speeches is undertaken; in the Chamber of Deputies and the Senate, at fairs and conventions, at the Academy, there is only one cry: "The land is dying, the land is dead, long live the land!" It is shown with what artistry France has, until now, balanced her agriculture and her industry, the one by the other: it is in this harmonious balancing of the productive forces that the secret of our happiness and our virtues must be sought. Let's not touch it, let's not deprive the Good Lord of the desire to be French. Which means, of course: let's maintain the numerical superiority of the country people over the workers. "When the ruling class exercises absolute power," writes Mr. Sauvy, "it is populationist . . . When, for one reason or another, the ruled acquire rights and, as a result, the rulers acquire duties, the question changes its aspect . . . The rule being no longer absolute, the limitation of the number of births becomes, if not necessary, at least advantageous."

The father killed the excess workers; the son is persuaded to prevent them from being born. Excellent advice, except that he has to carry it out: in a period of industrial boom, the multiplication of workers serves the interests of production. At the beginning of this century, the proletarians were frightening at a glance because they were too numerous; but the true source of their new power is that they are not yet numerous enough; the call for man power places value on them, provokes the raising of wages, limits the practical rights of the employers. Between 1871 and 1910 the annual number of strikes went from 267 to 1,073, and the percentage of successes wavers between fifty-five and sixty percent. The oppressed enjoy the advantages of both number and scarcity. And the anarchists join the employers in the field of birth-control propaganda, only because they are making Malthusianism a weapon of the class struggle.

The French capitalists are betrayed by their own capitalism: this slave-type regime forces them to exercise a discriminatory power on the mass; but at the same time it makes the task impossible by continually augmenting their man power needs. Caught between the contradictory requirements of rule and gain, the employer tears his hair: how can he maintain profits without increasing production? How can he sterilize the proletariat without provoking a rise in wages? How can he make France a great industrial nation while conserving for it the population aspect of an agricultural country?

The answers are implicit in the questions, but our capitalists, caught between fear and the lure of gain, hesitate to look for them there: which is why one still finds two currents in the France of 1914, one "populationist" and the other Malthusian, each of which corresponds to one of the terms of the contradiction. To all appearances, populationism was bound to win: the Government made it an official doctrine; but this was hardly more than a hoax. Really to combat the fall in the birth rate, it would have been necessary to begin by obtaining a lower cost of living; and since the bourgeoisie was firmly resolved to do everything possible to prevent that, the "population policy" of our ministers was reduced to a declamatory hubbub and to ineffectual measures.* Meanwhile, everything indi-

---

* Who then supports populationism? The industrialists? Not on your life: they found in economic Malthusianism the means of adjusting the man power supply and demand. No: it is the big landowners, the military and the priests. These backward types still think they are under the *Ancien Régime,* in the time when La Morandière advised the leaders "to multiply their subjects and livestock"; they have not noticed that the bourgeoisie was losing all its powers one by one and that it had entered into its phase of *relative domination.* Big industry gives them cause for satisfaction nevertheless: their noisy populationism will mask its underground work of depopulation.

cates that the bourgeoisie had secretly chosen the other solution. Surprisingly enough, it chose it *for itself*. The sudden proliferation of the outskirts of the city seemed to provoke a collapse of the urban birth rate. As if, having failed to castrate the poor, the rich had castrated themselves: bourgeois sterility strongly resembled self-suppression,* Paris became the tomb of the race. About the same time, the *Comité des Forges,* while boasting of continuing "the magnificent progress of the preceding years," made its first trials of economic Malthusianism. Everything was set: in 1914, nothing remained but to construct the infernal machine which was to bind by a reciprocal conditioning the abortive schemes of industry to those of the bourgeois family. In order to persuade the employers, nothing less was necessary than the great shocks of the war and the postwar period. The elite perceived that civilizations are mortal: "Poor France, it has been bled. What will the universe do without her?" The universe didn't give a damn, as we all know, but these academic lamentations hid a real terror: and it wasn't because of the war or of coal; between 1917 and 1921 the employers had arrived at the certainty that the final victory would go to the proletariat. Not today, nor tomorrow, perhaps, but slowly, surely . . . it was an atrocious patent fact: yes, yes indeed! Those bastards were going to win. In seventy years, the bourgeoisie had learned nothing and forgotten nothing and all the perfumes of Arabia could not wash the blood from its hands: it suddenly found itself *the same* as in

* A strange situation. The bourgeois households (except those which belong to religious circles) generally practice birth control in all its forms, and abortion. But this same bourgeoisie supports by its votes a government which punishes by imprisonment (sometimes even by death) birth control practices. The contradiction would be enormous if care were not taken that bourgeois women are very rarely implicated in the trials of the abortionists. Hardly anyone is seen in court other than salesgirls or working women. Everything happens in appearance as if the ruling class were Malthusian for itself and populationist for the ruled classes. *But that is not true*: for the ruling class ought to show an equal concern for infantile mortality; now it is known that it goes so far as to seek children in the wombs of working class mothers only to let them die like flies afterwards. The employers do not wish that there be *lots of* workers; they simply wish to take away from the proletariat the control of its births in order that the adjustment of the man power supply and demand operate automatically within the infernal machine which they have set up.

1848, *the same* as in 1871, with the same men confronting it, the ones who were massacred in the Commune, who were going to have to be killed in vain for the third time. This time they would win: and no one would pity the bourgeoisie, since it had not, in its hour of glory, pitied anyone else. Our employers saw themselves lost, bourgeois France began to speak about itself in deeply emotional terms. About itself, that is to say, about the human race; for the bourgeoisie, to predict the end of capitalism is to predict the end of the world: since the worker is only a beast, the fate of man is in the hands of ants: when these prodigious hymenoptera take power, we will lose our worldly goods, our lives, our honor and all these delights which, only yesterday, were worth dying for; the new lords will feed us to the lions, the kingdom of man will sink into the past. And let's not count on history to do justice to us, even after the event: the ants will rewrite it. Our future is cancelled by this appalling catastrophe which will continue to destroy us after our death and which makes us in advance, in our own eyes, living dead or, rather, errors which have been explained and corrected.

At the same period, on the same continent, anger and fear were engendering fascism everywhere: it was, if I may speak in this way, the "healthy" reaction. If the Italians and the Germans, a century late, began the Saint Bartholomew massacres all over again, it was proof that they counted on winning and that they believed in capital. In the midst of these madmen, the old French bourgeoisie, burdened with years and crimes, looked defeatist. Napoleon III, the attempted *coup* of General Boulanger, the killings, the slow-death camps: the bourgeoisie experienced it all and, finally, it could say that none of it led anywhere. Capitalism produces its own death; the proletariat resembles the Lerne hydra: cut off a head and ten new ones will sprout. You might as well not bother to cut off these swarming heads: it is better to try to find the way to make them, all of them, half-die. When the bourgeois of the South and East yelled: "To arms!" the French bourgeois answered: "Temporize;" when the foreigner yelled: "Pillage and kill! Massacre!" ours answered: "Undernourish!" Yes, it is about time in our country for them to build the machine that will go around in circles: since the progress of capitalism leads it to its own destruction, progress will be stopped; since worldly goods must sooner or later pass into other hands, they will arrange to produce only the necessary and to consume all that is produced; since the twilight of man has been announced to us, we will prolong his decline by manufacturing a twilight economy. Since competition drives towards producing more, competition will be strangled; since, on days of riots, people from the working-class suburbs invade the streets of Paris, brakes will be put on technical concentration to slow down social concentration. We must, in short, stop history. For a moment. A very small moment. Our bosses intend to retard the cataclysm by a few decades in order to have time to die in peace. That doesn't present any difficulty so long as one accepts the ruin of the country: for it is not a matter of acquiring new strengths, but of knowing how to use our weaknesses and of reinforcing each one by all the others. Does the market tend to shrink? Perfect: its strangulation will be completed by raising prices. Do prices tend to rise? The tendency will be accentuated by restraining production. Are raw materials lacking? An excellent reason for the foreigner to take control. Are children scarce? They will be made scarcer still if parents are reduced to despair; economic Malthusianism bases itself on social Malthusianism and accelerates it: a child costs money before it brings in returns; it is a new enterprise and necessitates new investments; when the whole of France has an aversion to modernizing equipment, people are not going to amuse themselves by needlessly renewing the human material. And then what? Frequently, economic revivals are accompanied by population upheavals: people wanted children because they were participating in a collective undertaking whose outcome the children would see. But we are waiting only for the deluge: why have children who will be drowned? Instead, let us persuade the worker that France is going to die, that the fate of the son will be worse than that of the father: it is the best way of opening his eyes to his own interests. Thus, in the midst of the fascist uproar, our bourgeoisie organizes a slow suicide which will spread out over perhaps a half-century. When threatened, it first reacted by failure-behavior; then it took hold of its behavior and transformed it into defensive strategy. It was playing a losing game, it will therefore play "loser wins." Our revolving economy will revolve more and more slowly and, one fine day, it will cease to turn altogether. But we will be dead; if the Russians take it into their heads then to lay their hands on our beautiful France, they will find only carrion and will be properly cheated. French Malthusianism is to fascism, its Italian-German brother, what defense is to offense, passive resistance to action, feminine to masculine, pessimism to optimism—in a word, negative to positive. In both cases, the leaders must reestablish absolute domination over the led: but the Nazis sought to establish their power on the strength of their repressive apparatus; the French bourgeoisie draws its power from a depressive ultraconservatism which reduces its class enemy to impotence.

We have seen the disarray of the employers in the face of the numerical growth of the proletariat: "If it gets any bigger, it will eat us; if it becomes smaller, industry might lack hands." Malthusianism renders these fears needless: production stagnates when productivity tends to augment; the conditions for technological unemployment are present; the *containment* of the working class then seems desirable from every point of view. It is Malthusianism again, moreover, that furnishes the means of achieving this *containment.*

The proletariat increases in an exaggerated manner because the workers have too many children and because rural inhabitants leave the land in too great numbers. Economic ultraconservatism will permit the regulation of both factors.

First of all, births: from 1935 on, the employers won all down the line. Up until then nothing had worked: those crude peasants obstinately kept the fecundity of beasts. But a few years of depressive economy sufficed to provoke the collapse of the working-class birth rate: this time they understood; they abstained, just like the bourgeois. People have sought to find the cause for this sudden recourse to Malthusian practices in the internal evolution of the proletariat. This is not false: the productive class has become more homogeneous and the workers' sons are more numerous in it than farmers' sons. But the former have fewer children than the latter only because they have endured longer the ordeal of city-bred misery and despair. It will be granted, of course, that they become more and more the product of this technological universe which they are producing and that little by little they are learning the *techniques* of life and death: the fathers were subject to the fatalities of the body, the sons know how to control it. But the control of births is only a means and one which can serve very different ends; it cannot explain by itself the sudden and stubborn sterility of the new generations. It does not suffice to know about Malthusian practices; it is still necessary to want to use them. Shall we seek the reason for this "abstentionism" in the inhuman requirements of mass production? If you wish. But, in this form, the explanation remains insufficient since the same falling off of the birth rate is not registered in the advanced capitalist countries. The work of the semiskilled worker is always arduous; for it to become entirely unbearable, new norms must be applied within the framework of a depressive economy. Instead, ask the working-class couples why they don't have more children: the answer is obvious: "We know our own sufferings too well to want to inflict them on others." Condemned to live in the universe of repetition, they imagine no other future for their sons than their own past. Our criminal bourgeoisie becomes an abortionist; it pursues with its tidy methods the work of its fathers: instead of massacring, it forces the adversary to decimate himself with his own hands.

Next, the rural exodus: it must be slowed down or compensated for or both. Nothing could be easier today: it is well-known that the peasant is not lured by the deadly candle flames of the city, but pushed and driven towards them by the excess of his misery; let us guarantee him a misery without excess. The great emigrations of the nineteenth century are rich in lessons. The first, around 1860, was due to the concentration of lands and to the consequent transformations of farming methods. Industrialists invented the peasants' market; they manufactured and sold plows and chemical fertilizers: the yield and the price of land increased, the demand for man power decreased, innumerable day-laborers were thrown out on the highways; others followed them, less badly off but with no more hope of one day becoming landowners. The lesson was understood: Malthusianism puts a brake on the mechanization of agricultural techniques in order to preserve small land holdings. It is known that transport takes up more than half of the time devoted to farming. Perfect: we will show the farmers a very special solicitude by putting tractors beyond their reach and by keeping for them a good 800,000 kilometers of broken-down roads. Let them go on foot, let them scratch the earth's crust with their old tools, let them plant with their bare hands: it is the best guarantee of social stability. It is true that social phenomena are circular; and that it is just as much the smallness of the land holdings which retards the mechanization of techniques: the small farms are too tiny to profit much individually from motorization. Thus, the Malthusianism of industry finds its justification in the scarcity of demand.* But what if the peasants nevertheless banded together? If they took it into their heads to buy tractors in common? "In this domain," say the specialists, "nothing will be done without their banding together." But the point is that they do nothing: the regime has everything to fear from the social transformations that machines would introduce into rural areas. Fortunately, there is habit: our peasants are nowhere near coming to agreement. Their particularism is deplored, but it is protected undercover. The State does all that it can to save the precious peasant ignorance: in 1949, the Minister of Agriculture received 471 million francs for agricultural education as against 14 billion to the Minister of National Education for technical education and craft apprenticeships. As a result, we lack 10,000 teachers. Thanks to this carefully maintained deficit, in France, two to three percent of the people in agriculture receive a technical education; in Denmark, ninety-five percent. So there we are, completely at ease: the hoodwinking system becomes the goal of the hoodwinked. The machine revolves.

The other great exodus of the last century—that of 1880—was

* Even so it must be added (putting the threshold of profitability of tractors at 38 acres) that about 500,000 tractors would be needed. We have 130,000.

the consequence of foreign competition. Our agricultural economy remained half closed down; the development of communications put America at our doors and the New World dumped its food products on our markets. Prices collapsed: Our farmers took to the roads once again. Nearly a million men abandoned the soil. In order to force the others to remain where they were, protectionist measures were very hastily resorted to. But afterwards? How could the recurrence of the disaster be prevented? By increasing the yield? It would be necessary to mechanize: progress would be exiled by one hand only to be reintroduced by the other; in order to prevent the exodus of 1880, they would be preparing for us that of 1860. And then? Take advantage of the climate to specialize in luxury farming as England specialized in high-quality industry? Impossible: to specialize farming is to educate the farmer. And then you would be sure to get what you want to avoid: an exodus. In order to approach foreign markets, it would be necessary to mechanize, motorize, increase the yield, reduce man power, and the peasants would leave their village. Damned peasants: at the least progress, they hit the highway again! Fortunately, Malthusianism provides the means to tie them to the land: since progress drives them off, they must be protected against progress. Let them produce wheat, more wheat, nothing but wheat, at the highest price, by the most thankless labor, with the most backward technique: the call for man power will be all the greater the weaker the productivity of each worker.* An Atlantic wall is raised against outside competition, France is isolated from the world markets; as to internal competition, it is easier still; destroy it; since the big farmers of the North and West cannot put a brake on production as conveniently as the industrialists, the Government will help them: it buys their excess products only to distil them. In short, France makes a bonfire of its harvests and each Frenchman,

* In the United States during the last ten years, the productivity of agricultural workers increased five and one half percent per year. If one achieved in France, for the next 20 years, an annual increase of the same magnitude, the income from agricultural production would go from 2,500 to 3,500 billion *but* the number of workers would decrease by about thirty percent.

his stomach empty, pays to see the smoke. The State swallows up billions in the scheme, but the goal is attained: it is in France that bread costs the most* and that the farmer is the most ill-remunerated.† For this was the goal, no doubt about it: by maintaining our agricultural prices above world prices and our industrial prices above our agricultural prices, Malthusianism engenders and preserves through a continuous process of creation, that absurd and suffering monster the French peasant, whom a self-serving propaganda tries to pass off as wise, who kills himself working in order to earn nothing, thinks he possesses a plot of land of which he does not even have the usufruct, defends the interests of the large landholders and votes every five years for his misery through fear of becoming even more miserable. This man of nature does not know that he is an artificial product and that his destiny, like that of the workers, is manufactured in the cities. But he is pitted against the cities by being reminded that his creditors live there, and above all he is pitted against the workers by being shown that their demands provoke the rise in industrial prices. If the peasant began to produce more and more cheaply, if he called for an increasing number of tractors at decreasing prices, he might come to realize one day that he and the industrial workers have common interests: which is precisely what is not wanted; stability requires that the laboring classes be separated by barriers of misunderstanding and hatred: convinced that it is necessary to divide to rule, the big employers support in the countryside at our expense a horde of noble savages whose votes back up their policies.

One must not ask too much: Malthusianism restrains the chronic exodus of the rural inhabitants, it does not suppress it. Of 1,000 workers, in 1905, about 480 were in agriculture; only 370 were still so in 1930; in 1953 only 329. Emigration still exists; but its nature changes and it becomes oriented towards the minor administrative jobs. This is another effect of the depressive economy: in

* In 1951-1952, 2,800 calories cost in Germany 55,900 francs, in France 96,000 francs.

† The gross income, for two fifths of our farms, does not exceed 300,000 francs per year.

debt up to his neck, dying of hunger on a mortgaged piece of land, the peasant wants security for his son; he will make a civil servant of him. And then above all, technological progress gives rise to or develops a new class, whose rapid growth will counterbalance, then check, stop, and surpass that of the proletariat: the salaried middle class. It is well known that Colin Clark established, for most of the industrial countries, a statistical correlation between the per capita national income and the proportion of unproductive (or indirectly productive) wage earners in the active population. To adopt his terminology, the secondary group and the tertiary group* increased together and in the same proportions up to the First World War; this was the period in which capitalist industry was constituting both its cadres and the bulk of its man power. After 1918, the growth of the tertiary accelerated, while that of the secondary slowed down. The universal development of offices and of administration corresponded to the effort of enterprises to reorganize themselves according to changes in technological progress and in industrial concentration; they centralized services, "integrated" the different sectors of the business, eliminated bottlenecks, charged specialized teams with preparing and distributing tasks, with interpreting the confluence of factors and forecasting market fluctuations, and regulating distribution: the goal was to increase productivity by assuring control of production. Now, Clark's plan is turning up again in France. Except that it has become a caricature; in our country, production has stagnated since 1929, and the numerical growth of the proletariat received its cutoff signal about 1931, while the swelling of the tertiary kept becoming more pronounced.† This is the direct effect of Malthusianism: the manufacturer does not worry about increasing his

* Let us recall that, for Clark, the active population is divided into three sectors:

Primary (fishing, forestry, agriculture);
Secondary (extractive, power and manufacturing industries);
Tertiary (transportation, commerce, banks, insurance, administration, private services).

† In 1866, in manufacturing there were 10 white-collar employees for every 240 workers; in 1948, 10 for every 47.

working personnel, since he is not thinking of producing more; he increases his administrative personnel because he wants to rationalize the enterprise in order to produce at less cost. Result: an excess of 800,000 active persons in the tertiary and actual underemployment. If, in contrast, we want to satisfy the overall needs of the nation today, it would be necessary to raise production by forty-six percent: this is clearly impossible, but *primarily* because of the shortage of man power. Where are we to find the workers to construct the millions of lodgings needed? And if we give ourselves a leeway of ten years, of twenty years, how are we to fill the gaps of the secondary sector short of drawing off man power from the primary and tertiary? But the employers are very careful not to do so: they maintain a semi-unemployment in the "services"* and keep France in a state of chronic anemia in order to put a brake on the development of the working class forces. Malthusianism did not miss its mark: a backward agriculture, an excess tertiary and a deficit proletariat are enough to assure social stability. And, naturally, the employers are in the clear: underproduction provokes underconsumption, i.e., the shrinking of the market, which in turn justifies underproduction. All is for the best on the condition that we let part of the population freeze to death in the winter and starve to death all year long.

A government which sought to increase the annual rate of productivity—we have seen—would have to relieve the congestion in the tertiary; but the employers are completely at ease: it will not be accomplished tomorrow, and this draining off from the tertiary, although theoretically possible, is practically forbidden because of the *social* resistances it would arouse. Yet, the tertiary has its underpaid people whose salary is at best equal to that of a manual laborer: one might expect that these borderline people would not make any difficulty about passing from one sector to another if necessary. Well, it doesn't work that way: the job makes the employee just as the frock makes the monk. By his buying power, the white-collar worker is allied to the productive wage earner; he is

* Tertiary sector. Trans.

distinguished from him by the fact that he does not produce. The typist's work is an integral part of management activities: in this way, she considers herself integrated with the ruling classes. In all truth, her functions do not separate her from the worker as much as she thinks; of course, she does not *produce,* but after all it is she who gives materiality to instructions worked out in the offices. Thus, she seems to me very close to the typographer, who is a manual laborer. Conceptualization is the momentum of bureaucratic thought: thought denies the reality of things and its own reality, language denies the existence of the designated object: the bureaucrat keeps himself at the level of statistics, of possibles and of pure ideas, that is, ideas which do not contain the germ of further ideas. Thought will rediscover its depth only by rediscovering materiality; since it never transcends anything but objects, it will transcend itself only by receiving from the outside the objective character of an object. When she types a memorandum, the typist transforms the idea into thing, she brings about the reciprocal transcendence of the meaning by its materiality and of the material by the meaning. There is then in her work, as in that of the shipping clerk, or the postman, etc., a productive character. But it is precisely this character which the white-collar workers want to deny: they believe they are participating in the elaboration of orders and tasks and pass over in silence their real function, which is to transform them by inscribing them in reality. By their behavior and by their aspirations, these "economic weaklings" of the tertiary mean to show their membership in the upper classes which oppress them. But they only ape their employers, and their attitudes clothe a stubborn refusal to be assimilated with the productive wage earners. They have only a totally negative social reality, since they are not what they claim to be and since they reject all solidarity with those who resemble them most. It sufficed to effect a few deductions from the primary and secondary sectors to pit misery against itself by creating this white-collar proletariat which detests the true proletarians because the working-class condition horrifies it. In the framework of an expanding economy, the harm would be less great: even if, as a whole, the "services" continued to grow, the working masses would increase also; the augmentation of national income and the demand for man power would help revalue the productive sector and encourage changeovers, as in the United States, where vast floating reserves of man power are massed on both sides of the borderline and are always ready to invade the tertiary or to flow back into the secondary, according to the combination of circumstances. But economic ultraconservatism implies social ultraconservatism: of 100 sons of workers born a quarter of a century ago, 55 remained workers in large-scale and medium-sized industry, 10 returned to the land and work as agricultural laborers; 35 crossed the line, of which 21 went to increase the ranks of the white-collar proletariat. In other words, a young son of a worker in 1930 had 65 chances out of 100 to remain a worker; 86 chances out of 100 to stay within the less-favored classes. If we add to this the fact that the rural exodus has slowed down, that it is almost impossible for the lesser white-collar workers to raise themselves to bourgeois jobs, that the small employers are protected and kept at their post by the State and big industry, the inevitable conclusion is that our abortive economy has partitioned off social groups and made of France, if not entirely a caste system, at least a society in the process of stratification. The advantage is clear: Malthusianism is not satisfied with reducing the proletariat—it succeeds in isolating it. Of course, people still enter the proletariat; it still happens that people leave it: but, more and more, one is born and one dies a worker. And it is not enough to hold this dangerous class off at a distance: it is necessary to hem it in. In the last century, the bourgeoisie lived in a state of siege; today it contrives to besiege the working class group. Each clings to his position, to what he believes to be his privilege: the peasant his mortgaged land, the small employer his poor business, the minor white-collar worker his starvation job. The big boys direct everything; they would need only to make a sign in order to ruin these little people, but they will be careful not to do so; the little people are their allies, their soldiers. These men who differ from each other in every respect have a common hatred for the proletariat. Without that hatred, the small employer would realize that he is the victim and accomplice of the captains of industry, the peasant that his land flees from him and flows away like water, the white-collar worker that he is being exploited by his employer. But they see nothing: nothing but the demands of the workers, which make industrial prices rise and augment the peasant's debt, and which put the two-bit tradesman on the brink of ruin; they see nothing but the sombre abyss which attracts and repels them. French employers weigh down two thirds of the nation in order to reduce the other third to impotence.

They no longer seek to intimidate by massacres, but to weaken the combativeness of the workers from within; they do not hesitate to shut the proletariat into a no-exit situation so well devised that the proletariat strangles itself or tears itself apart if it tries to get out. The encirclement of which I was just speaking is so far only a totally external success. There is more: since production produces the worker and since Malthusianism is the dominant characteristic of our production, the French proletariat is its victim and its product: we will see how the proletariat is conditioned in its very struggle by the evil it must struggle against.

1. Our fathers tell us that France had its shock-proletariat between 1890 and 1911. And, in point of fact, it must be recognized that the working class conducted more than 18,000 strikes during those twenty-one years. Counting them by year, one would immediately distinguish high and low points. But both are in constant progression: the ranges pass from 261 to 1,025, and from 267 to 1,525. Nor does the percentage of successful strikes cease to increase: it was fifty-three percent at the end of the century, and sixty-two percent in 1910. This blessed epoch ended with the First World War: on an average, the post-war strikes have been more numerous. But until 1926, the annual minimums and maximums are in constant regression and, above all, the success percentage falls from seventy percent in the year 1919 to thirty-five percent in the years 1930-1935. After the 1936 tidal wave, the number of strikes remained very high, but the tendency towards regression picked up again and became more pronounced: it still persists today and the success percentages are below average. Are

we really to believe that the workers were more courageous at the time of revolutionary syndicalism, and their leaders more adroit, more devoted? And what would be, in this case, the cause of the change? The bourgeois commentators fidget at this question: "The cause, O my soul, the cause?" There is only one: observe the triumphal rise of the proletariat up to 1919, the blessed year when the worker had only to make a wish in order for it to be carried out, and consider what happened afterwards: the multiplication of failures, the recrudescence of misery, the collapse. 1920 was the crucial year. And why 1920? Because *it was the year of the Congress of Tours* and of the working class split; from then on the proletariat has had its cancer.

To say that the worker is losing his courage because the communist ulcer is eating away at him, is after all just too stupid. And yet it is *true* that a certain weakening of his action could be observed. Let us return to the facts and see what they reveal. First of all, we notice that the annual number of strikes and their success percentage increase with industrialization up to 1912. We have noted, on the other hand, that this ascending curve included a few drops: there were times when strikes became less frequent, and each individually had less chance of success. The general curve of prices presents the same picture: a period of expansion does not proceed without minor crises. If we compare the two curves, it is obvious that the *low points* of both correspond exactly. From 1919 to 1935, the tendency is reversed but the relationship does not change:* strikes increase with the rise in prices and decrease with their fall. The meaning is clear: in periods of rise, the worker is differently *situated* in society; he is the object of a demand. This signifies that the national income is in full upswing and that the call for manpower would suffice to provoke the wage rise. If the working class tries to add to this rise through social agitation, it is because it demands a share of the collective enrichment. In other words, the proletariat *passes to the offensive* and draws its combativeness from the confluence of circumstances. Moreover, the competitive system

* With one reservation, which we will make further on.

allows the workers to consolidate their victories: the concessions which the workers wrested from the employer could not be taken back; if the employer had sought to compensate for the wage rise by manipulating a rise in prices, he would have been lost: he had either to renounce his profits or produce more: the *praxis* was adumbrated by the movement of the economy: snatched up by currents which threw him into full battle, the worker found himself acting again without having decided to act, and the efficacy of his acts was directly proportional to the expansive force of our industry. The proletariat carved out a future for itself in the future of capitalism. We know now that this happy period was to end with the 1918 Armistice. But *praxis* creates its own image of itself by projecting into infinity the immediate future which has engendered it: workers and employers, by simply moving to the extreme, had projected in front of them the myth of progress and the reformist illusion. It sufficed that the proletariat pursue its conquest: it would constrain capitalism to produce ever more, and the proletariat would draw ever nearer to the point of taking power. This is what Jaurès expressed around 1902 in terms which seem shocking to us today, but which expressed the common hope:

> It is impossible for the trade unions to organize, to spread, to become systematized without soon intervening in the functioning of capitalist society . . . And the day when the workers' unions, even by inspection, even by overseeing, intervene also in the setting up of mechanization, the day they advise, the day they impose on the employers such and such a machine, such and such a technical apparatus, they are collaborating with the employers in the management of the capitalist machine, whether they wish to or not. And indeed, I am not angry at the proletariat for this collaboration which is a beginning of the takeover.

Thus the real but finite future of liberal capitalism was prolonged by an illusion of reality all the way to infinity, and the worker mistook it for his own future. This false perspective stirred up the workers' combativeness, while at the same time disposing the exploited, through the mirage of reformism, towards collaborating with his exploiter. The workers had not forgotten the former Saint Bartholomews, but to the extent that the bourgeois world yielded to their action, the slogan of revolutionary syndicalism became a dead letter. Revolutionaries and reformists scarcely differed from each other any more except in language: when the Revolution appears at the end of continuous progress, what distinguishes it from simple evolution? The proletariat remained hostile to politicians and to platforms, but it was inclined to come out of its voluntary exile, to infiltrate the enemy, to "make itself felt." It had learned that the social phenomenon is, as Mauss says, a total phenomenon. But the objective truth of its struggle is that the struggle integrated the proletariat more each day into capitalist society and that it was to entail, finally, the subordination of the union organizations to the State.

During depressions, on the contrary, the proletariat fights with its back to the wall. Could its courage have been taken away from it? Certainly not. But if its combativeness is measured by the number of battles waged, it must be admitted that its combativeness decreases. This is because the strike has lost its efficacy. The unemployed constitute reserves on which the employer does not hesitate to draw; and then, if his business is going poorly, he will use the existence of social conflicts as a pretext for closing it. Yesterday, the worker had his say on everything; today, if he protests, he is thrown out in the street; blessed if he at least spoke up before being fired. Yesterday, he was an integral part of the factory; today, he feels that he is being tolerated there. It is not he, of course, who undergoes this devaluation, it is his labor power. This doesn't prevent his feeling assailed in his human reality. He thought himself indispensable: they repeat to him now that only chance or the employer's benevolence keeps him in his job and that there is, in a word, a kind of injustice in giving him work when so many others are refused any. By dint of hearing repeatedly that he is lucky not to be unemployed, the worker tends to consider himself an unemployed person who was in luck: in short, in times of crisis it is unemployment which gives work its meaning. Now, the unemployed person is a product of disintegration, a passive citizen who has been driven back to the borderline of society and who is stingily supported in doing nothing in order that people will not say that he was left to die of starvation. Whether potentially or actually an unemployed person, the worker feels *superfluous:* the crisis strips him both of his powers and of his responsibilities. He had the illusion of "collaborating" with capitalism: he now realizes his impotence; it no longer suffices to fulfill properly the work contract: if he wants to keep his place, he has to *deserve* it, to become what the foremen and the employers call a "good" worker. Moreover, the employers take advantage of the situation in order to select the personnel: they will fire the "hotheads," the union members, the militants; they will keep the others, those who are kept from protesting by resignation, fatigue and family responsibilities. Thus a kind of leavening process of the working class goes on: the best militants disappear, exiled into the no man's land of unemployment. They lose both their means of action and their contact with the masses: among those who, in spite of their relative powerlessness, remain capable of exerting pressure on the employers, the proportion of those who are resigned tends to increase. The worker has lost the illusion of collaborating with capital: only yesterday, through his action in support of his demands, he was contributing to the expansion of industry; at present, he undergoes the effects of the depression without being able to stay it: his progressive integration has brought him to share the responsibilities of his exploiters; exile frees him but isolates him; he loses all contact with the society which excludes him: that is what makes him particularly hostile to political demonstrations. "The consciousness of the working class," writes Lenin, "cannot be true political consciousness if the workers are not habituated to reacting against *all* abuses, all manifestations of arbitrariness *whatever the classes* which are victims of it, and to reacting properly from the social-democratic point of view."[14] He is right no doubt, but it is infinitely easier "to inspire political revelations in the masses" in a period of industrial boom than in a

[14] *Oeuvres choisies,* Edition de Moscou, I, p. 22.

time of crisis: between the masses and the ruling classes all ties are loosened, especially that of social struggle; antagonism tends to give way to a relationship of pure juxtaposition.* Let us not go concluding that the proletariat has lost the memory of its infinite task: the truth of the matter is that the confluence of circumstances deprives it of any future by forcing it to stick to its immediate interests: it *was* fighting to conquer; it *is* fighting to preserve. Never has the truth appeared so clearly: each class pursues the death of the other; if capitalism intends to safeguard its interests, it must keep the proletariat below the subsistence minimum. Far from pushing industry to produce, the humblest demands risk driving it to ruin. And, in point of fact, if the crisis gets worse, it can lead to the Revolution, that is to the blow-up of an economy sapped by its internal contradictions. But this perspective itself often restrains trade union action: when the circumstances are not favorable to large-scale movements, a local strike risks being repressed by force or ruining the enterprise.

The lesson will not be lost: the employers use the preceding observations as a basis for artificially achieving the objective conditions of workers' discouragement. Does the number of strikes increase with production? Then they will prevent production from increasing. If it falls below a certain level, are insurrectional disturbances to be feared? They will make sure that production doesn't decrease either. It will suffice to maintain the national economy in a state of latent crisis. A paradoxical consequence of what is called the iron law of wages is that the classes reflect each other: progressive employers, a shock-proletariat; stagnating employers, a fatigued proletariat. In order to darken the workers' consciousness, our industrialists have chosen to dim themselves; they hope the atrophy of production will be lived internally by the

---

* It is a question, of course, of the *social* relationship: the economic tie remains that of exploitation. As to this mere contiguity, it must not be understood as a true and permanent relationship with the employers but as a transitory form which the class struggle takes on when the workers' combativeness tends to approach zero.

proletariat in the form of generalized anemia. Thanks to their practices, in fact, there is both too little and too much of the French proletariat. For an economy which would propose to fulfill all the needs of the nation by mass production, the proletariat is not large enough: Malthusianism thus keeps it in a state of underdevelopment. But for an economy which claims to have made itself depressive through fear of depression, the working class is liable at any moment to be too well supplied. In point of fact, crisis is our unique perspective, and the fear of crisis conditions everything. By surrounding itself with small business concerns as a safety device, large-scale industry suggests that catastrophe is at our doors; the State succeeds in convincing us by the extravagance of its precautions: it is not a question of making this catastrophe disappear entirely, but it can be deferred by an incessant vigilance. Our sole hope is apparently in the perpetuation of ultra-conservatism. Certainly, there is work for everyone but that is because the nation imposes cruel sacrifices on itself in order to *prevent* unemployment. The worker would be the first victim of an unfavorable combination of circumstances; he is therefore the first beneficiary of governmental concern; if it ceases to bar foreign products, he will find himself on the street again; and if food products alone were let in, it would be the ruin of our farmers, the peasants would move to the cities again, and would swell the proletariat at the very moment when the industrial markets would be bearing the consequences of the collapse of agricultural prices. That is not all: take the employer himself; his wage earners derive their employment from his benevolence. If he were to use foreign or colonial man power recklessly, discord and competition would be likely to divide the working class; if he perfected his manufacturing procedures without increasing production, the proletariat would be hit by technological unemployment. *De jure* the French worker is an unemployed person; he is not such *de facto* thanks to protection by the public powers and big business. He is therefore given to understand that our economy can collapse at the least puff. Let him strike if he wants: he has been warned that he has everything to lose.

He must also be convinced that he has nothing to gain by it. On this point, Malthusianism has done wonders; the method was perfected around 1936 and still serves today. According to the Matignon agreement, "real wages should be readjusted according to a decreasing scale beginning at fifteen percent for the lowest wages and going down to seven percent for the highest wages." As a matter of fact, it is not impossible that the total increase, under mass pressure, rose to twenty percent. The Government and the unions suggested to the manufacturers that they compensate for the increase in expenses by a production increase, but the employers played deaf. Backed by the two-bit tradesmen who claimed they were poverty-stricken, they deliberately raised prices. From May to November 1936, for industrial products alone, the index of gross prices indicates a rise of 35 percent. This rise continued throughout the Blum experiment; it always remained higher than the rise of wages. In February 1937, Léon Blum himself declared in a speech to the civil servants that: "The rise of the cost of living in the last eight months makes a wage earner's household bear greater expenses than the advantages which all the measures taken in their favor have been able to procure for them."

From there on, they played loop the loop and the famous "infernal cycle of prices and wages" was set up. It goes without saying that it has been presented to us as an inexorable economic law. But this is a pure lie, and there is neither law, nor cycle, nor hell. The truth is that the "mass of consumable incomes" cannot increase if production does not increase: the money-printing plate has never made anyone rich. Readjusting wages achieves only a displacement of wages: the question is at whose expense this redistribution will be made. In a liberal system the employer must put up with the new expenses; in a system of monopolies, he will have them borne by the consumer. The advantage is double: they pit the middle classes against the proletariat; they divide and rule. And then they hoodwink the worker: whatever the rise in the nominal wage is in fact, buying power does not vary. Everything changes and nothing changes; what they grant with one hand to the wage earners, the other hand takes back for their own pockets. After the popular victory of 1936, it didn't take the employers two years to bring the buying power of an hour's work back to its 1929 level. Under the occupation, it fell lower still, and today, ten years after the liberation, it has not regained its 1938 level: for a quarter of a century, in spite of diverse fluctuations and bitter social conflicts, the worker's real wage has not budged: it ceased to increase at the same time as the national income and will begin again only when national income increases. That's the conjuring trick which disconcerts the workers, and I don't think I am insulting them in comparing them to those courageous bulls that charge the cape ten times and suddenly stop, disappointed at having met only a come-on. The worker does everything he can, he imposes hardships on himself in order to win the strike, he achieves victory exhausted, and all this just to witness a general price rise which puts everything back in place. Everything is done to convince him that it wasn't worth his trouble: some manufacturers push impudence to the point of hastily raising prices in the cafeteria in order to be able to post the new prices the very day when the wage earners have got their increase. No more than an instant was needed to reverse the situation. Without a crisis and without massacres, the employers have worn out the workers' combativeness: the worker loses all hope of winning; let him work on wages if he wants to, he hasn't done anything if he doesn't block prices; but he knows very well that he will block prices only if he takes power, and the other classes seem totally determined not to let him take it. Must it be said that the proletariat, as in periods of crisis, is cut off from its future? No: but we have seen that this future is first of all that of capitalism.* Now, the depressive ultraconservatism in our country gives to our temporality its two contradictory characteristics: repetition and involution. Repetition is the immediate appearance: the days follow each other and resemble each other. For three centuries, the sons were better nourished and better housed than the fathers, but during the last twenty-five years,

* Quite simply because the revolutionary undertaking, just like the reformist undertaking, develops within the temporal framework of capitalism.

nothing has changed and the mass of goods to divide up has not increased. If there are people who live better, it is because there are others who live worse. All Europe calls us misers: and, of course, this reproach cannot apply to the proletariat which does not even have the wherewithal to be miserly; but neither does it apply to the middle classes. The meanness is in the system; one must not see a national characteristic in it, but the collective situation which our lords have made for us. In the advanced capitalist countries, avarice is an individual chance-factor which the movement of exchanges upsets. But our Malthusianism discourages investments, and in our country money plays an eminently conservative role: since it is diverted from new enterprises, it drags us toward the older ones; we are afraid of risks because we are prevented from taking them and we end up detesting what is new. It is true that we hang on to everything; but that is because a future is being made for us which is an exact duplicate of our past. Americans throw things away before having worn them out: tomorrow products will be better and cheaper. In our country, the quality of merchandise will not change; it will cost more, that's all. How can anyone be surprised then that a French home resembles a magpie's nest? Wedding gowns, worn suits, outmoded hats, empty flasks, crumpled ribbons, bashed-in boxes, pieces of string: there are in our closets enough vestiges and monuments to retrace the history of half a century.* It seems that we insist on holding on at any price to a past which is falling apart: but the fact is we are afraid of tomorrow.

This eternal recurrence hides a continual degradation: everything is being worn out; people replace things parsimoniously and above all patch them up. The country is mildewing underneath: old houses in old cities, worn out machinery in old factories, old land and old habits, populations growing old, oldish children, children of old people. Meanwhile, the other countries, launched of an immense adventure, raise their steel walls around us.

* On the appeal of Abbé Pierre, one saw astonishing flotsam and jetsam suddenly emerge: blankets, heating apparatuses, old clothing, etc.

It is they who are rising, of course: but it all looks as though we were descending. When everything is changing, it is necessary to change in order to remain the same. In insisting *in the first place* on not changing, our economy engenders its own death, and it is this death which becomes our future: they repeat to us every day that our grandeur is behind us and that we are getting further and further away from it; they praise to us some kind of a pleasant mode of life which we haven't known, which our fathers knew, perhaps, when the equipment was new. Ours is the time of recrimination and regrets; France is Jeanne the Madwoman in bed with her putrefying husband. Bourgeois thought has fallen into prophetism: people are pleased to speak of Europe in "terms of destiny;" they predict the deluge, but it is only a way of covering up the desire to die in peace: the deluge, yes, but after us. They tap on the walls, they sound out the floorings: it will all hold up until the final moving day.

The workers labor and fight in this debilitating climate. They are not in despair; and they are not contaminated by the infamous desire to die peacefully, since they are not even allowed to live in peace. But in this leaden future which is being fixed up for France, how would they not see their own future? The world of manual labor has always been more or less one of repetition. At least the worker preserved, in a period of expansion, the hope of improving his lot; at least misery and fury drove him, in a period of sharp crisis, to throw off the burden that was crushing him and to attempt revolution. But everything conspires today to convince him that his lot will not change, regardless of what he does. Benevolence is pushed to the point of explaining the situation to him several times a day: what does he expect? Doesn't he know that the national income is stagnant? Of course, a more just distribution of wealth would be desirable; the big employers would be willing to grant him certain satisfactions: unfortunately nothing can be done without ruining the small employers. And don't they also have the right to live? Ergo: nothing will budge, nothing can budge. Why should the proletariat be revolutionary? It has something to lose. And why reformist? It has nothing to gain. The worker does not fall into these traps; but, all the same, he cannot help recognizing the degree of his powerlessness. True, he still believes in the Revolution; but he only believes in it; it is no longer his daily task; he has lost the proud certitude of bringing it closer by his own efforts. He used to see in the ever increasing number of his local victories a proof of his power over the universe; but Malthusianism, by blunting his weapons, has stripped him of his hold on the world; he proved that he wasn't afraid of the employers —even the toughest—or the State, or the C.R.S.; but his principal enemy is a faceless, bodiless being that he can't manage to get hold of: *price*. In the course of these last twenty years, the unions have elaborated little by little the notion of the "subsistence minimum": and that of the "sliding scale." People have sought to see in these new ideas progress for the working class movement. But they were, quite to the contrary, born of Malthusianism: the ultraconservatism of our economy forces the worker to fight in order to maintain the *status quo*. That is what makes possible a better understanding of his present aversion to political demonstrations. For the political and social goals of the proletariat are progressive by definition: when the proletariat is in a position to impose its will on economic terrain, political action arises of itself: it is the meaning of the advances achieved in the day-to-day struggle. But when union action drags its feet, when the worker is reduced to the defensive, political ends set themselves apart in relation to economic ends; they are likely to remain up in the air: precisely because they are *advanced* positions, the worker considers them from afar as hopes or desires, but he remains entirely cut off from them and he no longer finds the paths which could bring him closer to them. He is endlessly shown the repetition of his jobs and of his efforts; if he persists in putting the Revolution last, how can he imagine that he is preparing it? The world changes and France does not budge. The French proletariat wonders if it has fallen outside of history. In China, a new society is being organized; in the U.S.S.R., the standard of living is rising. The worker in our country hears this news with mixed feelings; it exalts his courage because it proves to him that social progress is possible, it depresses him because it seems to indicate that he is standing still, separated from his Russian and Chinese comrades by a continuously increasing distance and that salvation, if it ever comes, must come to him from outside. I will come back to this: but, at the moment, if we are to understand the worker, let us recall what we experienced under the occupation, when we were waiting for the Allies to win for us a war which we did not have the means to win with them.* Thus the Malthusian strategy permits the employers to keep the initiative: the depressive economy has command, from the outside, of the workers' *praxis,* it roughs out the possible operations, it determines their characteristics, it delimits their range and meaning; it determines the ends and the chances of victory. As soon as the worker gets involved in this prefabricated action, it clamps down on him: he discovers himself imprisoned in a contrived space which imposes on him its paths, its curvature, and its perspectives; the discouragement of the proletariat is a product of industrial underproduction; it subjectively expresses the objective limits which the structure of the economy imposes on *praxis.*

2. Malthusianism, then, seeks to dishearten the worker. But that is not yet enough: one must divide in order to rule.

Marchal has shown that between 1890 and 1936 the number of strikes increased and decreased at the same time as production. But he was the first to reveal a remarkable exception: from 1920 on, both the frequency of strikes and their success percentage were in full decline; however, until 1929, our economy remained in a

---

* There was the Resistance, of course—and believe me, I do not underestimate the importance of its action; and there was also the invisible passive resistance of the masses: all of that counts. There are today the Communist Party and the union militants; there is the enormous weight of the masses and the action which they exercise from a distance—be they inert—on all the social milieux. But the Resistance grew out of our military defeat; and the present organizations of the proletariat derive their principal characteristics from the great working class ebb which begins with Malthusianism.

state of expansion. The fact is explained by working-class dissensions, and this is not wrong. But where do these dissensions come from? Ah! I am told, from the war, from the socialist betrayal, from the Russian Revolution, from everything except from the Malthusianism which was not yet in practice when they appeared. Granted: union pluralism precedes industrial stagnation, and our Malthusians found the proletariat cut in half. But who says that they did not exploit this opportunity to the hilt and perpetuate a temporary state by reducing production?

The pre-World War I hierarchical proletariat was the product of the steam engine. The latter replaced muscle, but not skill; it remained *dependent*: it had to be kept up, regulated, directed, watched over. The lathe relieved the worker from moving his tool and from applying it to the piece to be cut out: someone still had to prepare the job, fix the position of the piece, the angles of the cut, the speeds, etc. By its very imperfections, the lathe defined the lathe operator: there are special profiles which the machine could not give and which had to be obtained by hand work and effected by means of auxiliary tools. The operation, and consequently, the operator, preserved in part an artisan character. Society trained the man the machine required: it conferred professional knowledge and technical experience on him through an apprenticeship of many years; competition selected the best afterwards: those who showed proof of tact, or an ability "to size up," of bodily dexterity, of initiative. But it was expensive to make a skilled worker: in a liberal capitalist system, it is the parents who must assume the major part of the costs. The peasants who have just left the land and the sons of unskilled workers do not have, for the most part, either the means or the will to do their apprenticeship.*

Thus the requirements of the machine go so far as to prescribe the manner of recruitment. The skilled workers are sons of skilled

* In *Travaux,* Georges Navel shows the difficulties that the son of an unskilled worker still met about 1919 in order to become skilled. He and two of his brothers were obliged to fake in order to become assembler, metalworker or fitter without working their way through an apprenticeship.

workers or of artisans; this aristocracy includes a few newcomers but most of its members have access to it primarily by birthright. To be sure, the elite worker is exploited right along with his comrades: but he differs from them because his competence singles him out to run a machine, he is the producer *par excellence*. As the principal agent and principal witness of the transformation of raw material into a manufactured product, he becomes self-aware in the fashioning of the inert thing. For him, apprenticeship represents much more than technical training: he sees in it a revolutionary initiation and a *rite de passage* which grants him access to his caste and to the working world.

The machine, too, assures the unity of the work group, or rather it is assured by the complex and synthetic operation that the skilled worker carried out by means of the machine and with the assistance of the other workers. In a mechanized enterprise, at the beginning of the century, out of one hundred workers there were about twenty "machinists" who had completed their four years of apprenticeship and who devoted themselves to installation and adjustment; there were about 60 drillers or punchers, lathe, stamping and milling machine operators, skillful and competent workers but who were far from having the former's training, finally about 20 unskilled workers who lived apart from the machines and who took no part in the manufacturing. The machinist directed both his machine and his men; the semiskilled workers who surrounded him he called his "accessories," whom he had "do odd jobs" for him; the unskilled workers, too, obeyed him: they spared him the dirty jobs. This technical hierarchy was underscored by the hierarchy of wages: the skilled worker earned seven francs when the "work horse" earned four. During this period, people began to speak of "the masses" to designate the working class, and they were wrong: the masses are amorphous and homogeneous, the proletariat of 1900 was profoundly differentiated, the hierarchy of labor and wages was met again intact on the social and political terrain. The simple adding up of the unskilled workers themselves cannot suffice to constitute "the masses": it is by abstraction that one could separate them from the other workers, and each of them is more narrowly tied to his shop comrades than to the other unskilled workers of the factory and the city; the working class is constituted by a multitude of solar systems, small structured groups that gravitate around a machine. These work teams communicate via the top: the form of the trade-union apparatus is determined by the composition of the working class: in 1912, France had more than six million manual workers and the C.G.T. only 400,000 members. Nonetheless, strikes were tough, expeditious, and disciplined, and they succeeded most of the time. That means that one militant was in general enough to pull along about fifteen nonunionists. In the struggle for their demands, the skilled workers kept the authority they enjoyed during work. Not all of them, however, since only one out of three joined the union: the best among them, those who had had the courage to give themselves a general education and who added to their revolutionary will the clearest consciousness of the workers' condition. To the steam engine corresponded a hierarchical proletariat which in turn produced a skeletal unionism with the shop as its base, the enterprise for its battlefield and the elite worker as its militant.

It seems that those were the good old days: a quarter of a century after its demise, our fine friends discovered revolutionary syndicalism and never cease to hold it up to us as an example: in the golden age of the Congress of Amiens, the bureaucracy did not exist; the union apparatus emanated directly from the proletariat and resided in it as a simple internal principal of organization; the defense of the workers' interests was assured by the workers themselves; one was militant without leaving the shop, hence without losing contact with the concrete problems of the enterprise. In point of fact, the Bergsonian general staff of the C.G.T. made itself the champion of spontaneity: it was Pelloutier who evoked a "mysterious bond" uniting the workers' organizations, and Greffuelhe who praised "the spontaneous and creative action" of French unionism; the union Self (*Moi*), in sum, plunged its roots into the inner Self (*Moi*) of the proletariat.

Before the First World War, the class struggle had a certain something.

Of course, this is stuff and nonsense: the *élan vital* of the working classes concealed the dictatorship of the skilled elite. The "active minority" scorns what it already calls "the mass" and detests democracy. "It is not," says Lagardelle, "the heavy and backward mass which must express itself here, as in a democracy, before undertaking the struggle; numbers no longer make the law. But there is formed an active elite which, by its quality, carries the mass along and orients it in the paths of combat." Let us translate: the "upper" stratum of the proletariat takes the responsibility of setting forth both its own demands and those of the "less favored"; this elite aspires to be sole judge of the good of all and seeks less to understand the popular resistance than to break it. I will not do the injustice of claiming that these admirable fighters have betrayed their class; if they distrust their comrades it is because they suspect them of being more sheeplike than revolutionary. They have maintained constant concern for reconciling their interests with those of the unskilled workers, and, at the beginning at least, in a prosperous country in the process of industrialization, these reconciliations were not too difficult. They became more and more infrequent in the last pre-war years. The workers' struggle has two sides to it: for the active minority, it is a concrete experience and an instrument of liberation; for the majority which follows the active minority, it often remains an abstract imperative. And when the militants involve the unskilled workers in an action for their demands, one can well say, with our fine friends, that the working class united in action and that its unity remains immanent. In fact, more and more frequently the militants struggle on two fronts: against their comrades and against the heads of the enterprise. At the top, however, one finds a handful of militants whose views are broader and who proudly call themselves "active minority": against the particularism of the elite, they aim at defending the general interests of the class. But when it tries to convert the skilled workers to industrial unionism and to centralization, this minority goes against the current. The working-class aristocracy remains favorable to "anarchistic administration" and to craft unionism. The Pelloutiers, Pougets, Merrheims, Monattes would have lost the game without the sudden conversion of industry.

1884: the first practical transformers made their appearance. Ten years later the electric motor competed everywhere with the internal combustion engine, and encouraged mechanization: technological progress gradually reduced the part of the worker in manufacturing, which led to the progressive downgrading of skilled manual labor. The new lathe produced new lathe operators: it needed only a flick which was transmitted by itself to the executing mechanisms. Suddenly, between the unskilled workers and the near-skilled, that unknown person, the semiskilled worker was discovered: he acceded to the machines like a skilled worker and fulfilled his function without serving an apprenticeship,* like an unskilled worker. He had already been around, of course, but no one had noticed him. Where had he come from? From everywhere: he might be a country lad who had just arrived in the city, but most often he was an unskilled worker from another industry. As early as 1900, in Saint-Etienne, in certain shops of the *Manufacture d'Armes,* "there are 50 machinists out of 250 workers; all the others are former miners or former weavers;* they have in their hands improved machines which render professional knowledge useless."[15] These newcomers were still timid: they had neither the time, nor the will, nor the strength to organize by themselves; they called for the help of the skilled and militant elite. In 1912, Merrheim, at the national C.G.T. Congress at Le Havre, attributed this speech to a metalworker from the East: "How can you expect us poor metalworkers, who are tired in the evening when we get home, to concern ourselves with the union? Those who could concern themselves with it, the technical workers, have created craft unions."

---

* Or after a very short apprenticeship.
* Mechanization was already very advanced in the textile industry. The weavers were semiskilled workers who had changed machines.
[15] Quoted by Collinet: *Esprit du syndicalisme,* p. 24.

Obviously, their demands were modest: and if they called for the right to join union organizations, it was with the fixed intention of delegating their powers to the elite. But the elite paid no heed: it bitterly defended aristocratic unionism against the newcomers. Rather than merge with the metalworkers and the moulders in order to form an industrial union, the Federation of Machinists, in 1910, preferred to leave the C.G.T. In 1900, there were 51 industrial unions as against 34 craft unions; in 1911, there were 142 as against 114; the proportion did not change. During this time, without skill, without union experience, without political instruction, the semiskilled worker was left to the mercy of the employers' propaganda and oppression. I recall the principal features of this new proletarian who had been suddenly engendered by modern machines and techniques of organization.*

Decided in some upstairs office, with regard to other operations being carried out simultaneously in the enterprise, the rhythm of his work imposed itself on him as an enemy force and governed him from the outside; his fatigue resulted less from a muscular expenditure of energy than from a continual nervous tension, a constant effort to adapt to pre-established norms. At the end of a day, his fatigue would stick to his skin; it accompanied him all the way to his sleep and he would find it again on awakening; this chronic weariness has become second nature to him; it is the very manner by which he senses his body. It is written on his face and is evident in his gait; it limits his powers and makes of him, in the proper sense of the word, a *diminished* man.

The degradation of work carries with it the devaluation of knowledge; the employers do not like the worker to be educated; nor above all to be intelligent: intelligence is harmful to output: the semiskilled worker and the machine achieve such a perfect symbiosis that an idea in the one is comparable to the breakdown of the other. Yet total lack of attention is impossible: distraction

* It goes without saying that it is not a question here of putting semi-automation on trial, which would be absurd, but of showing its effects *within the framework of capitalist production.*

and forgetfulness would provoke as many disasters as would lucid thought; it is necessary *to be on the job,* a vigilance without content, a captive consciousness which keeps itself on the alert only to be better able to suppress itself. But if the worker cleanses himself of his own thoughts, it is in order to make room for those of others: ever since the rationalization of industry consecrated the divorce between conception and execution, he does not know the meaning of his acts. People steal them from him, or condition them from the outside, they decide in his place on the goal and the scope of those acts. The very moment he makes himself the agent of production, he feels himself acted upon; in the depths of his subjectivity, he experiences himself as object. An involuntary accomplice of the employer, he strives to forget the little that he has learned because understanding would make his condition intolerable for him. He takes refuge in passivity because he has been deprived of all initiative; since he has been stripped of his thought, how would he know that ideas are the products of men? He gets used to seeing in the order established by the technicians, an external fatality of which he is the first victim. The social history of the rationalization of industry can be summed up in two formulas. At the end of the last century, Taylor said *to* the workers: "Don't try to think; others will do that for you." Thirty years later, Ford said *of* the workers: "They don't like to think for themselves."

The mechanization of work alters human relationships. Before 1914, the proletariat was a constellation. This aristocratic structure did not exclude solidarity or a man-to-man bond which vaguely resembled vassalage. Between the semiskilled worker and the "elites," solidarity of work was broken: the skilled worker would determine the task of the unskilled worker; that of the semiskilled worker was decided by the man in the offices; that man decided it from a great distance and for everyone, without ever seeing anyone. Today the semiskilled worker has contact only with other semiskilled workers; moreover the machine interposes its inflexibility between them: each perceives the existence of his neighbors in the form of the collective rhythm to which he must adapt himself; the *other person* makes his appearance with the delays, the mistakes or the failures: in the mechanical universe, another person is an error entailing a loss of earnings. The semi-automatic machine is the instrument *par excellence* for massification: it blows apart the internal structures of the proletariat; there remain homogeneous molecules separated from each other by an inert and inelastic medium.

By isolating him from his comrades, fragmented work sends the semiskilled worker back to himself; but he finds in himself only a general and formal essence: what he does, everyone can do, therefore he is the same as everyone else, and his *personal* reality is only a mirage. Meanwhile, imperious needs bring him back to the pure subjectivity of desire and suffering: hunger, pain, fatigue push him to the preference for self but without justifying that preference. Why you rather than me?—Because I am I. —And who are you? —The same as you. The unjustifiable subjectivity enters into conflict with the objective interchangeability. On an individual level, it leads to a profound feeling of inferiority; on a collective level, the classical forms of the struggle for demands have had their day: the appearance of these workers who have no professional value, who are *replaceable,* and obsessed by the fear of being unemployed, risks making strikes ineffective.

What is noticeable at first, in fact, is not so much the promotion of an unknown worker as the elimination of the old ones. The machinists whom the 1907 crisis threw out on the streets were not to be reintegrated; in 1913, during the strike at the Renault factories, the skilled workers held out longer than the others; they knew they were irreplaceable; the employer would ultimately have to give in. The employer did not give in: he replaced them with machines, with untrained workers; it became apparent to everyone that the skilled worker had had his day. Meanwhile, the semiskilled workers multiplied and unionism vegetated, was demoralized and deprived of its principal weapon; to these new men, without a tradition or a past, the old militants no longer had anything to say. And then suddenly, in August 1914, the war opened the eyes of the unionists: they discovered the masses; it was a rude surprise when they saw them issuing forth from the earth shouting: "On to Berlin!" Twenty years of propaganda only to end up in this madness? "What's left of our action?" a militant wondered. "What's left of our anti-war meetings?" And another one: "In a railway stock car, with other men who were bawling 'On to Berlin,' I sensed the bankruptcy of the C.G.T., the bankruptcy of the educators, the intellectual bankruptcy of the country." And Merrheim: "The working class was raised up by a formidable wave of nationalism," and Monatte: "The wave passed, it carried us along with it." Unknown, then suddenly discovered, the masses made necessary the creation of a mass unionism, of a mass party, of a new propaganda and a new ideology. Incapable of fulfilling these tasks, revolutionary syndicalism suddenly discovered that it was outworn! The old apparatus of the working class fell outside of the movement; the war caught the leaders without the masses, and the masses without protection. These young crowds, victims of the gap which separated their productive activity from the real content of their hope, could not yet be for themselves what they were in themselves (*en soi*): their radicalism, their instability, their fury soon followed by discouragement quite simply expresssed the fact that the new condition of the workers was unbearable; the fascinating myth of the war was to mislead their revolutionary aspirations for a while and make them aware of the violence within them: but this violence remained captive, alienated.

War, again, was to result in demystification. From the war, not from the circumstances of production; it was not the union leaders, it was the Somme, it was Verdun that tore their illusory self-image to shreds. "When I met them again at Verdun," writes Dumoulin, "they were angry at everyone: at the journalists, at the deputies, at the socialists, at the Parisians, at the police, at those in the rear. The strongest impression, the clearest among them was that of hog-wash, of lying, of exaggeration, of error."

When they poured back, in 1919, drunk with anger and distrust, the masses were available. Just about everywhere in Europe, revolutions depended on the encounter between soldiers and workers. In our country, two million demobilized men mixed in with three or four million factory workers. An unstable mixture, an explosive one: new militants swelled the cadres of the C.G.T. It seems that the Revolution was possible and that the bourgeoisie was ready "to make the greatest sacrifices to the proletariat." But the strike of June 1919 proved that the masses were not ready. How could they have been? Who had prepared them? On June 2, the Parisian metalworkers quit work; the strike spread to three unions in Seine-et-Oise; there are 130,000 strikers, 80,000 union cards are handed out. A semi-political, semi-guild strike: There are specific grievances, but also "a great anguish . . . a general sentiment which concerns the entire proletariat." The strike was directed at first by a *Negotiating Committee (Comité d'entente)*, a union organism which had just been created. But the great crowd of new union members—more than half of the strikers—was distrustful of all delegates, invaded the premises of the union meeting, called its own representatives "sell-outs" and finally elected an Action Committee (*Comité d'action*) which was to replace the Negotiating Committee. The Negotiating Committee abdicated its authority to the Federation of Metalworkers, which took over the strike. The Action Committee burst into the Federation's offices on June 22, insisted on attending their meetings, and dubbed the leaders "dispensers of hog-wash." Nevertheless, the Federation wanted a general strike. It asked for a meeting of the Coordinating Committee of Union Federations (*Cartel interfédéral*). The latter refused to extend the conflict, but advised the strikers against going back to work without having obtained guarantees. Now, as early as June 26, the Action Committee itself, drawing inferences from a discouragement which long preceded the Coordinating Committee's decision, had given the order to stop the strike. The defeat was total; people returned to the machines without having obtained anything: the masses had found themselves at odds with a bureaucracy whose prudent methods and long-term forecasts disconcerted them, and they had elected a Committee whose incompetence and turbulence had compromised firmness. The event has the value of *a clue*. A recent product of the new mechanization, the masses needed a leadership and a discipline appropriate to their fundamental structure; they rejected the unionists who had rejected them before the war, they would have condescended to submit themselves only to an iron hand implacably fighting the constant unbalance of mass formations. Where could such an authority have been found in 1919? The leaders of the S.F.I.O. and of the C.G.T. blamed themselves, justified themselves or made confessions; they were in agreement only in their condemnation of the newcomers. The June strike furnished them with new "whereas-es" to back up their sentence: one of them spoke of "Committees of Disobedience and Indiscipline." Another deplored the fact that "the instincts of the street crowd which howls and lynches have been brought into our meetings . . ." For a third, the worst disaster was "to have met in France a revolutionary situation without a revolutionary spirit in the masses." Blum was to say in 1921: "We know what unorganized masses are . . . We know behind whom they will march one day and behind whom they will follow the day after . . . Those who would have marched behind you one day might be the first to push you to the wall the next . . . The Revolution will not be made with these packs which run behind all horses."

And yet one had either to give up making the Revolution or to make it with "these packs." As for being unorganized, they were so without any doubt, but this was quite simply the proof that they needed an organization. Unfortunately, they could not organize internally because they had failed to become cognizant of their own needs. Torn between a dying aristocracy and a multitude which was wearing out its revolt in disorder, the question was whether or not the working class would be reduced to impotence.

No: these discords seemed temporary; the situation could not fail to evolve: of course, the organization was not going to emerge suddenly from the anarchic crowd, but already the youngest militants of the C.G.T. and of the S.F.I.O. were approaching the Kienthalians and the Socialist opposition; their war experiences had led them all to condemn the Second International; they had decided to put themselves at the service of the masses and to give the masses the apparatus they needed.

And then, above all, people thought that the movement of concentration was going to continue and that it would finally eliminate the workers' aristocracy. In order to persuade oneself that the semi-skilled workers would finally constitute almost all of the proletariat, it sufficed, about 1925, to glance at the statistics furnished by the Ford Company:[16] in this enterprise, one worker out of a hundred still merited the name of skilled worker; out of ten workers eight were semiskilled. This relentless downgrading was appalling: it brought the proud militants of revolutionary syndicalism down to the level of those subhumans whom Marx speaks of. But, on the other hand, it eliminated the unskilled worker. And above all, it gave back its strength to the workers' movement. When this so homogeneous "neo-proletariat" had found its cadres and its formula for battle, its cohesion would be more rigorous than ever and workers' unity would cease to be merely a word.

People had reckoned without our Malthusians. By stopping the movement of concentration, they put off unification indefinitely. Large-scale industry absorbs no more than forty-five percent of the workers, the rest are divided among 500,000 enterprises. Naturally, the most important establishments are not always the best equipped: in the automobile industry, the construction sector is much more highly concentrated and much less automated than that of accessories. All the same, the average enterprise does not have the means to push automation; the small enterprise remains manual. In 1948, of the 3,677,000 workers in manufacturing

[16] Percentage of workers	43%	36%	6%	14%	1%
Length of training at Ford.	not more than a day	from 1 to 8 days	from 1 to two weeks	from 1 month to a year	Up to six years

Table from Julius Hirsch: *Das Amerikanische Wirtschaftswunder.* Reproduced by Friedmann: *Problèmes humains du machinisme industriel.*

there were 1,306,000 skilled workers, 1,320,000 semi-skilled, and 1,051,000 unskilled workers. The first two categories just about balance each other.* The third is very divided: in printing and in construction, where skilled workers are by far the most numerous, the archaic structure of the proletariat is preserved: the unskilled worker works under their orders. In the iron and steel industry and in textiles, it is the semiskilled worker who dominates: the skilled workers are separated from the manufacturing process; they form maintenance and installation teams which no longer have any contact with the other workers:† the semi-skilled and unskilled workers thus form an almost homogeneous mass, primarily because of the fact that a few hours or a few days suffice to change the latter into the former. It must not be thought that this upheaval causes the proletariat to benefit from a new experience: on the contrary it provokes a break in experience and a bifurcation of the historical *subject:* the working class, to the greater joy of the employers, runs the risk of remaining cut in two almost equal chunks, which have neither the same structures, nor the same values, nor the same interests, nor the same techniques of organization and combat.

Duality of Values

The skilled worker has always based his demands on the qualifications necessary for his work. He is the true producer, the sole source of all wealth: he transforms the raw material into social goods. The idea of a general strike, so popular before 1914, grew out of this proud self-consciousness. In order to bring down bourgeois society, the worker has only to fold his arms; if he demands ownership of his instruments of labor, it is because he is the only one capable of using them. Besides, in small enterprises, his technical knowledge is rarely below that of the employer; the union group has *skills* and therefore feels entitled to control production: it will transform itself quite naturally, right

* 35.5% as against 35.9%.
† Often the sites of *manufacturing* are situated several miles from those of tool-making for the plant.

after the Revolution, into an organ of management. Since its rights flow from its merits, this aristocracy is not far from considering itself the sole victim of capitalism. At the Federation's Congress of 1908, a speech by a machinist expressed the general feeling: "To deny the professional value of the worker is more or less to grant extenuating circumstances to capitalist exploitation." Whence a peevish mind would conclude without too much difficulty that the exploitation of the unskilled workers is not, after all, so criminal. The working-class elite did not go that far: but it is true that it considered its helpers as "dead-weights." Did it acknowledge them rights? It is doubtful. Let us say that it saw in them the permanent objects of its generosity. This humanism of labor is ambiguous: one will readily admit that it goes a step beyond the humanism of wealth. And yet it is only a stage; if one stops there, the multitude will remain excluded from humanity. It is necessary, you say, to merit being a man. That is fine as long as one can *acquire* merit. But what are you going to do with those who do not have the means for acquiring it?

The new proletariat cannot claim the least merit, since everything has been brought into play to make it understand that it hasn't any. Yet fatigue and misery overwhelm it: it must die or obtain satisfaction. On what, then, will it base its demands? Well, precisely on nothing. Or, if you prefer, on the demands themselves. The need creates the right. With the appearance of the masses, an overturn of values took place; automation radicalized humanism. Let us not take the semiskilled worker for a proud man conscious of his rights: he is "a subhuman conscious of his subhumanity" who demands the right to be a man. The humanism of need is, consequently, the only one that has all humanity as its object: the elimination of merit blows up the last barrier which separated men. But this new humanism is a need itself; it is lived *hollowly* like the very sense of an inadmissible frustration. For the skilled workers, man is complete, all he has to do is reorganize society; for the unskilled worker, man is yet to be made: he is *what man lacks,* what is *in question* for each one of us at every instant, what, without ever having been, continually risks being lost.

Everything would be for the best if the humanism of labor had progressively been obliterated by the humanism of need: and that is what would have taken place if Malthusianism had not stopped the industrial revolution. Today the two humanisms coexist and this coexistence muddles everything: if the former becomes set and establishes a position for itself, it becomes the enemy of the latter. The masses, on the other hand, are secretly contaminated by the ideology of the workers' elite. They have no shame before the bourgeois; for the best of them, no matter what he does, will never *merit* the privileges he enjoys; but the skilled workers belong to the proletariat, they are exploited just as the semiskilled worker is, and if they live a little better than he, this difference appears negligible as soon as one compares their standard of living with that of the bourgeois. And, above all, they claim to owe these slight advantages to their merit. Is that true? I said that they were, for the most part, sons of skilled workers: but after all, that is not inscribed on their foreheads. The semiskilled worker tells himself that if his parents had imposed a few sacrifices on themselves, they too would have been able to put him through an apprenticeship. Or, perhaps, he reproaches himself for having lacked will, perseverance. The apparent inequality of conditions stresses in his eyes the inequality of values; if the skilled worker derives his worth from his operation, the semiskilled worker is worth nothing since he is, by definition, replaceable. In short, he is ashamed before those who ought to be his comrades in arms; his combativeness is likely to be thereby decreased. In order to free the masses from their feeling of inferiority, it was necessary to eliminate systematically all the pre-war socialist values; it was necessary to make the masses understand that they were offering all men the chance to look at man and society *in their truth,* that is to say, with the eyes of the least favored. Since technological evolution eventually downgraded labor, that ultimate superiority of man over man, it was necessary to show to this young barbarism, against all ethics and all elites, that "superiorities" are mutilations, that the only human relationship is that of *real,* total man with total man and that this relationship, travestied or passed over in silence, exists permanently within the masses and exists only there. But to the extent that the multitude is penetrated by this radical ideology, the skilled workers, who see their *worth* contested, hold doggedly to their positions. The aristocracy becomes aware of itself when it is attacked: during the last pre-World War I years, as a reaction against the rise of the masses, well-intentioned theorists baptized minority unionism "knight-errantry," and sought to make of the militant a new Knight Templar: a benevolent despot, the skilled worker agrees to devote himself to the masses, but he refuses them the right to defend their interests by themselves. The post-war period brought about a new leavening process and revolutionary syndicalism disappeared. But not its spirit: even in the C.G.T.U. of 1921 to 1927, the craft unionists were still resisting the Communists bitterly. From 1919 to 1934, Jouhaux's C.G.T. was forced to become bureaucratic "as a result of the growing complexity of union tasks," but the union official represented only the workers' elite and the masses remained outside the organization. In 1936, Sémard declared, at the Congress of Toulouse: "Two principle ideologies continue to confront each other in the workers' movement and in the union movement. These two ideologies are those of Proudhon and of Marx." Jouhaux rightly answered him: "Since 1909, I have never heard militants who took the floor to set forth their points of view avail themselves of Marx or Proudhon." He was right *formally* but in fact he was laying a smoke screen. For the two tendencies Sémard was speaking of are not *in the first instance* Marxist or Proudhonian: they exist in the French proletariat outside of any philosophical or political culture. Ask a Communist militant what he thinks of "human *dignity*:" he will shrug his shoulders. Is it by chance that, under Jouhaux's reign, the Federation of Metalworkers and the C.G.T. declared themselves in favor of the scientific organization of labor, provided it "does not violate human dignity"[17] and that these same words recurred in 1945 in a declaration of the C.F.T.C.? The "dignity" of the skilled worker is the superiority of his operation. He is *already* a man (since he is proud of his work), *already* free (since the uni-

---

[17] National Congress of Metalworkers, 1927. Cited by Collinet, *op. cit.*, pp. 60-61.

versal machine leaves wide room for initiative). In the name of freedom and dignity, he demands a more just society which will recognize his worth and his rights. The *masses* are not worthy; they can't even imagine what freedom is: but their simple existence introduces, like a splinter in the flesh, the radical demand for the human in an inhuman society.

Duality of Interests

It has often been noted—and I will not labor the point—that the mass submits to a rhythm of work which is repugnant to the skilled worker. In the Citroën plants, the strikes of 1926 and of 1927 pitted the toolmakers against those on the assembly line. The unionists—all skilled workers—wanted to lower the norms of output; the semiskilled workers wanted to step up the pace: since, in any case, their work was a curse, they felt that it might as well pay. Their piecework earnings perhaps equalled the hourly earnings of the skilled worker: it was a revenge. At its birth, work on the assembly line and on semi-automatic machines was condemned by the representatives of the proletariat: but, in the long run, it produced new workers who lived off mechanization, and, willy-nilly, were obliged to declare themselves fully in favor of it. There is no doubt, in fact, that the "neo-proletariat," by its very function, responds to the requirements of mass production: it became evident in the United States when the manufacturers, under the prodding of competition, sought to widen the domestic market and take on the masses as customers, by increasing output in order to lower costs. That certainly does not mean that the masses work for themselves: between the semiskilled worker-producer and the semiskilled worker-consumer is interposed the screen of profits and exploitation. But it is no less true that the raising of the standard of living accompanies the increase of productivity. In 1949, for one hour of work, an American worker produced four times more than a French worker. The same year, the national per capita income rose to $1,453 in the United States as against $482 in France. The interest of the semiskilled worker in our country is not to intensify his effort or to increase the number of his working hours: for the same effort and for the same number of hours, he must demand the progressive augmentation of his productivity. But that implies nothing less than the abandonment of Malthusian practices: it means renewing plant equipment and pushing concentration, efficiency and automation. Now, the fate of the skilled worker depends on the maintenance of archaic forms of production: in a way, he had a stake in Malthusianism. Certainly, the rise in his living standard can compensate for the skill-downgrading of work and the smashing of the hierarchy of wages: but the privileges of the elite are at stake, its pride, its "joy in work" and its dignity, that is to say, the consciousness of its superiority. Thus, the demands of the masses tend to break up the present cadres of our economy; the elite, on the other hand, moderates its demands in order not to provoke changes that would be fatal to it.

Union pluralism

Professional skill in the worker requires and develops judgment, initiative and a sense of responsibility; it also makes him irreplaceable. The employer—at least in the small enterprises, where automation is nil—still remains rather close to his personnel, which is made up mainly of skilled workers. The latter, by the very delicacy of their operation, are able to exercise a delicate and continuous influence on the employers; "contact" and tension are maintained by a perpetual confrontation of the workers' aristocracy and the industrialists. At the level of the enterprise, this elite, to the very extent that it is difficult to replace, can obtain much by the simple threat of a strike, and, finally, since this threat remains constantly implied, by negotiation. The skilled worker has aces up his sleeve: he can discuss and bargain; he uses violence only as a last resort. He advances and retreats, threatens and becomes conciliatory again; he adjusts to the employers' attitude, to the situation, to the ever variable relationship of forces at play, all *in words*: words which are in reality neither sound impulses nor acts, but *chips* which one puts on the gaming table and which one can equally well withdraw. Before passing to action, the skilled worker can take back his bid as many times as he wants; reciprocal blackmail and threats, promises, breaking off and resumption of negotiations: these abstract and almost symbolic maneuvers often spare a trial of strength; a compromise solution turns up at the right moment. The skill of the unionist enables the union to preserve its freedom of maneuver.

Let us add that this elite is homogeneous: doubtless the movement toward centralization gave birth to a bureaucracy. But the rank-and-file militant can consider himself a potential leader, he does not yield to his leaders either in experience or in theoretical knowledge; he exercises an effective and permanent control over them; inversely, the leadership cannot be mistaken about the feelings of the rank and file: the union members speak up, express their views, the currents of opinion *make themselves manifest*; they all contribute personally in establishing the broad lines of union action. Permanent contact between the leaders and the rank and file results in constant pressure of the worker on the employers: thus, the two conditions for a union *policy* are brought together.

With the masses, the chances for negotiation diminish. Downgraded, work alone ceases to be a means of action. As long as the motors run, the "human factor" seems negligible. At the same time, the worker, deprived of the guarantee which skilled worth gave, and the leadership, move farther and farther apart, finally to lose each other in anonymity. In this sense, the new condition of the proletarian tends to break the continuity of his action: in order to exert pressure on the decisions of the employers, the resistance of the workers has to cross a certain threshold before it is even perceived as such. In a word, the strike—that is to say, violence—is their sole recourse. But the nature of this "specific weapon of the workers"[18] has changed: the skilled worker is indispensable; in order to block production, he has only to stay at home. He is exercising violence: but this violence is legal, and then—in principle at least—it tends to remain abstract and apparently passive. By the same token, the employers' reac-

[18]Léon Jouhaux. Lecture at the Institut supérieur ouvrier, 1937.

tion must be contained within certain limits; the employer can, if he wins, multiply the sanctions: he will have trouble making blood run. But the semiskilled worker, as a producer, being anyone at all, can be replaced by anyone at all; it is therefore not enough for him to quit work, he must prevent others from working. After twenty years of uncertainties and waverings, the masses have found the new weapon, the only one which has been adapted to their condition: the sit-down strike. This was to violate the most sacred of bourgeois rights, and to expose oneself, consequently, to the intervention of the C.R.S. Summonses, tear-gas bombs; if that isn't enough, they shoot. Shall we say that the masses are more stubborn, more "vicious" than the elite? That would be absurd. The truth is that technological evolution has radicalized violence: in order to defend his wage, the semiskilled worker must risk his skin.

For the same reason, the masses have no other defense than mass action: it is a matter, through concerted operations conducted at the national level, of obtaining collective bargaining agreements which pertain to whole branches of industry. But these operations are possible only if the masses stick to a single movement, to a single set of directives. Now, as we have seen, it is a mistake to characterize the masses by a sort of primitive unity: they are molecular scatterings, the mechanical aggregate of isolations, the pure product of the automation of tasks. Doubtless the archipelago structure is a purely imaginary extreme of massification: in reality, the disintegrating forces come up against numerous obstacles. In particular, when social tension loosens, the mere presence of the union apparatus—this nervous system—preserves for the proletariat a "residual tonus." Thus, the working masses can hardly pass for an army on the alert; to be sure, the class struggle does not cease for an instant: not for an instant does the worker cease to undergo violence and to oppose it by his simple human reality. But the activity of individuals in no way proves that the masses are themselves active. It is a mistake to consider them as a collective *subject* with "psychological" motives. The comportment of the mass is not psychological at all, and the worst error would be to compare it to the behavior of individuals. The man of the masses is anyone at all, you or me; and his personal attitudes have no importance. In himself, he is a single conscious agent, but the forces of dispersion oppose his neighbor to him as an *alter ego* that reflects his own powerlessness and doubles his isolation, thereby neutralizing his activity and producing a collective whole that reacts like a thing, like a material milieu where the stimuli are propagated mechanically. The masses are the object of history: they never act *by themselves,* and every action of the working class requires that they begin by suppressing themselves as masses in order to accede to the elementary forms of collective life. One does not have the right to speak of a "pressure" they exerted on their employers; and their influence can be only negative: the employers know that exploitation beyond a certain threshold counteracts the massifying forces and is likely to provoke a rapid crystallization of the working masses into a proletariat. But, as for what concerns the day-to-day action of the militant, the contradiction is obvious: he agitates the masses-object in order to transform them into proletariat-subject; he tries, wherever he is, to suppress their granular structure in favor of organic unity. Now, unity can be achieved only if it exists at the outset in some fashion: each one, seeing his isolation in that of the other person, can escape from it only if the other escapes; in a word, wherever one is, the beginning has to be *elsewhere.* In the large industrial concentrations, the mode of mechanical propagation can, at the outset, take the place of unity. That is what is called imitation: it cannot be considered as a collective action, but it is that anonymous movement which makes action possible. It is up to the militant to transform the involuntary tide into a precise operation. It must be added, however, that imitation itself presupposes a certain prior unity. It is true that the "laws of imitation" govern only the social sectors which are in a state of permanent disintegration:* what I imitate in my neighbor is not the Other, it

* The members of an integrated grouping differ by their function (and, consequently, by their situation) in the very measure that they are bound by the law of the group: diverse within unity, why would they imitate each other? They cooperate.

is myself become my own object; I do not repeat his act because *he* did it, but because *I*, in him, have just done it. In short, I must perceive his situation and his needs as *my* situation and *my* needs in such a manner that his behavior appears to me *outside* like a project springing forth from my head; the imitator and the imitated are at one and the same time interchangeable and separated, and imitative behavior is the result of a dialectic of identity and of exteriority; the semiskilled worker being anyone at all, the mode of propagation of grievance demands throughout the masses will be contagional because each sees the other come to him as anyone at all, that is, as himself. To the extent that massification engenders both isolation and interchangeability, it gives rise to imitation as a mechanical relationship between molecules; and imitation is neither a *tendency* nor a psychic characteristic: it is the necessary result of certain social situations. Even so, it is necessary that these purely mechanical links be based on a prior synthesis which permits at least the *confrontation* of imitators and imitated, even if it is the purely material unity of habitat or of place of work. At the very least, what is necessary is the unity of danger run or of hope felt. Now, the relative scattering of French industry favors the employers. Distance does not suppress the contagional propagation: it raises its threshold; from a distance, the *same* becomes the *other;* in order that the unity of the situation be perceived, it is necessary that the urgency of the peril increase: only exceptional circumstances will reveal to the dispersed masses the concrete and present unity of the proletariat. In 1936, to cite only one example, the political triumph of the Popular Front set in motion the contagional propagation of social movements: the masses learned of their unity by perceiving it outside of themselves in the alliance of the three people's parties, and they reacted almost mechanically, by the identity of their behavior; if the movement had not been checked, it would have transformed itself sooner or later into revolutionary action.

The circumstances which bring about the crystallization of the masses into revolutionary mobs can with good reason be called "historical": they arise from the social, economic and political transformations of the continent; which amounts to saying that such circumstances do not arise every day. Thus, the passage from the state of a mass to the primitive unity of the mob necessarily presents a character of intermittence; the masses are affected by an inertia which prevents them from reacting to subtle excitations: one cannot expect of them those rapid movements rapidly stopped, those demonstrations of force and those operations of detail, those feints and those maneuvers which would permit them to exert a continuous pressure on the opponent without entering into open struggle with him. Moreover, the primary crystallizations can maintain no equilibrium: the mechanization of work stole the workers' future: if they budge, it is because their *present* condition is unacceptable, it is because they glimpse the possibility of modifying it right now. One cannot expect them to wear themselves out sustaining a long-term endeavor: in addition to the inadaptability and the discontinuity which characterize mass movements one might also mention a certain instability.

Let us not, above all, conclude from this that the "neo-proletariat" is more reformist than revolutionary: quite the contrary. It is true that the masses can be mobilized only in the defense of immediate interests: but, when they get going, they want everything right away. Bourgeois propaganda has persuaded them that the least change in their condition will precipitate a catastrophe. Thus, day-to-day reality becomes in their eyes a rigorous system of prohibitions. But what wrenches them out of their mass state is a still more fundamental impossibility: that of continuing to put up with their unanswered needs. Before this major impossibility, all prohibitions collapse and change becomes their most immediate possibility; hopelessness engenders hope, the crystallization of the masses into a mob engenders the belief that anything is possible. The skilled worker can limit himself to *a few* demands; the masses want *everything* because they have nothing. A concerted action, based on years of experience, in full possession of its techniques and its tradition, conscious of being a long-term undertaking, can limit itself for the moment to a specific objective. But since the masses do not have a collective memory and since their "awakenings" are intermittent, their action is always new, always begun over again without tradition or prudence. Nothing limits it, neither fear of failure nor reflection on history; it establishes itself in its pure essence, as sovereign efficacy and absolute power to change the world and life. By the same token, *all* needs become apparent at the same time. The expression "minimum subsistence" means just what it says: below this limit is death. For the man of the masses, to live is merely not to die on the spot. In a "normal" period, the worker can satisfy only a very small number of needs: those which, unsatisfied, would involve his death; and since the forces of dispersion have penetrated him with the feeling of his powerlessness, he must exercise a permanent censorship over all needs which are not *vital*. Half repressed, half masked, these needs are none the less constantly present: it is simply that they are not recognized or named. But when a quick deterioration in his standard of living suddenly puts the worker in danger of death, a popular movement arises and the masses are transformed; immediately the relationship with the possible and with the impossible is reversed, and needs come to light because action can satisfy them. When everything is possible, it becomes intolerable "to live at the subsistence minimum." From there on, the popular movement always goes further unless it is broken by the armed resistance of the employers: each of its successes is an encouragement to demand more; ever more radical without ceasing to be immediate, it necessarily challenges the very basis of society. For half the French, wages oscillate around the subsistence minimum; if it were necessary overnight to increase their real buying power by one third, bourgeois France would be blown to pieces. It matters little then whether strikers or demonstrators intend to make revolution: objectively, every mass demonstration is revolutionary: they begin it *in order not to die* and they continue it *in order to live*. And then, even if it were possible, within the framework of capitalism, to satisfy certain of their demands by a sustained policy, by a labor of ten years, of twenty years, the fact is that they do not have time to wait: a bourgeois who is ill-housed can be patient: he is cramped for room, that's all; a family of workers are piled on top of one another in a slum: they must move or die. But the lodgings they are promised do not yet exist: how can they move short of occupying those which exist already? In order to obtain entire satisfaction, the revolutionary mob must take power.* That would be fine if misery set the crowd in motion only at times when power was for the taking. But how can one believe in that "pre-established harmony"? It is true that every "movement of the masses" is a beginning of revolution; and sometimes the circumstances which determine a popular action can also weaken the resistance of the ruling classes. But the heroic and bloody history of the proletariat suffices to show that the conditions for a workers' victory are rarely present all at once. Furthermore, the proletariat represents only a third of the nation and the masses are only a fraction of this third. In order that they win one day, it is necessary to prepare for their triumph. To make alliances within the working class and, if necessary, outside of it, to draw up a plan, to work out a strategy, to invent a tactic—this is precisely what they are not capable of. Consequently, the role of the militant will change entirely.

In the first place, he is a functionary. Collinet puts it very well: "The mass cannot by itself participate in union life; it places its confidence in the official militants, judging them by the immediate results which they bring to it." But why does he go on to describe to us afterwards an ideal militant who would serve as intermediary between the leaders and the masses? Of course, it would be fine if this militant devoted his day, like the comrades, "to purely technical and professional work," while at the same time raising himself through a succession of rites above his specialty in order to judge professional problems, raising himself above professions in order to envisage "social problems in their generality." Unfor-

* And when it has taken power, its leaders must *at the same time* exert themselves to satisfy the mob and to struggle against its impatience. A new dialectic is born: in point of fact a long-term undertaking is necessary in order to achieve what the crowd demands immediately.

tunately, this individual who is both "rooted" and "detached" has nothing in common with the contemporary semiskilled worker; he's an old acquaintance and Collinet, calling him by a different name, is quite simply presenting to us the skilled unionized worker of 1900. Let us not be surprised when he confesses as an afterthought that "the militant is rare and unstable among the semiskilled workers." That certain men can be rooted yet detached is possible: everything depends on status, health, leisure, culture; in a word, on the type of work. But for those who lie crushed under the weight of the earth, it is not possible to soar above it at the same time. At first sight, there is not in principle the least difficulty in a semiskilled worker's making an excellent militant: the only serious obstacle would seem vulgar and circumstantial: it is fatigue. Only there it is: this fatigue is not an accident; it accumulates without melting, like the eternal snows, and it *makes* the semiskilled worker. Of course it will pass: when the hours of work have been reduced or automation has been pushed to the limit. But the semiskilled worker will pass with it. And we are not dreaming about the possibilities of American industry or Soviet industry nor about the human condition in the year 2000: I am speaking to you of 1954 and of Malthusian Francc; I am speaking to you of workers undermined by fatigue and misery *at the same time*. As early as 1912, the metalworkers cited by Merrheim complained of being too tired to concern themselves with the union and explicitly hoped that others would do it in their place. Since then, things have only gotten worse: in order to earn *as much* as in 1938, the worker must work *more*. He gets up at four or five o'clock, leaves at six, returns home at eight o'clock in the evening, eats dinner and goes to bed at nine o'clock. He complains bitterly of being deprived of family life: where do you expect him to find time to be militant? Besides, the work schedules have the effect of preventing union meetings, unless they are held on the job. Often it is necessary to provoke a work stoppage, if one wants the workers to speak up on a question which concerns them. As to the "rare" militants who meet Collinet's requirements, I can understand why they are "unstable:" they are obliged to steal time from their sleep and, sooner or later, they collapse. *Unless* they give up manual work and are supported by the union, that is by their comrades. To be sure, the militant must come out of the mass: but the point is, he comes *out* of it. Will you still speak, after that, of "Communist betrayal?" Come off it! This "bureaucratization" is a necessity in the period of *scientific management;* in the United States, where the C.P. has remained practically without influence on trade union evolution, all the workers' delegates from the big plants—including the shop stewards—are full-time union employees, paid by the union local or even by the employer. The division of labor that takes place between militants and workers within union organizations reflects only that which took place in the factory and which created the new proletarian; and the union "bureaucracy" is only the exact replica of the employers' bureaucracy. Since "others think for the semiskilled worker," since specialists in the offices of the enterprise take the responsibility of allotting tasks to him, it is quite necessary that other specialists, in other offices, think in counter-balance to this thought and determine the modalities of union action for the workers' demands. The elimination of man by man* in the factory must have its union counterpart; the "tandem of the technician and the semiskilled worker" must be complemented by that of the semiskilled worker and the professional militant. Is that unfortunate? Perhaps; but what can we do about it? The form of the union apparatus is determined by the structure of the proletariat. And then, these recriminations are irrelevant. Collinet shows his true lights when he uses the word "elite" to designate his teams of mediators: it is the name which the "active minorities" gave themselves in the pre-World War I period; our author certainly knows the masses and demonstrates a praiseworthy concern for their interests; but, when he seeks to judge them, he does not succeed in casting off aristocratic prejudices, and, although he is not a proletarian, he furnishes the means to understand workers' dissensions since he sees one part of the proletariat from the point of view of the other part. Yes, it is

---

* The expression is Friedmann's (*Où va le travail humain?*).

in the name of a former elite that he criticizes the new bureaucracy, and his understanding of the masses goes only as far as the scorn in which he holds them.

But if we accept the perspectives of a humanism of need, everything changes and the new functionaries are legitimatized by the need. They suit the masses better than any elite, because they do not have the contradictory obligation of defending both the general interest and an individual interest. People may insist that they too constitute an elite but that is not true: the elite worker is he who does the same work as his comrades and who is militant as well. He is *primus inter pares;* through his supplementary and unpaid function, he earns the right to be heard and believed in by his comrades. The union official on the contrary, is born of the division of labor: he does what his comrades do not have the time to do and, by this very reason, he no longer does what they do. Since they pay for his services, he has no claim on their gratitude nor powers other than those which they have delegated to him. There are risks, of course: and the tendency of the bureaucratic organization to consider itself its own end has often been pointed out; but, contrary to what has been said, it is in mass unionism that this defect is the least noticeable. Surely, it is necessary to abandon once and for all the romantic and participationist conception of an elite which plunges its roots into the deepest layers of the popular unconscious: the masses have no more unconscious than conscious, being pure mechanical dispersion; and it is certainly true, on the other hand, that they are incapable of exercising a permanent and detailed control over the apparatus. Must one conclude from that that they can be led wherever one wants? Quite the contrary is true: their very scattering shields them from all influences. The old bourgeois idea of the "leader" is so tenacious that today's political writers are unable to free themselves of it. And Mr. Burnham has said some surprisingly silly things on this subject. Collinet, much more prudent, does not refrain from writing: "The mass gives proof of explosive capacities. . . . But, the latter extinguished, it hands in its resignation to the cadres in whom the totality of union life is then summed up."

Now, nothing is less true: of course, the masses have neither the will nor the means to renew the cadres; they prefer to keep the leaders they have. But it is less from habit than from indifference. Before 1914, when a militant was elected to the office of union secretary, it was because he had merited the confidence of his comrades; but afterwards, he was obeyed because he was the secretary: in minority unionism, the source of authority is in large part institutional. Today's masses don't give a damn about institutions: primarily because a very large number of semiskilled workers remains on the fringe of the workers' organizations, following only those directives which they feel are consistent with their interests. The unionized skilled worker obeys because he acknowledges the authority of the leaders whom he has elected; when the semiskilled worker acknowledges the authority of leaders whom he may not have helped to elect, it is because circumstance have led him to obey them. Thus, action is equivalent to a plebiscite: the masses never revolt or protest or demand the renewal of the cadres, and one cannot speak of a pressure exerted by the rank and file on the union bosses: they follow or they don't follow, that's all. That means that they organize into an acting collectivity or they collapse and abandon themselves to the forces of massification. And, according to the results obtained, the union rolls increase or decrease: the cadres, of course, are not affected; but it sometimes happens that they constitute by themselves the entire union. Doubtless this instability favors an oligarchy of functionaries; but it is not true that it encourages routine: on the contrary, it obliges the leaders to correct their policy continuously. Of course, this ebb and flow cannot be regarded as *outspoken* satisfaction or dissatisfaction; but as involuntary signs and symptoms. No matter: they constitute in their way a rigorous though unconscious control; the masses control the militant as the sea controls the helmsman. He is the leader when they get moving; if they disperse, he is no longer anything. Even if he were more concerned with the apparatus than with his comrades, his particular interest is the general interest; his personal ambitions, if he has any, can be achieved only by inspiring in the masses a confidence that is renewed daily; and he will inspire confidence in them only if he agrees to lead them where they are going. In a word, he must be *all of them* in order to be himself.

No matter: in vain does he exist only for them, he has ceased to belong to them; he did share the condition of his comrades but, since he has been a functionary, he no longer shares it. How could it be otherwise? The masses are nothing but a false unity of isolations, masking a perpetual dispersion; if he had stayed within them, he would have been condemned to isolation and to ineffectuality like anyone else. In 1900, the differentiation of the proletariat enabled militants to remain in the class: the skill differences assured the hierarchy; the foundation of power was the bond which united the skilled lord to the unskilled vassal. The masses are sand: if I am only a grain, how can I give orders to other grains? The strange formal reality which is called "anyone at all" is only commutative isolation: I am anyone at all in the eyes of anyone at all; in my eyes anyone at all is me; in the process, this abstract character escapes me: it is always somewhere else; that would not matter if I could define myself by my individual activity; but since the semiskilled worker does anything at all, he is reduced to this abstract essence which doesn't even belong to him. This perpetual flight of my reality explains imitation, as we have seen: I imitate in order to recover my reality as a person, but this reality presents itself always as Other and as reposing in the Other; but if anyone at all seeks to command me, he changes himself into *someone* and I ask him for his qualifications. To be sure, when the masses begin to move, leaders come out of the ranks: but the point is that they have ceased to be masses and they have crystallized into some primary form of collectivity, the improvised leader of which concentrates and incarnates the diffused sovereignty: when they return to the dispersed state, the leader disappears. The apparatus remains: it justifies its permanence by its institutional character; but the authority of the militant is only an exile: if he gives orders to the masses in their own name, it is because he takes as authority their former or future unity, because he has made himself the repository of their intermittent sovereignty. He bears witness to their metamorphoses by reminding this multitude that it constitutes a terrible, violent, authoritarian society and one which exercised an infinite pressure on each of its members. In the process, the masses keep him at a distance: they do not contest his authority since they cannot set another authority against him and since their dispersed structure forbids their being a legitimate source of power; nonetheless, they do not *recognize* his authority: in point of fact it comes from *elsewhere,* from that integrated group which they have ceased to be. The unity of the proletariat—which the union apparatus permanently incarnates—remains an abstract order or an unattainable ideal rather than a living synthesis; there is even a kind of anti-unionism of the masses: the workers always tend to distrust these officials who, however dedicated they may be, do not totally share the workers' condition. When the forces of massification prevail, the presence of the apparatus prevents the total disintegration of the proletariat without assuring it the total cohesion of the class; it keeps the working-class population in an unbalanced state which continuously oscillates between purely mechanical juxtaposition and organic composition. Stirred up by an urgent current, the masses will become a collectivity again; in the union organization, they will begin again to see their emanation and the visible badge of their unity; in rediscovering their diffused sovereignty, they *will* acknowledge the authority of the officials;* it therefore matters little whether or not the majority of workers have union cards: one follows orders and one judges by the outcome. It is velocity which binds these discrete particles together; it is *praxis* which integrates them while differentiating them; it is the apparatus which carries out the mediation between all and each. But the origin of the current remains extra-union: it is hunger, anger or terror which sets things in motion or, sometimes, as in 1936, it is a hope that suddenly bolts from the blue. With-

* More or less. And in all great popular movements one observes latent or open conflicts between the improvised leaders and the union officials. Most of the time, it is the "*permanents*" who finally prevail: they have more experience. Still they must place their competence at the service of the real interests of the workers.

out the union organism, the movements would perhaps stop: its presence keeps up the semblance of unity which permits their contagional propagation; its newspapers and its delegates overcome distances, put the Strasbourg worker in direct contact with the worker of Perpignan.* But the union organism by itself is incapable of producing movements; it gets them started only when it has caught up with their true cause. On the other hand, it is responsible —in a certain measure—for their force, their amplitude, their direction and their efficacy: it is up to the union to enlighten the masses about their own ends and to accelerate or slow down local developments in relation to the general evolution. Still, it must be well informed about the economic confluence of events, must know the social situation and the relationship of forces confronting one another. Above all, it must be able to foresee the workers' reactions: is this new movement sound? Must it be supported by all the resources of the union and must the worker be urged to commit himself totally to it? Or is it only a grass fire which would be best left to die out? How can the union decide, if it has not gathered information, conducted surveys and consulted statistics? The masses continuously *give signs*: it's up to the organizer to interpret them; there is no longer time to invoke some vague knowledge

* The following facts show the importance of information and the role it can play in slowing down or accelerating a so-called spontaneous movement: in 1936, the first sit-down strike broke out in Le Havre on May 11; the 13th at Toulouse, the workers of the Latécoère factories stopped work and stayed in the factory. But these two strikes remained unknown in Paris: the union press didn't breathe a word about them. Alone, in the bourgeois press, *Le Temps* mentioned them in a few lines and without details. May 14, at Courbevoie, a new strike on the job. Silence in the press. Finally on the 20th and especially on the 24th of May, *L'Humanité* brought the three strikes together and stressed the novelty and the identity of the methods of combat. The same day, 600,000 demonstrators marched in front of the *Mur des Fédérés,* called out by the Socialist-Communist Joint Committee (*Comité d'entente*) and the C.G.T. The workers learned then simultaneously of their new power and the new methods of struggle. Now, from May 26th on, the strike movement spreads to the whole Parisian region and from June 2nd on to all of France. The role of *information* is well defined by these few dates: the almost total silence of the press postponed by twelve days the propagation of the movement. As soon as the newspapers mentioned the first three strikes, the movement became general. Toulouse and Le Havre were put at the gates of Paris.

which supposedly arises from rootedness, no time to base decisions on some kind of creative intuition: being object by nature, the masses become the proper object of the organizer* and there is a technique of the masses as there is one of navigation. The following text from *Force Ouvrière* is characteristic:

> ". . . In our opinion, there is no question that they [the strike movements of 1947] were caused by the material difficulties of the great mass of small and medium wage earners. . . . There is no need for an accelerator to start a vehicle that has halted on a slope. It suffices for the brakes to be released. As to the particular characteristics of this movement—because each strike operation has its own—we should bear in mind what the technicians of the nuclear sciences taught us, namely, that the origin of the atomic bomb resides in the release of a phenomenon of chain reaction by which the disintegration of matter is accomplished and propagated."[19]

The frankly mechanistic character of these images makes a striking contrast with the "organicist" phraseology of the pre-World War I period. The role of contagional propagation and the extra-union character of the causes of the movement are recognized explicitly. But above all, these frightened unionists (they were soon to leave the C.G.T.) frankly admit their powerlessness: one can brake, dam up a movement; but if the brakes go, or if the dike breaks, the car rolls to the bottom of the slope or the water spreads out over the lowlands. One recaptures in these pages an echo of the terror felt by Blum and the old unionists when confronted by the masses: the secession of the F.O. is an "every-man-for-himself" operation.

Centralization, bureaucracy, technique: these features of the new unionism are imposed on it by the nature of the "neo-proletariat." And it is this nature again which will upset union tactics by bring-

---

* Which does not prejudice, naturally, the personal relations which he can have with the workers.

[19] June 12, 1947 issue. *Force Ouvrière* was still part of the C.G.T. and Jouhaux's position was ambiguous: he was willing neither to approve the strikes nor to condemn the strikers.

ing to them three new characteristics: maintenance of social agitation, extension of strikes whenever possible, an attempt to "radicalize" opposition.

Permanent agitation

The masses always lag behind or precede their leaders. But let us be careful not to conclude that they are stupid or that the bureaucrats are perfidious: we would fall back into psychologism. In fact, this gap is only the *temporal* projection of the spatial distance which separates the militant from his object; it is explained by the conjectural character of the technique of the masses. The rank-and-file militant is *facing* the comrades whose activity he is soliciting: he speaks *to them* and they listen; but it is not often that he can *talk with* them. A unionist, Guy Thorel, expresses himself in these terms: "Wander around the factories, visit the construction sites, chat in the offices, go to meetings which are well or sparsely attended. Listen to the voice of the militants and observe the mass: you will be struck by the fact that there is rarely a dialogue between the militants and the mass. There is a monologue of the militants and a great passivity on the part of the mass. Often the militants are not able to penetrate this passivity. The mass listens but says nothing. And if you directly question someone in the mass, you will not often obtain any reaction that might enlighten you."[20]

That will not surprise anyone: these men are alone together. Separated by fatigue and misery, which one of them would have the audacity to speak in the name of all? Brought together by the common awareness of their isolation, which one would still venture to speak in his own name? The militant remains a stranger to them: he does not yet reflect their power and their unity. Yet, it is up to him to make conjectures on their frame of mind, on the effect his speeches have produced, on the objective possibilities of the situation. Admitting that his diagnosis is correct, the transmission still alters the messages transmitted: the "centrals" receive information second-hand, they rarely have "direct contact" and, when finally the top reassembles all the pieces of information at its dis-

[20] Appeared *in Esprit,* July-August 1951, p. 170.

posal, the synthesis which it carries out is itself only a reconstruction the probability of which, in the best of cases, cannot exceed that of a scientific hypothesis before experimental verification. Naturally, it will be tested: but since the action itself takes the place of experimentation, error is expensive and can lead to a disaster. In many cases, fortunately, it is not necessary to wait for the outcome of the conflict to perceive that the struggle was doomed from the beginning; the order will soon be followed by a counter-order. But, precisely because the mass is *other* than the militants, the apparatus is likely to isolate itself by demanding of the troops what they cannot give on the spot; and, in order to rectify their error, the leaders are likely to put themselves in the tow of the led. Of course experience, judgment, personal qualities intervene at all levels: but "authoritarianism" and "sheepism" are still the Scylla and Charybdis of union action; the officials steer the movements by successive approximations: a turn of the helm to the left, a turn to the right. That is why the essential task of the militants is "to maintain contact with the masses." These words would not have made much sense in the days of unionism of the elite. Can it be said that they do not make any more sense today? After all, it is characteristic of molecular dispersion to make contact impossible. Contact is made with a group, through the intermediary of its representatives, but not with a sum of discrete particles. If the militant wants "to contact" the masses, he must first of all give them a semblance of organization. Is this a vicious circle? No, for he must affect them continuously by a kind of collective excitation in order to keep them on the road toward solidification. And since action alone can churn them to the point where they "set," directives will be multiplied in order continuously to stir up the beginnings of action: even if these beginnings have no follow-through, they bring individuals together, they provoke emotional currents, they allow the testing and controlling of the workers' combativeness. The employers and the skilled elite will use this as a pretext to reproach the bureaucracy for preferring disorder to the true interests of the workers: the "good" unionist, according to them, acts at the right moment, conducts his action cleanly and neatly in order to obtain limited results, and terminates the struggle at the moment when these results are obtained. But this precise and discriminating struggle, which begins and ends in an orderly way, is possible only for the elite unions which are *activity through and through.* The inertia of the masses, on the other hand, is such that movement comes to them from outside; inertia therefore implies its counterpart, agitation, the goal of which is to maintain by a perpetual process of fermentation a rudiment of collective life that is perpetually threatened by death. Without agitation, the great popular movements would be more hesitant, they would take longer to come into being and they could be put down more easily.

Extension

The semiskilled worker is "interchangeable;" competition has given way to monopoly: for this twofold reason, the strike can no longer succeed at the level of the enterprise; it must extend to the entire branch of industry or to the whole nation. As a result, in each individual factory, decision is out of the worker's hands. Or rather he still decides, but under pressure: before the First World War, he evaluated a local situation, he weighed the risks, he entered into action for concrete reasons. Today, he is asked to involve himself in a movement which transcends him and whose significance he perhaps only glimpses. The militant serves as an intermediary between the whole and the parts. The apparatus has become identified with the movement which is starting: thus, the local official speaks *in the name of the whole;* each one of his listeners is still isolated in the mass but they are given to understand that the proletariat is recomposing itself everywhere: they need only yield to the general involvement and escape isolation. Even before the integration is completed, they experience the coercive power of a primary collectivity on the way to recomposition. This can't be done without profoundly altering union democracy, in the classical sense of the term. As soon as the collective subject*

* I mean by "collective subject" the *subject of the praxis* and not some kind of "collective consciousness." The subject is the group *brought together* by the situation, *structured* by its very action, *differentiated* by the objective requirements of the *praxis* and by the division of labor, at first random then

manifests itself, it is recognizable by the pressure it exerts on its members. Decisions are made at high heat. Of course, it is necessary to deliberate and the masses intend to decide freely what line of action to follow. But they know that the efficacy of their action will be proportional to the integrating power of the group. Each one can speak his mind; but, in order that a proposal be sustained it is not enough that it be *practical:* since the danger of breakdown persists permanently within the unity, it is necessary that the proposed motion effect *the agreement of all.* If an opinion fails to reinforce the collective unity, it will slip away and disappear without leaving a trace, forgotten by the very ones who first expressed it. It will be said that the same thing happens in parliamentary assemblies, since the minority bows to the decisions of the majority. But that is not at all true: it bows, but it continues to exist, juxtaposed to the majority as its permanent temptation, and it retains its aspiration to become the majority one day. In the masses, the majority eats up the minority. Or rather, there are minorities *in motion* which appear briefly and disappear as soon as they are counted; and the unity is continuously refashioned by the elimination of opponents: if they resist, someone will go so far as to do violence to them: in the eyes of the group, the dissident is a criminal who prefers his individual sentiment to unanimous opinion, a traitor who, rather than admit his error, accepts the risk of breaking up the workers' cohesion. Our government has learned to take advantage of the situation: it has imposed the practice of the referendum and extended voting rights to non-union members.

---

systematic, which the *praxis* introduces, *organized* by the leaders which it chooses for itself or which it discovers for itself finding *in their person* its own unity. What has been called "charismatic power" proves well enough that the concrete unity of the group is *projective,* that is to say that the unity is necessarily exterior to the group. The diffuse sovereignty assembles and is condensed in the person of the leader who subsequently reflects it to each one of the members; and each one, to the very extent that he obeys, finds himself, vis-à-vis others and outsiders, the repository of total sovereignty. If there is a leader, each one is leader in the name of the leader. Thus the "collective consciousness" is necessarily incarnated: it is for each one the collective dimension which he grasps in the individual consciousness of the other.

It claimed, of course, to be protecting the rights of man. In point of fact, it sought to loosen the collective ties. This hoax illuminates the abyss which separates a bourgeois democracy from a democracy of the masses. To vote by a show of hands is to yield in advance to collective pressures; but the secret ballot plunges the masses back into their original dispersion. Each one, finding his isolation again, expresses only what he thinks by himself because he can't know what he would think *in a group;* just a little while ago, at the meeting or in the shop, he *saw* his thought being formed, he *heard* it, he *learned* it from the lips of his comrades; now his opinion, if he has one, is no longer anything but his ignorance of the opinion of others. By claiming to save the person, our ministers have caused him to fall back to the level of the individual. These elections foster inertia: the decision to struggle is taken in common, at white heat; enthusiasm is contagious; but in the voting booth, doubt arises again. Each one, fearing the others' backing down, becomes again just anyone at all. One example among a thousand: in November 1947, the Citroën workers decided to strike on the job. The police intervened and had the plant evacuated. Whereupon the public powers organized a referendum. The goal was obvious: the workers were being made to vote on a semi-failure. The C.G.T. immediately enjoined them to abstain. The referendum took place: out of 10,000 eligible, there were 3,821 who abstained: these were the tough ones, the ones who refused to capitulate. And, quite naturally, they were the ones most hostile to this form of popular election. Of the voters, 1,201 voted to continue the strike: although they were in agreement with the abstainers on the objectives and tactics, they did not follow the orders of the C.G.T. because they wanted to make use of the right to vote, even if it was the Government that guaranteed it to them.* In all, 5,021 supporters of the strike. In favor of going back to work: 4,978 votes. Now, the strike began without a prior vote; but it was obvious that people would not have dared to make that deci-

* One could suppose—but the details are lacking and it is only a conjecture—that it is a question of skilled workers: they are both "hard-core" and supporters of an election system which guarantees individual rights.

sion on so slight a majority. That is, the 5,000 "hard-cores" carried the others along; the hesitant ones joined the group for fear of remaining alone: the opponents kept quiet, abandoning their opposition because they recognized its ineffectiveness. Thus there are two different ways of stating the case: the employers are free to claim that the second is the only valid one: in fact, they are both valid, but they correspond to two quite different states of the group. It is true that the evacuation of the plants dealt a serious blow to the strike supporters. However, without the referendum the strike continued: and the indecisive ones, not knowing a way to stop it, declared themselves in favor of it; the vote revived the hesitations of the "softies" and gave back courage to the opponents. Thus, the strike expressed the sudden integration of the group, and the election provoked its partial disintegration. The unity of battle is a primary formation which is established in passion and often maintained by constraint. The union officials are *dictatorial* to the degree that the group chose them to exercise dictatorship in its name over each one of its members.

Radicalization

Never do the masses mandate: they do not vote for programs; they indicate the goal to be attained; it is up to the militant to find the shortest path. And their demands are so simple that the achievement of them at first seems right at hand: food, housing, the repeal of a rotten law, the end of a war. In point of fact, their most elementary desire is separated from its object by the universe, and can be satisfied only by long and exacting labor. Food, housing? We have seen that it would be necessary to produce more, and, as a consequence, to give up Malthusian practices entirely, which implies, *at the very least,* that another majority should be formed and that a new government should impose its will on the big employers. The "spontaneist" illusion encourages good minds to believe that the people's exigency is a policy package: it would suffice *to remove the wrapping* to find the means of satisfying it. That is not so: need is only a lack; it can be the foundation of a humanism but not of a strategy. By demanding food, the masses force their representatives to struggle against Malthusianism; but their demand does not imply *by itself* a condemnation of Malthusian practices.* Thus, the militant takes the responsibility for the permanent conflict which sets the revolutionary movement, the tasks of which are infinite, over against the revolutionary *élan,* which postulates the ends all at once in order to call for their immediate realization. Since the masses cannot budge without shaking society, they are revolutionary by virtue of their objective situation: in order to serve them, the officials must elaborate a revolutionary policy. But, by that very action, they oppose themselves doubly to the masses. The precise and limited objective which the officials propose to attain at a given historical moment is both too far off and too specific in the eyes of their troops. Too specific: to the extent that the end proposed to the masses is only a means of attaining another means, the masses do not always recognize therein the absolute ends in the name of which they have agreed to fight and to die. Too far off: to the extent that this end is only a tactical outcome, it moves away from the immediate satisfaction which the masses are demanding. For them it is one and the same thing to demand bread or the establishment of a humane order: but they will not conclude from this that they must be for or against the sliding scale. In a word, the very essence of the masses forbids them from thinking and acting politically. Without any doubt, the policy of the apparatus is the practical and temporal expression of their requirements; and, since they represent the very forces which can carry out the revolutionary undertaking, it will be said that they are the means of this policy insofar as they are its end. But, since by definition strategy remains foreign to them, one cannot claim, properly speaking, that they *make* this policy, but rather that they are its instruments. Naturally, the leaders refuse to *manipulate* their troops: they ceaselessly exhort, ceaselessly explain and seek to convince. But the difficulty does

* Or if one prefers: *objectively* the satisfaction of these demands is incompatible with the maintenance of a depressive economy. But they can be posed *subjectively* without the workers knowing anything about Malthusianism.

not come from the leaders or from their relationships with the soldiers: it simply makes manifest the fecund contradiction which opposes the immediate to the deferred, the moment to duration, the need to the undertaking, passion to activity. Convinced that it is absolutely impossible to mobilize the masses for remote and abstract ends, the leaders constantly make use of what is called the "double objective"; they support the more general and more distant objective through an immediate and concrete objective, and they never neglect to point out, behind the objective close at hand, a remote objective which constitutes, so to speak, its political significance. Thus the leaders will explain to the wage earners that the increase in the buying power of their wages is tied to the end of hostilities in Vietnam and to general disarmament. In a certain sense, this so disparaged use of the "double objective" is only a manner of *explaining* history: one discloses to the masses the remote consequences of their grievance actions, one teaches them under what general conditions their particular grievances will be redressed. And there is no doubt, in fact, that in present circumstances the proletariat must impose disarmament if it seeks to raise its standard of living and that, reciprocally, it slows down "the war effort" each day to the extent that it defends its wage against the bosses. But the ill-meshed character of popular action, its "unevennesses," its instability, its sudden stiffenings, its unpredictable collapses have the effect of highlighting the "politicalization" of unionism. A successful strike appears as a total fact; its political significance is not separate from it. An unsuccessful strike is the opposite: did the workers go back to work because the union treasury was empty? Never mind: it looks as if they repudiated their union bosses; and what have they repudiated if not the "politicalization" of the strike? The apparatus remains up in the air, completely abstract; its "distance from the masses" is accentuated; it takes on in the eyes of everyone the aspect of a politico's bureaucracy. The leaders told the masses: in struggling for your wages, don't forget that you struggle *also* against war. Defeated by hunger, the masses temporarily abandon the struggle: people conclude from this that the masses don't give a damn about disarmament.

The splitting up of the proletariat corresponds to a breaking apart of popular sovereignty. For the skilled elite, sovereignty is based on merit, that is to say on competence, energy and education: the unskilled worker is "sovereign," for his part, only to the extent that he is included, involved, registered. For the semi-skilled worker, sovereignty emanates directly from the masses and only from them; sovereignty is of a piece with the movement by which, under the pressure of external circumstance, the masses come together as *a body*. The working class is torn by a conflict of powers.

Union pluralism is therefore, an effect rather than a cause: of course it helps to increase the workers' divisions, but initially it only reflects them. Before 1936, Jouhaux's C.G.T. grouped, essentially, skilled workers, civil servants, public service and white-collar workers; in the main, "the elite" of the secondary and a few elements of the tertiary. After the 1936 fusion, which was carried out at white heat and under the pressure of events, these militants became worried: they were already talking of colonization; as the war drew nearer, they hastened to recapture their freedom. After the Liberation, the numbers of the C.G.T. swelled again; the C.F.T.C. alone confronted it; organic unity was the order of the day. But almost immediately the former militants of the Jouhaux C.G.T. complained of no longer feeling at home. "They were like strangers in their own home," wrote Bothereau in 1947. The phrase is revealing: the C.G.T. of 1945, in spite of its venerable name, had all the characteristics of a new organization and one that was still seeking its path; but the workers' "elite" persisted in considering it a very old institution and one which belonged to it: the "elite" welcomed newcomers as if it were at home and deplored the bad manners of its guests. Of course, these militants did not dream of accusing their comrades from large-scale rationalized industry: it was the Communist leaders they accused; without them, union unity would have maintained itself automatically. But the reproaches they addressed to the C.P. primarily struck at the masses. The Communists, they said, prefer unorganized workers to experienced militants: the former were easier to manipulate than the latter. But isn't that harboring resentment against them for representing the masses rather than the elite? You say that the new leaders resorted too easily to violence, that they fostered a pointless agitation in the factories which harmed the interests of the proletariat, that they gave evidence in negotiations of an intransigence which risked causing the negotiations to fail? One can well imagine that this barbarity scandalized alert militants. But the violence, as I've shown above, arose from the situation itself; agitation is only a perpetual struggle against the continuous action of the massifying forces; as for intransigence, it has two principal causes: first of all, the condition of the semiskilled worker is intolerable; then he does not have the possibility of *maneuvering;* because violence is his only recourse, it is in a climate of violence that he asserts his demands: the plant is occupied, the C.R.S. will perhaps have it evacuated; they will shoot if people resist; the situation is not propitious for compromise: a great deal of courage and anger are needed to impel the workers to stand up to the dangers; the masses, therefore, and for good reason, regard the employer as the enemy; concessions and reconciliations are considered betrayals: they demand everything as long as they hold on; if their forces abandon them, they fold. Have the Communist leaders stifled union democracy? Which one? The only one ever practiced was aristocratic. The "elite" has forgotten that a democracy can be authoritarian if the authority emanates from the masses themselves. The union "dictatorship"—if it really exists—is imposed on the minorities in the name of the majority, but it would be absurd to believe that it can be imposed on the majority itself: the masses can be neither mobilized nor manipulated, they decide on action when they are transformed into an acting community by the play of external circumstances. You say the "Communist" unions are politicalized? The fact is that the existence of the masses as such is incompatible with the economic and social system which produces them. Let me be clear:

I do not claim that the present structure of the C.P., its objectives and its methods are entirely and exclusively determined by the objective demands of the semiskilled worker; this party has its history, its own dialectic; it is conditioned by the world. But I maintain that these accusations aim primarily at the masses: it is the masses whom the militant of the elite condemns by proxy; they at once frighten and fascinate him: tomorrow the automation of jobs may reduce him to the ranks of the semiskilled.

The representatives of the masses in turn accuse the F.O. and the C.F.T.C. of playing politics "on the sly," and they are not wrong. When everything is tied together, Malthusianism and misery, the rise in prices, rearmament and the Marshall Plan, to reject the policy of the C.P. is to carry out that of the Government; besides the C.G.T.-F.O. relies on the Socialist Party and the C.F.T.C. on the M.R.P. ministers. To restrict the workers' demands to the economic and professional sectors is to seek to change effects without touching causes; it is, above all, to leave the hands of the parliamentary majority free. One wants to obtain the maximum within the framework of the system; one calls for piddling favors, and, in order to deserve them, one condemns communism in "apolitical" speeches and one receives "apolitically" the emissaries of the American trade unions. And yet the reproaches which the C.G.T. addresses to the leaders also strike the rank-and-file militant: after all, the Force Ouvrière, up to 1947, represented only a minority "tendency" in the C.G.T.; neither Jouhaux nor his lieutenants wanted to take the initiative of breaking up unity and it is the provincial militants who caused the rupture by threatening not to renew their union cards. At the meeting of the Friends of the Force Ouvrière, called together in haste, the leaders proposed a compromise: the "democratization" of the C.G.T. would be demanded of the "majority." In vain: the militants would have none of it, and the headquarters followed them reluctantly in the secession.*

* Last summer's strikes, on the contrary, permit us to hope for a rapprochement imposed by the rank and file.

Shall we say that the masses are entirely lined up behind the C.G.T.? That only the skilled workers are enrolled in the F.O. or in the C.F.T.C.? That would be an oversimplification. Many skilled workers have stayed in the C.G.T. through class discipline.* Others have joined autonomous unions. And then the religious character of the C.F.T.C. complicates the problem further: in certain regions, the current of de-Christianization has not yet penetrated the masses. Nevertheless, by and large, our division is still a fact: the C.G.T. polarizes the revolutionary tendencies of the mechanized proletariat of large-scale industry; most of the other unions represent the reformist tendency of a skilled elite struggling against skill-downgrading. In one sense, union pluralism is legitimate, since it is the reflection of a profound schism; in another sense it is a catastrophe for the working class, since the plurality of apparatuses increases conflicts by giving configuration and limits to each of the tendencies and by obliging each group to define itself by its opposition to the others. But, in any case, the schism has a more profound cause: it is the finest gift which the employers' Malthusianism has given to the working class.†

* The Printers Union (*Fédération du Livre*), by 28,000 votes against 18,000, decided in 1947 to remain in the C.G.T., in spite of a long reformist tradition.

† This Malthusianism is outdated today (1964). But it will take a long time before the social structures which proceed from it can give way to new structures and before the union struggle adapts to the new necessities.

A Reply to Claude Lefort

A Reply to Claude Lefort has been translated from the French by Philip R. Berk.

Translator's Note: The translator wishes to acknowledge the kind of assistance of Professor Michel Rybalka in the preparation of this essay.

Never have I denied the deep roots of the worker in society nor the objective basis of the working class. Nor have I ever thought that men were merely tin soldiers which one had to fuse together by applying heat from without. Solitude and union are for me complementary relationships whose harmony is the index of a society's unity. That certain limited groups should be solidly unified without mediation stands to reason. Why cannot such a "sociality" one day characterize society as a whole? Marx tells us that the communist society will reabsorb within its body and dissolve all authorities so that the free development of each will influence the development of all. But first this society must have dissolved its classes, the divisive principle, for it is the class struggle which tears apart the social fabric. When that rip begins, where will it end? Common sense would answer that in order for classes to oppose each other they must each have a unifying principle. But this is merely a commonsensical argument: a nation is only a "phoney dream"; it is composed of fragments; why could not the working class have a similar illusory coherence, made of innumerable conflicts? And does not this unity vary with the relative pressures on it? In wartime, the army's unity is dependent upon action, for action unites men, whereas suffering divides them. In any society you find activity and inertia in varying degrees: the reciprocal exteriority of its members—that is, their tendency toward disintegration—is a function of this inertia, that is to say, of those external pressures brought to bear upon the group.

Did I say that the inertia of the masses is their natural condition? The masses are not natural: they resemble Nature, but they are made; the exteriority of their components is produced; an historical status was imposed upon the proletariat at a certain stage of its evolution with the development of technology. This mass state is never stationary, precisely because there are and always have been political parties and means of communication. Did I place the Communist Party outside the working class? Then where would its transcendence come from? And if it transcended the working class, how could it act upon it? Could it transcend the masses when in fact these Communist cells are micro-organisms which grow in their midst, or could it transcend the working class when the masses are organized into a class by the Party itself? Where have I written that the Party was identical to the working class? It is as if I called a "bunch" the band which ties the asparagus. All the same, the band is outside; but the Party, I could say, using your language, is "that which permits the workers to act and to think together and to think themselves different from society." In short, the Party is a force of mediation between men. You believe this mediation to arise of its own accord among the workers, while I think it is, at certain times in the history of the working class, both natural and willed, an ambiguity in part spontaneously experienced by the workers, and in part willed by the militant leaders which creates the possibility of a dialectic in which the people are sometimes contrasted to the Party and sometimes united with it. Did I deny that the Party draws its strength from the proletariat? Will I surprise you by revealing that the Communists are as persuaded of that as you and I? The Party's role is to break the invisible barriers which potentially isolate the workers from each other. This does not necessarily mean that it gives life to dead men. It reconciles passions and interests, unites hopes and efforts, maintains solidarity. Through its orders each member is made aware of the common purpose; to obey it is to become collective. Doubtless, its orders would be ineffective if they did not flow in the direction of social currents, but for the Party to guide itself upon the actual trends of the working movement, there must *be* such trends, and for them to exist and become manifest, a measure of unity is necessary. If the bond slackens, the masses spread out and scatter, the ligaments relax and weaken, the entire group glides towards molecular disorder; but let it tighten and its colors and structure reappear and its movements are once again oriented. And since you are pleased to cite Trotsky, take these remarks for a simple gloss on what he judiciously wrote in his *History of the Russian Revolution*: "The parties and the leaders are not an autonomous element, but nevertheless a very important one, of the historical process. Lacking a ruling organization, the energy of the masses would vaporize like unenclosed gas in a cylinder. However, the piston is moved neither by external movement nor by the cylinder but by the exploding gas." After all, did you not agree with this when you wrote: "The political activity of the workers remained dispersed as long as the most dynamic elements of the intellegentsia did not allow them to crystallize into a single organization. But these elements *if left to themselves* would have no power whatsoever." But I do not agree. The working class develops, languishes, takes on new life unendingly, yet without returning to its original state. I hold that for it to reconstitute itself and survive, the working class, today more than ever, needs the help of a group which has grown up in its midst. Precisely that and nothing more. I thought it useless, dangerous and even presumptuous to construct a theory of the proletariat. I said that *today* the masses need the Party. But without hesitation you gratified us with your theory of the working class and with a dialectical reconstruction of the worker movement since its origins, whose aim was to show that the working class writes its own history, that it organizes itself progressively by its own means and develops its experience *spontaneously*. I must admit that you never explicitly used the word "spontaneously", but, as Saint-John Perse said of the sun: "It is not spoken of, but we feel its presence." But what name will you give to "the effort of the working class to behave as a unity and to affirm its total supremacy"? And to that "natural but not unconscious process"? But you want to maintain that the development of the working class is autonomous and that parties are only its transitory *expression*. And you want to prove that *against me*. Let us see how you set about it.

Marx said that the proletariat "produces the material conditions of its ascendancy . . . (which are) the cooperative form of work, the efficient application of science to industry . . . and because the transformation of individual modes of work cannot be developed except in common, the economic control of all means of production, joint social labor, the entry of nations into the network of the world market, etc." But while the productive forces are socialized, productive relationships remain individual. You conclude therefore that the simplest gesture of the worker at work is already revolutionary. On the one hand, the conditions of production, namely, the capitalist order, turn into hindrances for the productive forces, once work is socialized. On the other hand, the proletariat, by its daily work, little by little creates the "material conditions" which will permit it one day to take power. While producing capital, the proletariat also produces itself, capitalism's gravedigger. It would be absurd to distinguish the worker's industrial activity from his political activity, for that would be to confuse the purely abstract and negative goal of the proletariat, the overthrow of the bourgeoisie, with its positive and concrete goal: to organize progressively the new relationships to be established among men, to progress little by little towards a "restructuring of industrial conditions, etc." And furthermore if it is true that the proletariat, in the depths of its distress, produces its own course, then inversely, the insurmountable boundary of its liberating *praxis* is the present material conditions of production: "They must begin," wrote Marx, "by producing themselves the material conditions of a new society and no effort of mind or will can save them from this destiny . . ."

All is for the best: the proletariat makes its own history; it creates by the sweat of its brow that future moment when the question and the answer will be one, and when, as you politely say, it will be able to "restructure the conditions of production." And work of course has a value which I may accurately call "cultural." The worker produces himself in producing capital. Insofar as industry socializes production from without, the worker, from within, molds himself in his way of life, his behavior, his system of values and his experience, as a *socialist;* the organization of the working class for itself and in its struggle against capitalism progressively sketches what will be post-revolutionary society.

One could call this "class immanentism." If one wanted to expose the shameful finalism which is hidden under all dialectic, one would have to say that the working class is the most efficient way of realizing a classless society. It would require such a thankless effort to produce the material conditions of this society that humanity, wishing to eliminate all oppression, finds that it can only do so by making itself the oppressed proletariat. How could one exhaust oneself in producing surplus value if one is neither dupe nor victim? Profit would be in essence a trick performed by Reason. Of course, I am joking and you have said nothing of the sort. But if I were a "young owner," I would be of your party, for with your interpretation, you establish the foundations of a Marxism for all. Exploitation exists, but it is merely the objective structure of the productive system. And at bottom everybody finds it to his advantage: while the workers prepare for what in the long run will be the ascendancy of the classless society, the owner makes his daily profit; work and capital become friends; convinced of the ineluctable necessity for a classless society, your "Lefortist" owner sacrifices his honor to the revolution and defends the system, if need be, by force: he can aid his fellow workers simply by forcing them to produce the conditions of emancipation. This is not at all startling: you want to prove that you better serve the proletariat by establishing yourself among the intellectual bourgeoisie. If the argument works for you it will serve for others, and why not for the entire bourgeoisie?

Suddenly one feels that something is missing from your discussion. It seems that it is no longer Marx who inspires you but rather Engels, Engels who diverts dialectical materialism towards economism, who describes exploitation as a physico-chemical process*

* "Even supposing that all individual property is originally based on the actual work of the owner, and that, in the subsequent development of things, only equal values have been exchanged for equal values, we shall necessarily arrive, by the progressive development of production and exchange, at the present mode of capitalist production and the whole problem is explained by economic causes." (*Anti-Dühring* II, 10)

This text is directed against the "idea of violence" of Dühring, and in this and who believes that social conflicts arise not from the structure of the productive system, but from the evolution of this system.* It is Engels who shows us men produced by the system without showing us the system produced by men, and who reduces the human conflict to nothing more than a symbolic expression of economic contradictions. Hegelian universal idealism is intensified by an all-embracing tragic sense, and in Marxism too, there is the process of capital and the drama of man, two inseparable aspects of the same dialectic. You, on the other hand, adopt the point of view of economism when you discuss the employer: he is invisible, he does not exist. Your tranquil hatred is so radical that you have turned him into a pure object, the passive product of capital, and consequently, of the wage earner. So much I understand, but what is missing is the class struggle. Since the employer is only one of capitalism's loudspeakers, you cannot struggle against him, ward off his blows, nor counter his ploys; one runs the risk of neither defeat nor victory. When you say that the worker "struggles" against the middle class, you simply mean that by producing he influences the present form of production. This so-called venerable

---

perspective, it is admissible. For Marx as well, moreover, the free work contract creates two dupes: the owner as well as the worker. However, the nuance is otherwise: it is that capital is not a "thing," it is a relationship between men, a perversion of proper human relationships. That is the essential difference.

* "The relationship between the distribution for each given age and the material conditions of social life in the same age is so deep in the nature of things that it reflects itself regularly in popular feeling. As long as a mode of production finds itself in the ascending stage of its evolution it is cheered by the very ones whom the corresponding mode of distribution puts at a disadvantage. That is the history of the English laborers at the coming of large-scale industry. As long as the mode of production remains the normal social mode, the system of distribution is accepted . . . and if a protest is made, it is from the midst of the dominant class . . . yet among the exploited masses there is no echo." (*Anti-Dühring*, II, 10)

How can one understand then that "the struggle (of the proletariat against the bourgeoisie) begins at its very inception"? In reality there is never any struggle: there is an economic system whose real contradictions sooner or later become manifest. Protests, indignation, hatred, which are "only symptoms," arise "when the mode of production has already gone downhill, when it is half alive, when the conditions of its existence have in large part disappeared." And what do these reactions signify? That "its successor is knocking at the door."

class conflict, this civil war is reduced to an indefinitely augmenting pressure which the forces of production, each day more numerous and more socialized, exert on the old framework which contains them.

After that you are free to give to the proletariat all the intense humanity, the vitality and conscience that you deny the employer; you are free to be a Hegelian when speaking of the workers, a disciple of Engels when speaking of the owners. You have equally done away with the conflict as a real drama between men; these two mortal enemies are unaware of each other. Even if you come to recognize, regretfully, an "experience" distinctive to the ruling class and one proper to the proletarian class, you hasten to add that these experiences are parallel. How could they confront each other since they never encounter one another? Of course, the owner is a part of the worker's experience, but only as an impersonal determining factor, while in the life of the owner the worker is hardly more real: that is the *a priori* condition which makes capital possible.

Do you honestly believe in the class struggle? You find it difficult to answer. In a recent article you allowed a number of revealing sentences to come out. You reproach the Communist Party for putting the accent "on the necessity of struggling *against* capitalism, of overthrowing the middle class, of abolishing private property." According to you, these ideas are "abstract," their objective is revolution, a political episode, and not the organization of proleterian power. The Party aspires only to success in the immediate struggle, the working class shakes off its hold and while continuing to fight exploitation in all its forms, it seeks to define "the positive form of its power," which leads it back, of course, to your theories. One cannot put it any better: the class struggle is not the real drama which sets living men at odds with one another; it is an abstract structure of a richer phenomenon: *cumulative experience*. And you go on to speak quite naturally of the revolutionary movement as a "brake which the proletariat exerts on society." True, in any battle, there is an expense of energy, action on nature, production, destruction, hence a brake. Why then, however, should it be repugnant to define the battle of Pavia as a brake set by the Imperial army on the French forces? Because it would neglect the specifically agonistic element. If you reduce the struggle to a brake, you have underhandedly eliminated one of the combatants. No one will be astonished after that to see you invent that graceful euphemism for the Revolution: "A restructuring of the conditions of industrial production."

Now the proletariat is completely alone. By itself it can "write its own history." Instead of being the purely inert effect of mechanical forces, it produces itself in producing its product, and whether it increases output or goes on strike, it brings the hour of its deliverance ineluctably nearer. "The social experience of the working class progresses on all levels at once." In effect, the working class has *no exterior*. You also wrote: "The proletariat is not objective . . . it can only be defined as experience." And "the changes which affect the size, structure and mode of work of the proletariat have meaning only insofar as the working class assimilates them subjectively and translates them into its opposition to exploitation. That is to say that there is no objective factor which guarantees any progress to the proletariat." A fine expression. How early you learned to twist language to your purposes. You show the proletariat's unity by the unity of its experience, but the unity of its experience, progressively accumulated, presupposes the unity of the proletariat. No, you say, each in creating itself engenders the other; experience is proportionate to organization and vice versa. But it is just that which does not work: the proletariat is crushed by a perpetual present. The machine and its product exist in the present, having neither past nor future; the proletariat, "produced by its own product," appeared without a tradition and hoping to destroy all traditions. Marx calls the workers "new men," "the invention of modern times." The unendingly convulsive environment does not favor the formation of a social memory, and it is odd that you who cite the Marxist passage on the crises of the bourgeois age are not more aware of this. "A continual turnover of modes of production, a constant shakeup of the whole social system, a perpetual agitation and obscurity distinguish the bourgeois period. All the traditional and congealed social bonds dissolve, while those that replace them grow old before they can ossify, etc." And as if that were not enough, cataclysms from without shake the entire society and change the social structures. The profound alterations which affected the proletariat in the first years of this century would have been enough to destroy its social memory: how can you expect those new workers who arose around 1910 to adopt the aristocratic traditions of revolutionary syndicalism and of tradesmen? Certainly there was a change, but it was not a cumulative historical change. Besides, war added to the disorder: two million employees were mobilized, the female working force increased ten-fold, the young generation which entered the factories around 1917 never knew syndicalism. This fact was confirmed during the last war when all observers noticed that the young workers had almost no knowledge of the 1936 general strike. For them it was a matter of legendary and barely comprehensible events. Thus, if you want the proletariat, despite the number of inimical forces and good reasons for forgetting, to preserve its common memory and experience, you cannot count on experience itself to furnish it with the minimum of unity which memory requires. In a traditionalist society that evolves slowly, the circle would not be a vicious one, for experience evolves its own instruments. In a class continually in turmoil, whose organization is always behind that of the owners, what is needed are frameworks, guides, warranties of experience. Insofar as the past remains, even only as behavior, *exis,** or guiding pattern, it is preserved by specialized agencies. Just as it needs mediation between its members, the working class, far from being unified by its memory, needs mediation between itself and its past.

Leaving this subject for the moment, let us suppose that the formal conditions of this "cumulative experience" are given in reality. What would trouble me is this: you have spoken of two parallel experiences, that of the owner and that of the worker. I

* In Greek "*exis*" means "permanent condition," and is opposed in Sartrean thought to "*praxis*," or "activity."—Trans.

can as well add others: that of the peasant class, that of the middle classes, etc. And I see too that a bourgeois can express in his fashion the experience of the bourgeoisie, a peasant that of the peasantry. But you, Lefort, who are you? where do you fit in? How can you speak to us of the experience of this working class which "has nothing objective about it" and which "only deals with its own activity"? You probably count yourself among the number of those intellectuals "who have diligently been able to acquire the theoretical understanding of the movement." But, first, even that is not abundantly clear and you tell us yourself that Marx laughed at the social-democratic intellectuals who claimed to be the intellectual mouthpieces of the proletariat. How does one tell the wheat from the chaff? He says, somewhat naively, that these individuals must "have a real value" and that "they espouse the working class ideas." But he added, of necessity, especially if one admits your assumptions, that they would accompany the proletariat in its work and that they would become part of its "constitutive elements." He completed the picture elsewhere, by explaining that this new addition came from an *actual proletarization* of certain strata of the intellectual bourgeoisie. All right, a proletarized intellectual falls from his class, joins the proletariat, and adopts all its ideas. Only then is he worthy of serving it by communicating the theoretical understanding of his own impressions. You are not proletarized, as far as I know—no more, in any case, than a large number of young students who call themselves bourgeois. You have not fallen from your class since you keep company with other intellectuals and some highly cultivated workers, as did the republicans under Louis-Philippe or the radicals in the period of MacMahon. You do not accept all the ideas of the working class since the majority of workers vote communist while you are hostile to "Stalinists." Finally, you cannot claim that you verified the practical worth of your ideas in the course of a common action in which, involved with the workers, you participated since you never act at all. How then can you describe and define "the subjective experience" of the working class? The truth of a dialectical movement can establish itself in one of two ways. If one is oneself caught up in the movement, it is *praxis* which is decisive. Action and idea being one, the true idea is a successful action. If one is out of the action and immobile, as you are, then one must assume that his place is at the end of the historical process. Nor is it true that one could equally cite the same alternative for any intellectual whatsoever of the "left." Some, registered with this or that proletarian party, serve in the midst of the workers. It is *precisely* membership in the Party which serves as mediation: through the Party one can, with more or less success, change one's class. But above all, never let me be one to refuse to anyone a knowledge of the worker's world, however slight or incomplete it may be. This one leaves it, that one has relatives who work in a factory, and even if the third has only read theoretical works on the proletariat, he has at least learned and understood a minimum of abstract ideas. I believe that there is *communication* between groups and classes as between persons. They communicate *and* struggle. And moreover, the struggle itself is communication. The other party is there, immediately accessible—if not decipherable—and his experience is there, completing itself in my own or mine completing itself in his. All these imperfect meanings, badly defined and interrupted, which constitute our real knowledge, are taken into account there, in the other who perhaps knows the answers. There could be no experience nor class struggle if men were not for each other at once object and subject, and if I did not find the Other totally within me.* But you, you who pretend

* That does not mean that these experiences are *complementary* nor that they can fuse in a harmonious unity called "all human experience," as the pre-war idealists believed. On the contrary, they are for the most part incompatible, contradictory, one exclusive of the other. But that does not prevent you from finding them in the field of your experience nor from being directly threatened by the hatred of a colonial native, nor even that you could change perspectives and attempt to see yourself with another's eyes, that is to say, to determine your objective reality by relation to other systems of reference. But in any case while these values and these points of view, which are not yours although combined with yours, creep around everywhere to oppose you, and present themselves to you like systems of comprehensible relationships, they will always keep their irreducibility: always different, always foreign; immediately present, yet inassimilable. We shall soon see how, because you hold to this middle position, you go from one extreme to the other. After having spoken of "parallel experiences," you will not hesitate to sum up the entire experience of the Mediterranean world.

that these experiences are separate, you who live like myself on the income of capital and whose activity is unproductive, you do not have the right to explain the worker's subjectivity as if you were Hegel and it were the World-Spirit. Even then, one cannot understand how you will restore to us the moments of this foreign experience, for, in the *Phenomenology of the Mind,* it is in the last analysis, indeed his own consciousness that Hegel records. But how can one speak of the subjectivity of the Other, if it has no exterior? However, looking more closely, I see that in this subjectivity the interior is the pure interiorization of the exterior. The proletariat as subjective experience is identical with the process of production unwinding in the ideal milieu of subjectivity. For example, the objective status of the producer becomes subjectively "familiarity with the mode of individual production"—the constant change of techniques becomes adaptation to new tasks, a transformation of the idea of instrumentality. If the mechanization of production makes individuals *objectively* interchangeable, the working class acquires the sense of universality. The subjectivity of the working class is one with the mode of production grasped in the perspective of a past and of a future whose parts are organized in the synthetic unity of an experience. Thus you pass from total subjectivity to complete objectivity. Thought and its object are but one. When a Communist makes known the interests or the feelings of the proletariat, rightly or wrongly, it is *in the name* of the proletariat that he speaks. But I am very much afraid that you, Lefort, only speak *about* the working class: your truth is not successful nor could one say that it embraces total reality since history is continuous. If you refuse nevertheless to take your ideas for opinions, it is because you mistake your method for the progress of reality itself. And probably you repeat in a whisper the secret that Hegel spoke aloud: "Thought contains as a product of its activity the universal which constitutes the very ground, the intimate essence of the reality of the object." The working class, by producing, produces the idea for itself, and you, like a thought in action, produce the idea which produces the proletariat.

Now we can understand why you are so quick to grasp the proper relationships between the different meanings of working class experience! Now we can understand how the effect of the mode of work on the proletariat seems so simple, so clear and so sterile to you; and how you can laugh at the sorry empiricists who believe in the opacity of the world, that shallow stream. But let us try to take a closer look at this Absolute Knowledge that you pass out.

The originality of the proletariat as a class appears, according to you, in its role of producer. Let us see how the working class *creates itself* (as experience and as a unity) in so far as it labors. Let us, in other words, examine your system of interpretation.

First, you inform us of the capital importance of compactness. A denser class has a better chance of confronting in its entirety the bourgeoisie; the bond which it achieves among its members increases its ability to govern. You write with surprising assurance: "The degree of compactness of a proletariat is synonymous with the degree of its social existence." Why not? Only if, of course, social existence is defined as the degree of compactness. As for your remark on the bonds, it is a truism if you mean only that contacts are more frequent, but it is an error if you claim to judge beforehand the nature and the meaning of these relationships. Should one conclude that the working class of the U.S.A., where compactness is more pronounced than in France, "achieves a bond . . . which increases its ability to govern"? And does its history, from the I.W.W. to the unfortunate compromises of the C.I.O. and the growing indifference of the working class, have anything to do with the density of population? Is the passive obedience of Lewis' 400,000 miners due to density, and if it is, is that what you call self-organization? Bonds of course, but among whom? Would not the effects of density be changed by the presence of foreign workers, say, a large contingent of North Africans in France or a Negro population in the U.S.A.? You claim that one can ignore this, but only because you have arbitrarily overestimated the role of formal factors. But if one could see in compactness a fundamental structure of the proletariat, it would not act except in the direction of existing tendencies. Compactness will multiply the images of anger and the changes of riots, or the examples of resignation; in a time of equilibrium, it can be a simple factor of stability. It has been a long time since Costes defended his demographic thesis, and I am aware that "sociology has since made progress." He explained that "the growth of a unified population facilitates communication between the different segments of society and makes possible an accurate image of the unity of natural laws." They took him aside and explained to him that quantity could not produce social effects except in the framework of a society already organized and as a function of existing structures. Why then did you, who are so convinced of the progress of sociology, make the same error fifty-three years later with the same elaborateness? Since density only operates through existing environments and forms, will you say that it is a matter of a "permanent relationship in the framework of a social structure and cannot be interpreted as a product of history?" On the contrary, it is certain that compactness in a given region indicates a fundamental structure, one linked to the totality of production (industrialization, machinery, geographical distribution of resources, etc.). But the relationship of the proletariat to this compactness as a factor of its experience is conditioned in turn by a series of secondary or historical factors which can transform it without there being a change in the number of factories or in the importance of their personnel.* And it is true that Marx considered Britain as the lever of the Revolution, although he did not think it had a universalizing spirit or an insurrectional passion, which he held would probably come from France. What really seemed revolutionary to him in Britain was not the working class, but British capital.

Secondly, you discuss cooperation: "Cooperation in work unites their acts, organization makes the product the result of a concerted process." So you say. It is enough that this cooperation exists objec-

* For example, the appearance of machine tools and nationalization which stunned the working class did not noticeably hurry the very slow movement towards compactness which characterizes French industry.

tively for you to be assured of finding in it a correspondence between the mode of organization and the subjective experience of the proletariat. But it is you, you alone, who affirm the parallel. It *must* be so *because* your theory is true. You forget only one thing: exploitation. Cooperation is not felt by the worker as a good sign of solidarity: it may happen that he feels it in horror and rejection, like solidarity among victims, or in constraint, since it depends on the rhythm of others and their work; or it may be simply that he is not sensitive to it, as occurs in so many cases of mechanization. The third possibility is perhaps the most frequent: fatigue, the intensity of imposed rhythms isolate; and then the machine gets between men; "the inhuman" destroys human relationships. In the first two cases, one feels dependence. The worker is conditioned not only by the owner but by his fellow workers; in this stiff and external "solidarity," an alien movement, whose speed and frequency have been fixed from without, crosses his path, shakes him, and makes him feel that horribly inverted complicity of victims bound by the same chain. In any case, true cooperation is found elsewhere, between the owners, management and supervisors: all those salaried men who live on the income of capital, who share the ideology and certain interests of the bourgeoisie, who cooperate, plan and organize the work. Cooperation among workers is just the reverse of that: they help each other help the owner, but they do not help each other. Or rather they help each other in vain, they cooperate in vain. And I am astonished that you who like to cite Marx did not pay attention to the refutation he made of your theories in advance: "Their cooperation begins only when they work, but then they have already ceased to belong to themselves. As soon as they begin to work they are part of capital. In so far as they cooperate and are members of a productive system, they represent nothing more than a special form of capital. . . . The particular mechanism of the manufacturing stage is the collective worker himself, composed of many individual workers. The collective worker possesses . . . all the productive capacities and utilizes them—applying uniquely to their specific functions all his organs, individualized in the particular workers acting in groups. The more an individual worker is incomplete and even imperfect, the more he is perfect as a part of the collective worker. . . ." And here is the passage where Marx shows, against your theory of revolution without the class struggle, that the *Other* is present as a real agent of the development of production even in the elementary act of production itself, even in that gesture by which you would like the worker to become already revolutionary by the simple perception of the objective nature of his task: "In manufacturing, the division of work contrasts the workers with the intellectual forces of the material process of production like a foreign body, a power which dominates them. This split begins in the simple act of cooperation in which the capitalist represents before each worker the unity and will of the economic structure. It develops in manufacturing which makes of the worker an isolated and lame worker. It ends in big industry which makes science a productive force independent of work and assigns it to capital." I hope that these passages will remind you of what you keep forgetting: that the worker's experience is at once the experience of paid work and of oppression: "Alienation appears . . . in that my means of subsistence is also that of another, that the object of my desire is the inaccessible possession of another . . . that everything is in itself something other than itself. . . ." I agree that the worker is revolutionary from his first gesture, but because he totally experiences the world and the Other, because the Other is present in his action and in the objects of his desire as a hostile force which robs him, and because he cannot want to "restructure" his work without putting down at once the desire to seize power from the Other.*

Third: "Continuous technological upheavals (demand) that men acquire new human refittings . . ."

---

* The only certain effect that one can attribute to cooperation is perhaps that "military" discipline which, according to Lenin, has transformed factories into barracks. But that is precisely what you do not want to hear and you will soon explain that the militarization of the masses is the very sign of the bureaucratization of the directors. You wish to draw *spontaneous* solidarity from cooperation, like a rabbit from a hat.

There you are quite frankly odious. But you are excused because you lack imagination rather than heart: that is, you follow your ideas wherever they lead. You believe that Marx is romantic: but look how he speaks of those physical changes which you so jovially name "human refittings": "Manufacturing overwhelms the individual and attacks the very root of the individual working force. It cripples the worker, making of him a sort of monster while encouraging, like a hothouse, the development of his specialized capacities by suppressing a world of instincts and abilities."

Unfortunately the biologists and the psychologists would tend to support his ideas, not yours. You have read them, of course. Reread them then. But perhaps you are dreaming of the "cultural" influence of individual work. In this case, I regret to inform you that Anglo-American and German investigations will destroy your pretty dream: the cultural influence of individual work is entirely negative; it has liquidated professional culture, technical ability and that intuitive understanding of which the artisan was so proud; it has ruined curiosity, interest, the desire to teach oneself; it has produced various psychoses, dulling those who have not lost all spark of intelligence: they repeat the same gesture all day, dream or count in their heads or ruminate, chewing the same sentence over and over. Ah! And then there are also, as you say, those who "adapt": those are the ones who are really finished. They let themselves flow with the current: "After all, I don't have any responsibilities." As for "contributions to society," let's speak of them: summer, winter, long trolley rides home, extra hours. They go home, they eat dinner, they yawn, they sleep. Never mind, you are happy to learn that the proletariat, having discovered the interchangeability of workers, has risen to the perception of universality. But I am afraid that this is an error: Interchangeability is fear of losing one's job, the agonizing feeling that one is replaceable. The worker who strikes or who fears to strike certainly has the feeling of a strange contradiction: his immediate needs, his hunger, his fatigue, his distress show him his singularity; now he can no longer think that, for he is not a human being any more; only the idea of a universal commutability is left to him, if that is indeed how he imagines it. But I do not see that this contradiction can advance him much; and had you thought about it, you would have seen that it has been out of date since 1893. This universality of which you make so much was already understood before you arrived on the scene: it is quite simply the abstract universality of democracies. What does it have to do, may I ask, with the concrete universal of the "individual integrally developed" or the socialist community? How, above all, does this commutative universality resemble universal *reciprocity* which must create truly human relations? Not another word will I add about "the influence of social differentiation in the cumulative experience of the proletariat." There will be one day perhaps a redistribution of roles within the working class, but what one can now say is that the "second industrial revolution" has rather acted in a levelling fashion. One can note the tendency, although less pronounced in France than in many other countries, towards the elimination of extremes (laborers and skilled workers) to the benefit of the semiskilled workers. One still encounters, of course, many businesses with an archaic structure (a high number of workers) but, as long as the movement towards efficiency progresses, the working class will come to resemble the American working class in its composition: a small segment of skilled workers, highly qualified and very well payed, without professional contacts with the semiskilled workers, a uniform, increasingly homogeneous group; interchangeability leads in addition to the suppression of interprofessional boundaries. More at home in the concrete, the Communists have been quick to see the ambiguity of experience: the mass is fluctuating, apprenticeship is no longer necessary; for these reasons resistance to capitalism will be weaker. The worker feels his dependence all the more, being nothing but a cog: hence mass movements are possible. When resistance diminishes, dependence grows: given contradictory pushes, one must be strengthened, the other weakened: a militant leader is needed to aid his comrades in defining the sense of this ambiguous experience.

Moreover, it is not your "cumulative experiences" that make

one unhappy; in fact, I think that the proletariat profits from everything, as long as one means by proletariat the entire working class with its internal links and its sensitive organs. But in contrast to your schemas, your foolish consistency, your academic and simplistic conclusions (e.g. the manufactured product requires the cooperation of the workers, *therefore,* the workers will integrate cooperation into their subjective experience) I wanted to show that an experience is a living, totally embracing relationship, so that a moment presents itself to experience as a confused muddle of meanings and actions. First of all, facts are not as neat as you say: they must be reconstructed, then each of them is at once obscure and all too full of meaning, even if they be general and essential facts like coherence or internal differentiation. Obscure, because a fact is unaware of its own meaning; too meaningful, because a fact contains a large number of meanings, each of which might be taken for an autonomous totality. There is the fact produced by fatigue, hunger, bitterness—and the practical one related to work or to the productive attitude—and another fact which invests all the other facts with the universal existence of the Other, the inversion of human relationships and the alienation or the enlightenment through past experience, etc. All objective structures of the social world present themselves as an initial confusion to the worker's subjectivity. Nothing is elucidated, nor are there absolute *guarantees*: resignation (being crushed by the *Other*) and revolution (outstripping the *Other* towards the unlimited task) simultaneously illumine the situation, but their relationship is always in flux. Is it idealism, irrationalism? Not at all. Everything *will be* clear, rational, everything *is* real, beginning with that resistance to deciphering; but it takes time, and if active experience begins in receptivity and uncertainty, it is permissible, if not necessary, to ask for help. The deciphering *can* be achieved by an intermediary. Still, a party can only try its keys; it cannot force them. But you, hoping to make all mediation useless, present us with "the experience-which-contains-its-own-interpretation." The difficulties which we have already encountered bring us back to the usual idea of experience: an obscure mass of "consequences without premises" which require a number of men to decipher.

That is just what you reject. On the whole, I understand you: reality is opaque and difficult to grasp because we are situated in history. I imagine that the world is at first obscure for the workers insofar as the world and the worker in the world are obscure for me. But you refuse to be situated in time and place, for then you would lose your claim to Knowledge. Being situated would teach you that you are neither Hegel, nor Marx, nor a worker, nor Absolute Knowledge, but rather that you are a remarkably intelligent, young French intellectual who has ideas about Marx like those men had about women circa 1890. Of course, you agree to the proletariat's living its relationship to production and its opposition to capitalism as a stratagem, an effort towards unity, a progressive discovery of its tasks, but *on condition* that you are there to transcribe one system into the other so as to influence the objective of its subjective element, to describe the lived relations of the workers among themselves, the ambiguity of their relation to the working class elite, and to show subsequently how much these relationships, subjectively experienced by the working class, will lead to a reformist attitude. Using the "reciprocity" of perspectives you will be able to find in reformism *the meaning* of the internal relationship of the proletariat or in these relationships the *true* meaning—that is to say within the structure of Absolute Knowledge—of this reformism. In this, you resemble not so much the militants as those psychiatrists who establish correspondences between the objective conduct and the speech of the sick without wishing to enter into their delirium. Everything is clear: no one is situated, neither you in relation to social classes nor the working class except by relation to production. You deny in the same breath your own position and that of individuals who make up the working class: "Can we not ignore the individual when we speak of the group?" How can you ignore the individual? The working class is nothing but a universal experience of culture; therefore, subject and object are similar in nature. Empty thought and the solitary working class mutually sustaining their solipsisms will have a common experience of the universal.

You gave to your creature activity, force, consciousness and life, all gifts but one: inertia. Your proletariat has the right to be mistaken, to be less than omniscient, to fail, in short, to suffer. Obstacles, human limits, fatigue and fear you have relegated to individuals, while the working class itself is impassive. The bloody and sometimes obscure history of the working-class movement is but an epiphenomenon; you never speak of the risks, the disasters, the renaissances. Its predicament, opacity, moorings, bearings, passivity, all these qualities are connected; through them, man is the object of man, of the sun, of a dog. Don't you wish there to be a Lefort-object or an objectivity of the working class? Naturally you are not foolish enough to deny to workers their belonging to the real world; they can die of cholera or famine; you yourself mention the depersonalization of which the semiskilled workers suffer or the deficiencies in proletarian culture. You would freely admit that the massacres and the deportations of 1871 upset the composition of the proletariat and deprived it of its leaders. No matter: insofar as it is felt, the change does not affect the working class; it transforms individuals or, to be exact, small groups. But the proletriat will not participate in that except in so far as it integrates it to its own experience.

Yours is then a proletariat having all plenitude and positivity, like Leibniz's God, who acts and who reflects his action in himself. But weakness, the void, passion have taken refuge in each of its members, so that one can, without actual contact, decimate it from below and finally annihilate it by acting on the individuals who compose it. Will they not say that the active history of the proletariat-subject and the fluctuating history of working class movements take place on different levels? Doesn't this smack of Durkheim: doesn't your proletariat resemble that collective consciousness which "dependent on the whole without depending on the parts which compose it, enjoys, thanks to this diffusion, a ubiquity which liberates it?" But, on the contrary, you specified that "class is not a reality aside from individuals." The formula is certainly ambiguous like all those formulas of our eclectic sociologists—Durkheim too could make use of it. But let us agree that "Sociology has made progress" since the *Essay on the Division of Work in Society.* Class, according to you, would be "that which allows men to act and think in common," etc. A functional definition, in short, which points at a relationship. Class, then, is sociality, but what is sociality? It is precisely that which permits individuals to belong to groups—for example, to the working class. We return to where we began: the working class is a relationship, a constant process of self-organization and integration, an experience. I am hardly enlightened by all this. When you say: "that which permits . . . ," class becomes mediation; you make of it something neutral and that is very good. When you define it as "participation in a course of action . . . ," that is no longer the same thing, for this participation is only an abstract designation of the real fact of thinking and common action. At least the two preceding definitions have not obliged us to leave the terrain of the neutral. But when you write "the working class relies on a small fraction of itself," I no longer know what you mean and I anxiously wonder if you are not speaking metaphorically. And finally when I read: "the working class only deals with its own activity" I see that it is not a matter of metaphor and that you designate by these terms the subject of working class history—perhaps of all history. Is there any gradation or must we believe that these notions are roughly synonymous? Is acting on oneself in order to integrate structural modifications completely capable of being absorbed by experience? No, you will answer, the working class produces, and produces itself while producing. The class produces the man and the man produces the class, which is to translate into Marxist dialectic the nineteenth-century formula: doing while letting oneself be formed. But that is not the real question. What do I care whether it creates itself or is made. I would like to know how this pure activity of integration can be distinguished from individuals by its very direction and the aims of its *praxis* since it has no existence "outside them." Must one imagine an activity which is social and collective through and through, incapable of aiming at anything that is not collective, that is to say, similar to the objects of its experience (capitalism, production, etc. class interests, in the framework of a boundless scheme). But if that is what you ask it to be, the working class is nothing more than a verbal system, chosen to express collective *results*: you come back to "as if." The working class, such as I conceived it, probably united by the Communist Party, could, in its revolutionary movements, apprehend concrete totalities, that is to say, syntheses of the concrete and the universal: this strike, this claim. For I see it, in itself, like a concrete universal: unique since it was made with these particular men, in these particular circumstances—universal since it embraces an entire collection. In short, it is an enterprise whose real actions and thoughts are integrated in the real movement of history. But what does your working class do? It organizes itself: that means that with its universality it integrates morphological transformations which are themselves universal. As for structural changes, variations in size, evolution of the modes of work: these facts can be expressed by abstract and sometimes quantitative concepts; they are in no way *historical* in nature, for in order to situate them, one would have to date them from without. And the activity which will integrate these changes is itself abstract since it will spend the time in defining and applying formulas of regrouping and redistribution. For example, universality as the abstract meaning of interchangeability will be interiorized into a universal relationship between men, an even more abstract universality. Do you see that that is but *one* of the aspects of working class experience? That it also contains concrete, historical formulas of organization and concrete memories of great social events? But how can these different levels of experience exist together? And what are their relationships among one another? Moreover, most of your examples show us the transformation of empirical and practical contents, which are generalized and schematized while going from objectivity to the subjectivity of the working class. Nor does that surprise me. When, in order to escape the tough problems of the collective conscience, one imagines the unity of a group to be immanent, this unity is idealized in interiorizing itself and impoverishes itself in the process.

After all, what is your working class? What is its relation to reality? If you want us to believe you, you must show it to us and you must make us see events that could not be produced without it. And since it is active, you must prove its effective reality by the results of its action. You place the originality of the working class in its relation to production. According to you, we would encounter it at the beginning, present at the most elementary gesture of men at work. At this level, it would already be the integration of its immediate reactions, and likewise, it would not be difficult to distinguish the individual attitude from collective activity, for workers, taken one by one, work as they can; that is to say, taking into account their needs, their fatigue, their wages, current social conflicts, etc. But whatever their individual attitudes, the proletariat, their class, manifests itself by the unity of the collective movement which, by their work, pushes capitalism towards its next crisis or which, by means of their demands, exercises a harassing and harmful influence on the national economy. Thus, as Marx said in a passage which you cite, it makes no difference what the worker believes he is doing, the important thing is what he has to do. That is the *original unity* of *praxis* and, consequently, of the subject of *praxis*. By a double action, converging and simultaneous, the working class prepares the material and social conditions of the Revolution. You say that the working class is identical with that enterprise in so far as men participate in it and lead the struggle against exploitation. Two workers, even if they do not know one another, are linked by something more than a simple identity of condition: the very content of their acts is revolutionary *praxis*; their two convergent activities create the closed world of the proletariat.

If that is your proof, it is worth nothing. The *objectivity* of production is what the Marxist theorist or the capitalist or the thoughtful worker sees. Objectively, the worker prepares the next crisis. But "objectively" belongs to the world of economists and capitalists. As for him, he makes what they tell him to; he sells his energy in order to live. One can equally say that the producer himself produces bourgeois society and that the manager and his competitors hurl themselves towards the ruin of the order *while hiring the proletariat as its gravedigger.* From this point of view, the race for profits is the essential factor, for through the manager as intermediary and under threats, that is what will oblige the proletariat to become the simple instrument of this suicide. It will never be decided whether it is capitalism which is destroying itself by its own contradictions or whether it is the worker who "executes the sentence which bourgeois society brought against itself." In reality, these two interpretations are equally just, equally incomplete and incapable of being harmonized. This vicious circle reflects the existence of the Other and of alienation.

In any case, you base the existence of your class *subject* on a half-truth. And should you answer that this half-truth corresponds exactly to the *subjective experience* of the working class, I would not be satisfied. For the working class may feel itself equally to be actively producing the downfall of capitalism or working under pressure in order not to die of hunger.

Indeed, this supposed subject-unity is an object-unity. Or, if you will, the unity of the supposed *praxis* comes from the capitalist system itself. Working hours accumulate apart from the workers to increase productive capital. Inversely, the structure of a bourgeois democracy will give a particular physiognomy to an economic crisis which strikes it. And the very unity fostered by the crisis and the interdependence of its reverberations in the different sectors of national life will impose from without and through the mediation of the Other a certain objective unity on the claims of the workers. The English example is particularly meaningful since there the wage policy continues, even today, in a disorganized way. Unequally developed, unequally strong, different in origin, age and structure the trade unions limit themselves in general to defending the interests of their members, sometimes against other unions. A group which obtains a wage increase acquires thereby a differential advantage which can be thought of as a differential disadvantage to the other groups. Later other unions follow its example, still in a disorganized way; the original advantage, which was differential and positive for the most favored group, tends to disappear in the general rise of the cost of living. However, this tendency depends on different factors—the importance of the most favored group, its situation in production, distance, density, etc.—which will decide the rapidity of the extension. Where the group is of a lesser importance, the delay may be considerable: the acquired raise is maintained and the cost of living remains steady. If the group is of substantial importance, its example will be followed at once: immediately wages and prices will spiral and government intervention will be necessary. It is an example of what M. Lhomme in *Social Politics in Contemporary Britain* calls non-coherent politics, that is, "without planned coherence and in which equilibrium is statistical in nature." However, its effects have the structure of organized phenomena. The wage increase may be considered as the effort on the part of the working class to make wages remunerative. So that Lhomme himself discovered in union bargaining a *general* tendency ("the bettering of the worker's life, the major objective of union effort, is sought most often through wage increases") which is somewhat diffused by the plurality of factors (the individual structure of each organization, morale, etc.). It is to this tendency that their adversaries refer—for example, when in 1949 the *Economist* accused the unions as a bloc of playing the role of "economic aggressor." It is true that, independently of its members, each trade union may be considered a "decision-making unit." (On this level we *really* encounter collectivity and sociality.) But there are many places where decisions are made and they are quite different: some are conservative (in general the older unions), the others are more active (large unions which find membership in new industries). The principle of imitation which controlled the succession of reactions presupposes precisely a radical separation of the parties.* Without doubt they provide models for one another.

* Of course one can negate the *actual* importance of imitation. It is evident that need, the general situation, fear of work-stoppages and other forms of opposition to capitalism are much more important factors. No one goes on strike merely from a desire to imitate: but we speak of imitation because

But in so far as they are different from one another, their interests run counter to one another. For the least favored unions feel the differential advantage of the most favored as an insult; and inversely, the most favored fear that their success may start a general movement: a general wage boost would wipe out their advantage. The action of one union on another is therefore separatist for the same reasons as individual antagonisms. If the results are unified, it is because the incoherence of individual actions is unified by the synthetic reaction of a semi-coherent system: the parts of the economic system are united, or, if you prefer, the processes of capitalism are dialectical. Here again, one could say that the changes of detail are meaningful only in relation to the whole: several similar disturbances produced at different points of the "production-wage-price, etc." complex may produce a single reaction. Moreover, if the federated elements are unable to voice their demands,* at least the opponent's practice will unite them. Mortin does not think that there is a risk of inflation from the rise of wages in the U. S. A.; banks would refuse credit. In Great Britain, where banking does not have the same interest nor the same function nor the same relation to the government and individuals, the danger would be more troublesome.[21] If the unions become one united aggressor, it is because the banks decide to treat them as a single activity functioning at different points. And if they so decide, it will be because they are a social reality (despite antagonisms and as a consequence of the successful union of their members) and because they can by a single reaction avert scattered threats. On a higher level, the state will effect the final unification by placing action and reaction, the wage-price spiral, proletarians, managers,

---

it is an incentive mentioned by the unions themselves, hence both objective and subjective: legitimate demands were checked by defeatism, by an overestimation of management strength: "We will get nothing!" The success of one group, however, shows that a struggle is at least possible. More precisely, there is no *imitation,* but the first union move reveals to the others what their possibilities are.

* Everyone is familiar with all the attempts to establish a "national wage policy."

[21] W. A. Mortin, "Trade Unionism, Full Employment and Inflation," *Amer. Econ. Rev.,* 1930, cited by Lhomme, *op. cit.,* p. 188.

bankers and businessmen in the perspective of the national interest.* But in so far as demands constitute a problem for English industry and run the risk of causing a crisis or of constraining capitalism to *transform itself* in order to remain the same, that is to say, to ensure profits, economic aggression can, not inaccurately, be called *revolutionary*. That means simply that the worker cannot better his condition without compromising the socio-economic equilibrium of capitalism: everything happens *as if* a revolutionary group had been formed and was really engaged in a mortal struggle against the existing society and as if it used the worker's poverty and anxiety to achieve its aims. It is precisely the virtual existence of this group which they claim to discover in the coordination of popular movements, when this coordination is simply a reflection of the unity of the national economy. And it is this ideal existence which gives a strange credibility to the reproach so often made that political parties use social movements for political ends.

The synthetic unity of effects cannot prove the unity of an enterprise. On the contrary, it is the synthetic reaction of the adversary (government official, management, the banks) which gives to disorganized behavior an air of unity. Can one say that this *objective* unification of different popular movements will result in their *real* union? That has occurred: in France, governmental repression in 1831, by mixing republicans with the first worker's associations certainly hastened their alliance. But this borrowed unity is borne by workers as a class status. Work stoppages, dismissals, lock-outs, etc. suddenly disclosed their objective reality as an oppressed class. Put aside your fantasies, your "natural but not unconscious developments": these are but words. The truth is that the workers, in their prolonged alienation, experience their class in itself; they learn about their class as something which is in the hands of the Other. They learn about it as having been first

* This last remark does not imply any theory about the nature of the state. which remains to be drawn up. In any event, even were it the agent of a single class, it would still see farther than the groups which compose it. It would then dominate class interests as such and would effectuate exploitation on a national scale.

an object for the Other, and they become conscious of being *objects* above all; their essence does not belong to them. Their first movement to lay claim to their class and class consciousness is not the peaceful development which you describe: it is a struggle to tear their objective reality away from the Other, to reinteriorize their essence and to oppose the *working class in itself* to the self-conscious class which demands its integrity. There is, in effect, as you have noted, an experience of the self *as class* which develops with the evolution of the proletariat, but even this subjectivity must be taken from the enemy. The consciousness of the oppressed does not arise naturally, rather it *invents itself*. By a double movement which induces it to refuse being a thing and to proudly reclaim *for itself* the objective characters which are imposed upon it, the proletariat becomes conscious. Its subjectivity is at once the negation* of the consciousness of the Other and of its own objectivity.

There is not a word about that in your article: it is not your concern; you are only intent upon proving that the working class produces itself. But what remains then of those troubling coincidences, those observed regularities in social conflicts, the totalization of industrial products? Nothing. Looking in that quarter for working class unity, we have found the unity of the oppressors and of a government which obeys it. If you want to convince us of the actual existence of an autonomous proletariat, you must show it.

That at least you have seen, and that is why the brilliant philosopher suddenly changed into a sociologist. You *suggested* the proletariat, we had *suspected* its ideal existence, *glimpsed* its natural and dialectical evolution, both reformist and revolutionary. The only problem was that it has remained invisible. What one sees every day, in effect, is a sort of bastard proletariat, five million workers whose unity resides evidently in their mode of work, pay and life, in their demands, in their "patterns of life and action," etc., but also and most visibly in their manner of obeying (together

* By "negation" I mean that struggle in which it "seeks the death of the Other," and not the parody of negation by which you theoretically negate the bourgeois class.

and more or less well) the orders of unions and parties. They meet in Communist or para-Communist organizations; often it is the union's publications which inform them about the attitudes, even the existence, of other groups. In short, simple, pure observation is not decisive: it reveals simply a group of men with institutions, agencies and cadres. But you want to show that the instruments, the cadres, the specialized agencies are only the *expression* of spontaneous union; this is not right: your social genetics lead us to *class-autonomy*. But this autonomy must be found through divided rule and bureaucratic exploitation. You say that the class alone organizes itself. Then you must, despite appearances, make us see the failure of all these specialized agencies. The working class without the communists, the organizations without a free working class is like India without the English, Latin without tears, and the Revolution without suffering; it is like Nature without Man. Of course you show nothing since you would have had to suppress the parties and the unions in order to be certain that their disappearance did not entail any change.

What is more interesting is that you try all the same to refer to positive experience. And of course that is necessary. For you fail to explain satisfactorily that the stark contrast of activity and passivity, of unity and multiplicity has long been superseded by the eclectic concepts of an omnipresent sociology. In vain you resist the idea of synthesis which you find in Durkheim, the idea of totality which you seem to find in my article. As soon as you define class as "something else than the sum of individuals," the reason is clear. Class is the *relationship becoming mediation.* And since there is in fact a multiplicity of relationships, it must be the relationship of all these relationships. Yet that is not sufficient. Given a kaleidoscope I can speak of the relation of colors, but if I turn the kaleidoscope, the relation will change. In this case, the relations are the purely passive results of the induced changes. They are not unified, but are held together by their continuities; they are neutral. Your class relationships can be neither the result of an all-encompassing unification nor of the active relationship of communication and interaction, nor even the epiphenomenological relationship which flows passively from objective changes. You reply that it exists and is created, that it comes from a chance relationship, but hardly arisen it relates its terms one to another, etc. We know the stock answers; however, this "metastable" notion—which mixes doing and being so as to make inert exteriority seem like *praxis* and *praxis,* a mode of being—is far from satisfying all the tasks which you impose upon it. You want to show the borrowed, parasitic character of the Party's activities. But it is not the Party which unifies the working class, it is the class which unifies the Party. Therefore, we must expose the working class—and its activity unduly laid claim to by the Communist Party. Now, that is just what the "spontaneous" relationship could never show. Unemployment, for example, is surely, for a given period, a coherent and structured reality. But its unity, as we have seen, does not come from the workers who suffer from it; it is the very unity of the capitalistic process. You want to interiorize unemployment, make of it a part of the subjective experience of the working class, and you are right. Only this reinteriorization already presupposes unity in the form of a pre-existent activity of subjectivization. What then is needed? That you show us the workers together both as a multiplicity—that is to say, as exterior one to another—and as a power capable of incorporating all exteriority. Unemployment can be a relation between strikers if they go beyond the poverty which separates them towards an experience of the proletariat. Whose experience? Who is the subject? Experience of what? What is its class content? Will we say that there is a reciprocity of perspectives? That would be fine if it were only a question of meanings. For example, it is true that the suicide of an American from the Middle West can reveal a double sense to the sociologist; it is true that the *social* meaning is contained in the individual meaning, as the individual meaning in the social. It is purely and simply a question of methodological precepts, aiming at the reconstruction of a fact. But in the case which concerns us, the problem would remain unsolved if we limited ourselves to saying that the individual worker is a part of the working class (or that his consciousness is a part of the collective consciousness) as the class is a part of the worker;

we would have merely shown the logical relationship between the extension of the concept and its comprehension. In a structured social milieu which has its traditions, institutions, propaganda and culture, one can certainly imagine that for the individual reciprocity will be formed from birth by his surroundings, from which he will receive customs, techniques, culture, etc. But the social reality is in each and in all like a cultural "pattern" which has no life but that which is given to it, which *maintains* itself as a tradition, and never evolves like a purposeful movement. If the proletariat is a subject, if it writes its own history, it has another reality than this ideal unity. It is not a "pattern," it is a real unifying power. Hence you cannot avoid it; there must be a return to synthesis.

You try once again to hide this necessary procedure: you seem for a moment to be satisfied by vaguely structured relationships, by a diffuse presence of each in all, of a Bergsonian multiplicity of interpenetration which would be neither entirely sum nor synthesis, but could at any moment pass from one to the other. I am aware that our urban agglomerations are frequently in this state of colloidal suspension. And the resulting uniformity of the masses is never sufficiently developed so that the worker loses the feeling of belonging to an environment. But I also see that this "participation" is generally thought of as a consequence of socially organized work. And this work, at first glance, seems exerted on the masses by specialized agencies. The docker of Marseilles and the docker of Brest are united because there are parties, unions, newspapers, congresses that link their plights. It matters little then that the majority of workers can be formed by non-party or non-union members: information is communicated, orders circulate, collective sentiments spread from active centers, the action of minorities coalesce around the majority and carry the masses along. Common sense then sees in all this confused unity, which is unceasingly open to question, the residue of a constant effort of the working class elite to organize itself. From there, profound reactions are produced in the large body, currents are born which can influence the parties, the big unions and beyond. To prove your thesis, it is this activity of organization, leadership and induction which you must take from the specialized parts and give to the whole. If not, how could you write this: "a class crushed by exploitation . . . in order to organize itself must resolve innumerable theoretical and practical problems, thus finding itself obliged to trust its leadership to a minority while on the other hand its revolutionary activity and its communist aspirations assume that it suppresses all domination in its midst and that it inaugurates a new kind of collective action?" Or this: "The whole working class . . . perceives in its privileged element an anticipation of its fate." Or: "the movement of the working class to organize itself leads it to entrust to one of its elements the functions of representation. . . . ?" Or, in another article: "The feeling which the working class has . . . of its low cultural level?" And how can you speak of "the *total* experience of class" if you did not previously give it the right to totalize its experience?

In a word, your argument will hold only if you confess your secret organicism. And that is in effect what you do. Most assuredly you do not use the word, but you palm the thing off on us. The proletariat, you say, deals only with its own activity; changes exist for it only in so far as it incorporates them. Well, is that not exactly one of the first laws of organicism? "The effect of a stimulus," writes Goldstein, "depends above all on the meaning which this stimulus has for the total organism." And if you take exception to Goldstein, will you deny having read the Gestalt psychologist Lewin, noted for having applied the same rule to social groups? He wrote, just as you did but without your caution, that a "social situation is a dynamic whole" and that a modification of the parts exists for this totality only through a synthetic modification of the whole. And, more explicitly than you do, he applies to sociology the principle of readjustment: a social group changes in order to negate prior change, thereby reestablishing equilibrium. This leads him to proclaim the relative autonomy of each "gestalt": "Each one creates its own movement." Subjectivity, then, is the interiority of the group, defined as self-determination. The trick has come off.

But what becomes of your Marxism? And must I believe that it is really the *proletariat* which you describe as a "participation in a scheme of life and action, a *particular apprehension* of the milieu," in short, as "that which permits them to act and think together and to establish themselves as different from the rest of society."

Dialectics allows us to conceive of a historical proletariat-subject, the substance and the profound guarantee of the objective proletariat of sociology. This implies at once a dialectical reversal of terms: the existence of the empirical proletariat, producing factual proof, becomes guaranteed in turn. "Participation," "apprehension," etc. imagines the proletariat for itself as a cultural "pattern" uniting individuals; as for *praxis,* whose sense may escape the worker, ("it does not matter what he thinks he is doing") it is the proletariat in itself. And, since you make a distinction between the appearance and the profound reality, one could even wonder if the proletariat *praxis* is not, in your view, the intelligible character of your proletariat-jelly. But on the other hand, the subjectivity of the proletariat as a living participation in the cultural models of the working class becomes the *object* of the sociologist, while its profound objectivity as a historical reconstruction of the rational totality leads to the proletariat as a subject of history. The noumenal proletariat is a scheme, the activity of self-organization, present unity; but it does not manifest itself. The trembling proletariat-jelly manifests itself, but this variable mixture of viscosity and of powder can equally produce separation, powerlessness and solitude: all the mystical words in which eclectic sociology likes to express its foreboding of the ineffable will not prevent men from being united by solitude, by shared impotence, by resignation, nor avoid the possibility that their manner of being one-for-the-others can be precisely a mutual distancing, an antagonism, a repulsion. Look at Malthusianism: around 1935 it reached the working class, and the birth rate collapsed. It was a question of such clear general conditions that you are bound by your principles to point out their social character. Or else would you have us admit that there is, between the finite modes and the attribute, a collective intermediary, something like the infinite mode of Spinoza? Seriously, what would you do about this growing tendency towards childlessness? Can you say that abortion practices are revolutionary? That they represent a spontaneous defense on the part of the worker against the real lowering of his wages, as Karl Marx had already observed, and that they will result in giving new values to human merchandise? Such is your system: from the first you insist that capitalism is unstable and fragile; after that, whatever the workers do they will ultimately destroy it; therefore the proletariat is in essence revolutionary. But this time, you will not convince me so easily. Opposed at once by the government, the middle class and the Party, Malthusianism, preached by anarchic-syndicalism in the desert, bears witness today to a sort of lassitude, to despair and resentment. Social duties no longer exist towards either comrades or future generations: this genocide is a rejection of the future whatever it may be, a total distrust. It is—like rioting or a wildcat strike—a radical act which can only rise from the depths of a huge population. In this sense it is most certainly an act similar to revolutionary behavior but inverted, negative, refusing what revolutionaries affirm; in reality, it is closer to servile revolt* than to revolutionary action. This asocial conduct is really social in nature; it is a contagious reaction to a mode of collective life, it tends to propagate itself; it reveals to everyone that his life is intolerable and that it is a crime to "give life," to feed the machines with other lives. In the bourgeois class abortive practices remain asocial because they are hidden. Paradoxically, the Malthusianism of the workers does not hide itself: women speak of it among themselves, exchange advice, addresses, and above all they help each other. Abortion among the middle class, like suicide and eroticism, is performed in privacy, and the persistence of these practices betrays only the persistence of the pressures of dissimulation to which the individual is subject. On the contrary, the workers' abortions are a collective practice, a common suicide, and those who practice it are united by a kind of pity. This refusal to give life answers all your requirements: it is in fact "what unites in the understanding of the same mode of life and action . . . sharing in projects . . ." etc. Better still, it could be the

* Bastide has shown how black slaves in Brazil, out of both revolt and despair, practiced Malthusianism.

direct reaction of certain working groups to the real nature of mass production. Recall those nomad Indians of Brazil who allowed themselves to die quietly when the Portuguese wanted to settle them on farms. I wonder sometimes if "working class melancholia" does not have just the same causes. The Indians were not liquidated by slavery itself, but by the change in their mode of work and their style of life, different food and the forced transition from nomadism to the sedentary life. Does not the advent of mass production, the specialized and repetitive jobs of the assembly line, lead to an analogous maladaptation among modern workers? The interest in work decreases, fatigue increases, the worker's world falls apart; depersonalization, physiological warping, interchangeability rob the worker of all his incentive. Show us then, taking this example, that the objective conditions of production are transformed by the subjectivity of the proletariat into a revolutionary experience! No, there is no passage from empirical sociality to the working class which writes history.

The idea of *class* as a mere similarity of status and interests, such as the peasant class, and the idea of *historical subject* as a subjectivity forcibly imposed on total history, are both equally empty. We have seen that it is not enough to connect them in order to escape from verbalism. When you have united sociology to history, water to fire, and class as a style of life to historical subject as *praxis,* you will not for all that have created the proletariat. For it is nothing to have "rooted" it in society, in history, in the present situation, if you do not give it at the same time *passion,* that is to say the possibility of bearing up, of suffering, even of dying. In short, the proletariat has not only a relationship with its own activity, it has to deal as well with its own inertia and through it—with the activity of the Other class. For it is also through our passion that we have the painful and ambiguous experience of the real. Even successful action, by its failures in detail, by the rhythm it imposes, by the defense that it requires, and by the fatigue which it causes, reveals to us our inertia. Work, moreover, presupposes it; were it not for inertia man could neither make his tools nor use his abilities properly, as Marx has said. And you who reproach me for seeing "only the work which one performs upon oneself," how could you not see that work is *misery*. And if you see it why do you not show that this experience is also the experience of passion; it is only in this way that it permits a painful and equivocal "understanding" of reality. When Marx criticizes Hegel for having stood dialectics on its head, he does not merely contrast materialism to idealism: he wants to show that each moment of dialectic is a conquest achieved by effort and work, and if necessary by combat, against chance and exteriority. He wants to reintroduce into our most rigorously devised enterprises delay, disproportion, and constant distortion of our operations—in short, the permanent possibility of a disorder which shows the constant risk that humanity may destroy itself. And when Hegel speaks of the "moment which stands by itself," Marx sees above all that the very work of man, becoming a thing, manifests in turn the inertia of a thing, its coefficient of adversity; he sees that the human relationships which man creates fall back again into inertia, introducing the inhuman as a destructive force among men. We dominate the environment by work, but the environment dominates us in turn by the rigidified swarm of thoughts we have inscribed there. Marxist dialectic is not the spontaneous movement of the Spirit, but the hard work of man to enter a world which rejects him. Someone recently recalled how Brunschvicq blamed Hegel for not having introduced any *resistance* into his system. Without anything which restrains, succession remains a formal idea, an order. A concrete and real duration appears only with effort, waiting, patience and impatience. Time is the necessity of being early or late in relation to an enterprise: here we have again returned to the lump of Bergsonian sugar. But Hegelian time neither advances nor slows down; in its calm development things occupy the only place that they could occupy. Of course there are vestiges, conflicts which can slow the march of history. But let us not be confused; it is a question only of self-regulation; these fictional restraints will permit the Idea to manifest itself in all its facets; they are the deceptions of Reason. Hegelian dialectic necessarily relates to past time since one cannot *live* in it. It is only in past time that things are always in their place;

but Marx has allowed us to recover true dialectical time. Yet apparently accepting the premises of Marxism, you have eliminated the resistances of things and of men, and you revert to Hegelian idealism. You would have us believe that the subjective experience of the working class corresponds exactly to the contemporary order, or that the same reality is translated simultaneously and without distortion into two different languages, for the degree of subjective organization of the working class expresses the nature and the degree of the socialization of work. Through this exact correspondence you destroy reality for the sake of meaning.

I do not deny that the worker's experience seeks ceaselessly to adjust to the evolution of capitalism, that it has been able, at times, to correspond exactly to the worker's status taken in its totality, and that this harmony between the subjective and the objective may occur again tomorrow. I only say that this reciprocity becomes unreal if it is claimed that it will be realized spontaneously, for adjustment is not automatic, an effort must be made. I see in the working class movement a conscious and constantly renewed effort on the part of associations to catch up with delays, to hasten those evolutions that are too slow and to reach the level of managerial organization, sometimes by eliminating the intermediary stages.

Enough. I wanted only to give a very rapid and superficial sketch of this confused history, so full of delays and lost chances, in which the working class seems to exhaust itself in catching up with an earlier delay, whose path is often disturbed by exterior violence, wars, etc. and whose subject transforms itself rapidly without anyone being aware of it. I notice not only the changes in the rate of production, but also the political aspects of the situation; I see that one could understand nothing about this if he refused to envisage it under the aspect of *struggle;* I see that the leaders are nothing without the masses, but the working class has coherence and power only in so far as it has confidence in the leaders. As for the authority of the leadership, I see also that it is neither usurped nor illusory. The leader interprets the situation, illumines it by his plans, at his own risk, and the working class, by observing the directives, *legitimizes* the authority of the leader: "It is in *practice* that a man must demonstrate the truth, that is to say, the reality and power, the scope of his thought." I do not know why you cite Rosa Luxembourg and Trotsky, for I say nothing that they have not said and they say something quite different from what you say. It is not a question of showing the Communist Party dictating its opinion to the masses. The Party cannot be distinguished from the masses except insofar as it is their union, and through this very union they produce their internal currents. On the basis of these currents it interprets the *situation* of the working class in society and its present position in the traditional struggle that it heads. The Party shapes the social framework of working class memory, it is the sketch of their future, the agent of their action, the permanent bond which struggles against their dehumanization; it is the *perspective* from which the proletariat can find a new role for itself in society and in turn take for object those who would make of it an object: it serves as both tradition and institution. But the *content* of these empty forms will grow through the very effort which the masses make to unify themselves; it is by intimate association that particular interests become general, and isolated individuals become an enterprise.

For proof of this I need only the example of "creativity" which you yourself cite. The initial experience was a scandal: in 1903 it was discovered that trained workers were no longer irreplaceable. The strike lost much of its effectiveness; all the more reason for the semiskilled workers to have appeared defenceless. It took thirty-three years in France* for men to find a new solution, thirty-three years during which, after the failure of revolutionary movements and the general retreat of the proletarians, despite the poverty or perhaps because of it, are recorded a slowing down of social conflicts and the growth of the percentage of defeated strikes. Why, then, in 1936, when the external threats became clearer and a weak resumption of business began, why did the masses invent "the take-over of the factories?" There is no longer any doubt that the movement was "spontaneous." Is one then obliged to see it as an action

* Strikes within the factories occurred in Italy from 1918 until Fascism.

of the entire working class? We can determine here the *true* sense of this *spontaneity*: in actuality, the masses are normally structured, they have newspapers, they are influenced by the parties and unions; the crowd has a nervous system whose muscle tone spreads with diminishing strength. Now in this environment, which is already somewhat "centralized," one learns suddenly that universal franchise has elected 146 socialists and 72 communists to the Chamber of Deputies. In 1935 (on July 14, for example) there had been political demonstrations which had sometimes gathered more than a half-million people, and the July 14 Committee was "supported by popular enthusiasm." But one must remember that the Popular Front was a political union whose unity was created on the top level; local elections indicated a shift to the left by the electors, that is to say, by those citizens in the framework of democratic institutions. The Popular Front's rise to power, after so many signs, was considered by the workers to be a sort of promotion of the proletariat: in the person of its leaders, it was the working class which took over the powers of government; the solidarity of these two mass parties and their unity in action reflected its own characteristic unity; never since 1871 was the working class so completely conscious of itself. Now around the same time (May 11 at Le Havre, May 13 at Toulouse, May 14 at Courbevoie) three strikes broke out which were accompanied by the occupation of the factories. The press said nothing about it at first, but *L'Humanité* observed on May 24 that in the three conflicts the workers adopted new techniques of fighting; that same day 600,000 paraders marched past the "*Wall of the Federals*." Around May 26, the strike movement became widespread in the environs of Paris and in June it spread throughout France.

It is clear that the working class felt its subjective unity in so far as it saw its objective victory in elections, clear too that it extended in terms of further activity the victory of its political parties. In short, it interiorized its objective unity which was only the objective unity of its leadership. Its victory in the setting of bourgeois institutions, through its leaders, was lived in and by its occupation of the factories. The pressure relaxed, something was going to change, the worker could speak to the owner as an equal. They struck in joy *because it was easy.* That speaks eloquently of the force of that permanent repression, that continuous presence of the armed enemy, of which you seem unaware, of that active, deliberate, unambiguous counterpart of exploitation, governmental oppression with its police and if need be the army. These masses began to assert themselves because their leaders ruled France; and if they *invented* the occupation of the factories, they did so because for the first time they dared to do so. Doubtless they pushed the government farther than it wanted to go: when they unite, the masses have their rhythm, their style of thought and of action. But they were able to steer this action from one frontier to the other because they were constantly united by rallies, by speeches, by encouraging newspapers and they saw their unity as both a guarantee and a promise. In a word, it was *within the framework* of the accession to power by the elected members of the Popular Front that the masses, *already* united, manifested all their desires and their real will. You will say, perhaps, that the *Société Française de l'Internationale Ouvrière* and the Communist Party in uniting only expressed the proletariat. This is quibbling, for if expression could determine this immense tidal wave, then expression is also action. That is what I tried to explain in my article: "spontaneity" exists insofar as the class *already united* can go beyond its leaders, steer them farther than they meant to go and can translate into the *social* sphere an initial decision which was perhaps only *political.*

But how could you even conceive of what Trotsky called "the dialectic of the heads of the party and the masses" when you have decided *a priori* never to interpret the behavior of the proletariat as *passion?* How could you admit, for example, that the masses of 1936 gave a *social* interpretation to a *political* action: you are so afraid to acknowledge any activity by its "apparatus" that you reduce political struggles to secondary and intermittent phenomena of proletarian experience. "There are not two currents, one which proceeds by means of political demonstrations, the other through economic consolidation; there is an experience of the opposition which occurs constantly in the midst of and through the process of production and which more and more crystallizes into an overt struggle on a scale which involves all society, and which challenges the power of the state."

In one detail we agree: there are not two currents. But let us see what conclusions you draw from that.

From its inception, according to you, the proletariat exists; it lives its status of the exploited under the active form of an opposition to exploitation. Hardly born, it raises the question of the right of the middle class to govern. However, let us not believe that it rejects its condition: such a rejection would lead one to believe that it endures its condition, that its status is imposed upon it. Now really! "To reject one's status when it is by virtue of this status that the conditions of struggle and social revolution are given!" I know you quite well and yet you have really surprised me by this sentence. It is true that the worker has the right to strike; and production, which in the present order "empties the producer of his substance," produces the long-term death of capitalism. But from the fact that this intolerable situation contains in itself the contradiction which will (much later) terminate it, must one conclude that the worker has to accept it? One might as well say that the sick man wants his illness because it is the basis of his cure and the means of medical progress. The proletarian status is defined not only by manual work; it is also defined by the condition of being a wage earner; and when I said that the worker rejects his status, I thought I was repeating what Marx said a hundred times.[22] But you, you have dropped one of the principal themes of *Capital* because it disturbs you: it disturbs you that the hourly wage progressively destroys the man who receives it; that terrible progressive decadence which Marx foresees on each page of his work disturbs you. More than anyone else, Marx insisted on the degrading character of paid work; he showed how it undermines

[22] "The proletariat has of necessity the task of revolutionizing its conditions of existence. . . . The proletariat sees its impotence and the reality of an inhuman existence. . . . It has lost all authority, and revolts against its condition, a revolt to which it is pushed necessarily by the contradiction between its human nature and its vital existence which is the manifest, total and decisive negation of it," etc.

the worker physically, deforming him to the point of illness. It brutalizes him, debases him to the role of helot, exposes him to every deception. He dared write that Lassalle owed his success to the degradation of the German working class. Yet of this I find no echo in your article. However, when Marx spoke of this brutishness or when he called the worker a subhuman, he did not mean to insult him, quite the reverse, and it seemed to him that the only means of being a man today was to be "a subhuman, conscious of his subhumanity." He wanted to insist on the difficulty of the struggle, he wanted to show that the worker is crushed *from the first,* brutalized and weakened. Rendered defenseless, he is conquered in advance, circumvented by capital. What is remarkable is that little by little he will transcend this state exactly as man himself in several millennia rose from the bestial state. But you systematically forget that work is an "enemy power." Marx repeatedly tells us of the dangers of industrial production, even, despite his usual reserve in speaking of the future, to making recommendations to the socialist government: "Socialized producers rationally govern the metabolism between them and nature, submitting it to their joint control instead of being dominated by it as by a blind force." Marx urges them to transform "the isolated and specialized individual who merely fills a social function into a wholly developed human being . . ." All of that strongly displeases you, for you sense, I imagine, the difficulties which Marx encounters; you want to evade the argument that Andler and others have made against him, that he has two conceptions of the proletariat: one of which is catastrophic while the other implies a sort of permanent revolution. They have said that a hundred times: if the worker descends to the last degree of decadence, how then will he be capable of assuming the responsibility of the man in power when the final crisis derails the capitalist machine? Fundamentally, that amounts to saying: if the worker is passive, how will he be transformed into an active agent of history? But these two conceptions only exist in the analytic understanding of certain socialists. In fact, Marx saw the necessity of a constant effort of emancipation which needed to be all the more sustained as the working class saw its condition worsen further. In short, Marx's thesis has always been the reciprocal conditioning of both progressive (and *relative,* that is to say, representing the increasing diminution of wages *in relation to* surplus value) impoverishment and permanent revolution. To transform poverty into a factor of revolution, one must make such poverty conscious of its nature and its needs. But that is just what bothers you, for what is needed is precisely specialization. Right, a part of the working force will first join together to call the others to organize; the militants will unite the masses and instruct them. Mediation is necessary between the working class, an activity as a historical enterprise, and the masses, the passive product of production. There must be *someone* to transform into upward thrust the weight which drags the masses down, to transform suffering into demands. It is that which makes you lose your wits: if the masses are affected by a degree of passivity, then the Party can play a historical role—that is what you must deny at any cost. And you replace by a smooth evolution the tough struggle between the forces of unification and the forces of dispersal which is unleashed in the very midst of the workers. From its inception, the proletariat was gifted; when young, it already contested the validity of bourgeois power; this good subject, this happy native profoundly "rooted in nature and history" expanded under the gentle influence of daily work. Gentle and harsh, of course: there would sometimes be enough to make one lose heart, but he tells himself that he has assumed this heavy task in order to liberate humanity; and that gives him all his energy, as does that Latin proverb which he frequently murmurs: *Labor improbus vincit omnia.* However, he progresses until he is ready to restructure the conditions of industrial production. Then it will be Arcadia, original simplicity recovered in the heart of abundance. In short, we come back to the very sophisms which I denounced in my article: in order to discount the Party, one must deny the worker's passivity, or, if you prefer, have it swallowed up by activity. Then we will have that "natural but not unconscious development" which leads us insensibly from the proletariat-seed to the proletariat-flower, and at last to the proletariat-fruit.

All that is fine, and to avoid recognizing the effectiveness of Communist action, you rapidly substitute terms: you attribute the activity of the Communist Party to the proletariat as a whole, and you recognize in the Communist Party only a passive existence. This inertia is the one which *also* existed among the proletariat and which you palm off on it. But do you realize that you are going from Charybdis to Scylla? If the proletariat is autonomous, if it deals only with its own activity, if the parties and associations only passively express the degree of its organization, where does *error* come from? If you reject the right to explain the influence of Lassalle by the "brutalization" of the German working class, how *will* you explain it? For, in the last analysis, in error, in political mistakes, in mystification, there is non-being. But what is the source of this non-being if the proletariat is pure activity? You sense so well that you have come up against the old problem which ruins all dogmatism, you are so conscious of the difficulties in which you are going to drown yourself, that you try first to destroy the very idea of error. Let us take reformism: it seems to you impossible that it can be "customary," that it comes from mystification or betrayal. It is not, nor could it be, an "illusion" of the working class. Why? Because "ideology expresses certain real social relationships and the very ambiguity (of reformism) expresses the double social character of the worker's unity and diversity . . . The entire working class perceives in its privileged minority an anticipation of its own fate."

Splendid. But why do you add: "If reformism revealed itself for what it is it would not be equivocal . . ."? Does it not reveal itself for what it is? And that which the masses perceive as an anticipation of their own fate, isn't that, according to you, reality? Isn't the personal advantage which the privileged minority acquires what one calls an illusion? You say no: illusion is an error which is not based on reality: where did you learn that? If I mistake a tree for a man, this illusion is surely explicable by reality. It implies a certain organization of my senses, a certain structure of the field of perception, a whole disposition, a "behavior" which inserts me into the world in this place; the fear which I feel before this dark form is obviously the very meaning, the subjective expression of this whole. In this sense it is perfectly founded in reality, insofar as it expresses something which exists. However, I admit that it escapes us insofar as it points to *something which does not exist* (this non-existent man who scares me); but it is precisely this which has characterized the working class attitude towards reformism, at least as you describe it: its understanding of the present fate of the privileged minority as representative of its own future fate is in effect founded in reality. Insofar as it means *something,* it manifests the proletariat's "distance in unity." But insofar as it sees in this privileged minority an evolution which will lead it from reform to reform *under its leaders* until the final overthrow, it expresses something which does not exist and which has no basis in reality. And even if it should realize in its midst the indissoluble union of reformism and revolution, nevertheless the exteriorization, the alienation from its objective tendency, the projection of itself outside, the deflection of the movement by a minority which exploits it and that manner of seizing as a *necessary future* what is subjective *will,* all this would still bring us *precisely* to the *illusion of reformism.*

From Error we go on to Evil. The working class *is* always all that it can *accomplish,* the political struggle is intermittent, the subjective experience is expressed by a constant progress of self-organization; moreover, the proletariat only deals with its own activity and it has nothing in it which does not express it and is not based on real foundations. Then why aren't you a Communist? Since the Communist Party is not exterior to the working class, since it is not separated from the masses except by that "distance" which the exercise of power generates, it must represent the working class. And where would its influence on the working class come from if it were not exactly what the working class had made it? Others have accused it of representing the interests of a foreign nation, but as you are logical you do not make a point of it and you realize the hat trick which presents us with a "Stalinism without Stalin." All enemies and friends of Communism—and the Communists themselves—without denying the extreme importance of national factors, refuse to study the development of the European Communist Parties independently of their relations with the U.S.S.R.; opinions differ when it is a matter of evaluating the role of the U.S.S.R. and its influence on national politics. But you write tranquilly: "Stalinism can be interpreted in this sense *even before* its relationship to the existing government in the U.S.S.R. has been closely studied, but evidently the fact that it has been realized in another country has played a decisive role in the expansion and the consciousness of the Stalinist bureaucracy." You cannot admit that the characteristic evolution of Soviet society has influenced the internal structure of the French Communist Party: it would be necessary to recognize that the Communist Party partially receives its status from without; the proletariat would be directed by an ambiguous agency whose movement should be conditioned simultaneously by currents which sweep through the working classes and by the transformations of a foreign society, that is to say, finally by the Other and by world events. But in your monadology, the working class "has neither door nor window through which anything can enter or leave." So you have recourse to preestablished harmony: each proletariat produces its own Stalinism and if one of these bureaucracies seizes power in its country, an admirable propriety produces within each little national Stalinism an appropriate change; it is not a matter, moreover, of an alteration of structure: let us say that it will take less time to become what it is. The *outward* appearance of Stalinism-without-Stalin is felt *within* by the Stalinisms-without-Stalin in the form of a relationship of the proletariat to its own actions. However that is where the "reciprocity of perspectives" leads when one employs it without discernment: in the present constitution of the French proletariat you claim to find the U.S.S.R. on a small scale; inversely, the entire Soviet society seems an enlargement of the regional proletariats. In each of these you can find the dialectical movement of the other, but for each, you must remain on the level of self-organization.

What is the result of this monadology? It is at any rate paradoxical: you, declaring yourself hostile to "Stalinism," have denied yourself the means of condemning it, while I, for example, with many others who only use "common sense," do not hide my sympathies for many aspects of the Communist enterprise, yet I reserve the right and the means to appreciate it. What you refuse on principle I accept without difficulty. I admit that there are in the working class memory partially or temporarily unintelligible experiences whose key can be found in the hands of the Kominform or in those of another proletariat. Of all susceptivities, the ones which you fight the most are the passions which come to us from the Other and which suppose the intrusion of the Other in us: but I encounter in myself, in all men, in all groups and even in all classes, the presence of the Other, not only as a stranger to whom one is opposed in complicity, but as the objectifying power which penetrates us, divides us and makes us possible traitors in the eyes of the other members of the group. I understand very well the relation of the French Communist Party to the Kominform and to the U.S.S.R. Each group resents the Other in itself as its own inertia. Whatever constitutes the real dependence of the Communist Party on the Kominform, their relation necessarily implies conflicts, oppositions, concessions, accomodations, compromises. What is granted to the Other is present then in each as an inertia, as an opaque crystallization, as a layer of non-life in the midst of life. Of course we are not arguing fundamentals: I only want to say that the French Communist Party, subordinated, local, imperfectly informed about world issues, allows itself to be infiltrated by the activity of the Other, which then becomes an unconditioned source of its own activity. At the same time, the proletariat, when it respects the orders of the Party and of the *Confédération Générale du Travail,* engages in an activity which reflects at once its own tendencies, the political form which the Party gives them, and the more abstract imperative, farther from the Kominform. Insofar as the Party in the midst of the working class is the *subject* of its activity, there is in its subjective interiority a layer of objectivity and exteriority, and this subject cannot be a subject for itself, that is to say, "to deal with its own activity," except insofar as it is an object for another subject. The "distance" which is established between the proletariat and that part of itself which represents it does not come from the exercise of power alone. In the very midst of the proletariat, the Other is introduced through the Communist Party; the order given by the chiefs no longer aims at the workers in the immanence of the working class, but without objectifying them entirely it makes itself the conductive climate for a transcendent activity which at the deepest stratum of the working class appears as a certain *level* of its objectification (a level much more intimate than that of its objectivity for management). This purely formal description aims only at establishing *the existence of the Other* as an objectifying activity for the deepest of subjectivities. It remains true for all hypotheses; that is, it does not determine whether the relationship of the Communist Party to the U.S.S.R. is favorable or harmful to the interests of the French proletariat. I simply claim that one cannot find an answer to this question if one does not first accept the hypothesis of a constant interaction.

You reject this. Therefore you can only be silent. Those whom you call "Stalinists" would agree without hesitation that neither the authoritarian Party nor the Soviet state can be envisaged as the definitive form of proletarian organization. It is a question of temporary agencies, adapted to the present conditions of the class struggle, and which the proletariat will reabsorb when these conditions have changed. In return, you agree that the workers, for the most part, keep their attachment to the Communist Party. How could it be otherwise? It is "the characteristic movement of the class to organize itself which strengthens the process of social differentiation and the power of a working class minority." In Stalinism as in yesterday's reformism, the working class recognizes its reflection, its work, the temporary trustee of its sovereignty.

And yet you judge that this minority wrongs the working class. How can it? It draws all its power from the proletariat, which cannot turn its own activity against itself. All powerful as its voice, the ruling "segment" is only its voice: to harm it, to brake its development, it would have to possess an evil force which comes to it from the void. Since the proletariat only deals with its own activity, since you have been able to write that "the working class trusts a segment," etc., what sudden modesty prevents you from adding that it has elected by itself and for itself an authoritarian form of organization? You who see in wage earning and the inhuman harshness of work "conditions and means" to "restructure the conditions of production," why do you not show "Stalinism" as the unique, if harsh, means of giving military unity to the masses—or, in your language, as the expression of inflexible discipline which the proletariat imposes upon itself while absorbing its recent social changes? Oh! you will say, that is something quite different: do you not see that this bureaucracy exploits workers? Now here is your fairy tale. First, the differentiation of a minority. Second, the creation of a *distance* by the very fact that in the working class political and economic functions are not autonomous: bureaucratic authoritarianism. This is as true for reformism as for the Communist Party. Third, the minority "becomes a part of the exploiting system." It prepares a new organization which will transform the working class into an unconscious, regimented mass exploited by its own bureaucracy. Fourth, "reformism" characterized a minority who wanted to become a part of the exploiting capitalist system. "Stalinism" appears when capitalism no longer has anything to offer the "new men" of the working class. It will then lead the life and death struggle against the elite in power. It fights for the coming of a new form of exploitation characterized by the rule of the worker's bureaucracy and state management of the economy.

Reading you, I sometimes think that I am mistaken, that by accident I opened the *Social Contract,* because like Rousseau you confuse the real with the ideal world. For finally, this description, *if one applies it to the U.S.S.R.,* is not original, which is not to say that it is false. For a long time the Soviet government and administration have been seen to be linked to the Russian Communist Party as a minority (some say, a class—and you do not hesitate to use the word) which founded a kind of state capitalism and which, in this new framework, continues the exploitation of the workers. Simply, the critics of the regime—Trotsky, Serge, who, anyhow, had helped to build it—distinguished between what it could have been and what it had become; they relied on *historical* circumstances to account for this "degenerescence." The masses were tired, the resistance of the peasants turned to civil war, etc. Trotsky, moreover, while recognizing that circumstances dictated the bureaucratization of the Party, nevertheless conceived a certain margin of possibility within this very bureaucracy: there was the *good* bureaucrat—who might have been Trotsky himself—and the *bad* bureaucrat—who was Stalin. You have swept that all aside, for it was still too much alive, it rankled, and then, after all, the Revolution of 1917 was not your work. Hence, all power comes from the Devil; all authority exercised by a working class minority on the working class in the name of the class itself must *necessarily* transform itself into an exploiting bureaucracy. Fine, it is neater like that, one might say, embalmed. But it is self-evident that historical circumstances do not justify your point of view: for example, you get caught up in your stories about "distance" and you do not consider it possible that the present form of Russian experience can be dictated, even partially, by the *vital* necessity to intensify production. This Platonic description never takes into account the situation of the U.S.S.R. around 1920. Then an immense socialist country, threatened from without, its wealth ravaged by war, its industry, although it had made strides in the first years of the century, had a delay of a hundred years to make up. To intensify industrialization, develop productive industries, create new frameworks, establish a scientific organization, a technocracy which in its outlines resembles the final stage of capitalist societies: do you not think that these obligations were fundamental? And do you not agree that Soviet society, its existence threatened by bourgeois democracies, had to impose an iron discipline or disappear? Let us take another tack. At this stage of production, industrial organization is dictatorial and the division of labor attacks the very unity of the worker; for not one second, however, did you wonder whether the form of political power was not *everywhere* conditioned by the form of economic organization (which they improperly call technocracy). You show the bureaucratic minority dreaming of joining the capitalist bureaucracy in the framework of state control; but you do not even think that this minority of the proletariat could also form an authoritarian bureaucracy in order to *fight* the bureaucratic authoritarianism of bourgeois democracies. In short, you do not even think of showing that the fundamental necessities of production, at the present level of technology, determine *above all* and for each of the hostile classes the present form of the class struggle. Your "Stalinist" minorities are alone in the world; they deal neither with the exhausted masses, dispersed in the midst of dense populations and yet regimented, nor with economic, social and political necessities; neither with enemies from within or without nor with a specific predicament, that is to say, with the relation of the powers between themselves, with the U.S.A. and the U.S.S.R. You have defined Stalinism without taking into account any of these conditions; your only explanation is the general morphology of the proletariat. At a certain level of development, the working class produces an auto-toxin, "Stalinism," which can poison it if it does not succeed quickly enough in eliminating it. Nothing else counts. And even, you would have us believe, the *fact* of the Russian Revolution does not have the importance that is too often attached to it: self-poisoning took place without it, elimination will take place despite the Soviet bureaucracy, everywhere and first of all among the Russians. This episode has significance only for the Russian and Czech workers who discovered the truth all at once.*

But this last remark suddenly surprises me: How can that be? Must one be Russian to see through mystification? "Yes," you tell

* Here I hesitate for fear of betraying you: *do* they discover the truth or *must* they discover it? Could you tranquilly affirm here that you possess sufficient documentation to undertake the study of the "working class" in the U.S.S.R.? By valid documentation I mean: documents whose origin is clearly established, mainly first hand, judged by internal and external criteria, which can be correlated with other series of documents, and which permit either a general view of one sector of industry, or a detailed study of one industrial complex. And if you do not have that, what can you say? That the worker is exploited in the U.S.S.R.? By this you aim above all at the economic system. The discussion is open, but it is not that which occupies us at present. Our subject is rather whether the working class in the U.S.S.R. is opposed to exploitation, but the only proof you can furnish is that it is indeed opposed because it could not fail to be so without contradicting you.

me, "in so far as the ruling minority has not seized power, exploitation is not clear." And I see, in effect, that the French bourgeoisie does not share with the Communists either its capital or its income: Stalinism cannot exploit while it is "an opposition deprived of all participation in power." All right, then our Communists are not exploiters and it is their authoritarianism which you blame. They "turn the proletariat into a passive element . . . they send it into conflicts and alliances without worrying about its conscious evolution . . . discussion, elaboration, justification (concessions imposed on the proletariat) never leave the framework of a small minority of leaders." But the proletariat cannot be passive unless it determines itself: it cannot give meaning to the existence of the Communist Party unless it incorporates it into the experience of the working class. Moreover, does it not aim at the precise goal of overthrowing the bourgeoisie and seizing power? You say that is the very goal of Stalinism: a struggle with the bourgeoisie whose ultimate goal is the capture of the powers of the state. We agree, it is the Communist Party which must lead the working class to victory, yet you demur; first the radical opposition of Stalinism to the middle class "does not *a priori* express the revolutionary action of the masses" but rather the incapacity of the present bourgeoisie "to open a prospect of progress to the working class aristocracy and bureaucracy." Now what is this "working class aristocracy?" And where did you prove what you have set forth? Let us admit that a distance is created necessarily between the leaders and the rest of the working class: let us also admit that the ruling minority shows a tendency to think of its own interests; yet it remains to be shown that this tendency induces "bureaucracy" to "participate in the exploiting system, and, not finding what it was looking for there, is tempted to substitute a new mode of exploitation." After all, if you did not know in advance the conclusion that had to be drawn, you could conclude on the contrary that the failure of their attempt sends the leaders back to the working class and shows them the impossibility of distinguishing their own fate from the complete victory of the proletariat. Is that not how the workers discover the vanity of their antagonisms and, in order to transcend their impotence, substitute class interests to particular ones? What allows you to write that they will exploit the workers? The example of the U.S.S.R.? In order to be convincing, one must decide *a priori* to eliminate all historical circumstances; one must erect as a principle that the fate of a revolution depends uniquely upon the rulers and that one can accurately predict its course only if one knows the nature of the ruling elite; one must affirm that all revolutions directed by the Communist Party must end in a Soviet society. Or else will you lean upon the present characteristics of the French Communist Party and upon the nature of its authority? You seem to be thinking of doing so: you notice that it amounts to the same thing "to institute military-type relationships in a group . . . and to participate in the system of exploitation." But "Stalinism" does not participate "in the system" since, according to you, it only aims at overthrowing it. And "military" authority is linked to exploitation only in your mind, for if the working class submits to this authority, it is because the present circumstances of this struggle, the power of ownership and the size of the conflicts require that it submit to a dictatorial and centralizing power on the world level. Only you have your preconceived idea that the class struggle does not exist. If violence and hatred are found among the Communists, the working man is innocent of them; certainly he does not like the bourgeois but he has other things to worry about, and it is not hatred which makes him resemble the "Stalinist" but his concern to reorganize industry on a rational basis; in other words, he "participates in certain aspirations of the bureaucracy": in short, you confess, not without embarrassment, that the attachment of the masses to the Communist Party is not the result of an "illusion."

That brings us back to our subject: where does Error come from? where does Evil come from? How can the revolutionary masses submit to the counter-revolutionary action of the Party? The exercise of power creates distance. Excellent, but if the Communist Party attempted to treat the masses as a passive object, it would not be successful if the masses did not allow themselves to be so led. You cannot escape it: if the Communist Party is counter-revolutionary, then the working class must equally be so, according to your principles; if it is bureaucratized, then the working class has produced the bureaucracy as a moment of its experience and self-organization. Since you are not a Communist, it must be that you are making a value judgment on the Party. I am not going to correct you, for it is neither the time nor the place to defend or attack. What I want to make you see is that you have undermined your own position by replacing Trotskyite possibility with Hegelian necessity.

You say that you have not made any judgments; what turns you away from the Communist Party is that the working class is similarly turned away from it. It is in the process of experiencing its opposition to all forms of exploitation, including Stalinist bureaucracy. You reserve for yourself the role of illuminating it.

But how can you expect that they are going to believe you unless they share your Hegelianism? You say that the proletariat is trying a new experiment. How can you tell? By certain signs. Like you, we are familiar with these signs; the right wing press lists them every morning: the vague discontentment of 1947, the union schisms, the growing apathy, the rejected strikes and protest demonstrations, the refusal to go to the polls in the working class districts during the last local elections, the information that the Communist Party itself gives us on the decline of party membership in certain departments. But these facts must be interpreted. *Le Figaro,* which like you although for different motives, aims at dividing the working class from its leadership, would like to see in that a proof of a proletarian move. The newspaper sees it as the explosion of revolt after a long period of patience. Tired of submitting to an oppression which leads him to destruction, the worker stands up and says no. The Communist Party prefers to see this as an instance of *passion.* After a period of indecision on the part of the leaders, the masses were baffled; of course, they quickly add that "in most cases the workers made their own corrections." No matter: to absolve the masses, they blame the Central Committee and the Political Bureau; but in doing this they risk concentrating in them the entire activity of the working class. In short, we are dealing with contrary interpretations. Simplify them and you will have two banal images: the working class revolts against the bad shepherds who have led them astray; after steering off course, the proletarian ship seems disabled. Neither interpretation is entirely false and I do not think that one can interpret the present situation except as an inextricable mixture of action and passion in which passion temporarily dominates. But that is not your path: the proletariat has neither doors nor windows; it undergoes nothing. What we would naively take to be a profound but ephemeral discouragement, you would see as an active refusal and a new self-consciousness. Several months ago you were not quite positive, you were still questioning: "The antipathy of the most alert workers towards a new party is evident. Is this rejection merely a minor aspect of the workers' demoralization or does it have a deeper meaning?" But you have found very quickly the deeper sense and you recently showed it to us: the proletariat is in the process of drawing the conclusion from a new experience: "The working class cannot alienate itself from any form of structured and stable representation without this representation becoming autonomous." Coming back to itself, the working class understands its own nature more profoundly: it cannot divide itself, it will exercise power totally and as a totality or not at all. There we have the mainspring of your machinery. The workers may seem discouraged, yet when the good apostles propose to form a new party, they send them packing. The simplest way of understanding their attitude is to ask them what they have to say about it; it is true that we only know their conscious reason: no, they say, no more politics; we are helpless, we can change nothing. Or else they show a certain annoyance towards the C.G.T. or the Party, but they continue to support them, as the union elections show; and if they distrust the so-called revolutionary parties, it is not—to take them at their word—that they are aware of the working class as a whole but rather that they suspect that they have been sold out. Are there any other reasons for their behavior? Profound reasons? Perhaps, but no objective sign allows one to discover them. How can you be so certain? By virtue of a clearer and richer understanding? by some exigency of the object? by virtue of some sixth sense which gives you access to great depths? No: quite simply by virtue of your *a priori* desire to interpret common experience in a profound manner. You decided that depth was possible, in other words, that the immediate conditions of sociological experience could always be interpreted in terms of *praxis*. Everything happens then as if you wondered how these repulsions represent the proletariat as a subject of history. It is a matter, then, of projecting what is passive *into activity* and of establishing a system of correspondence between the negative realities and the positive realities so that the former appear the objective signs of the latter. And in fact when one has become accustomed to your system, one can read without cracking a smile the sentence that you once wrote on the working class avant-garde: "The reasons which prevent it from acting are a sign of its maturity."

But proof is lacking. Why should this correspondence exist since you have not succeeded in showing that the working class is *praxis* and subject? And even if you had established that there is an empirical proletariat and an intelligible proletariat, what permits one to believe that the correspondence between them is precise? Why is this discouragement simply nothing more than discouragement? Can you say that the loss of faith among the workers involves them in a movement whose sense is the abolition of all specialized agencies, all specific authority in the midst of the working class? One must be suspicious here. When Marx wrote: "It does not matter what the worker thinks he is doing, what counts is that he is obliged to act," he means that the objecive results of action may be very different from what was anticipated; and too, that action, strictly defined by the situation itself and by objective structures, better expresses the reality of the agent, his powers, and his function than the idea he has of his possibilities and his aims. Action preserves, in one sense, its practical organization; it always corresponds to a goal as to a dialectical unity of its means, although it becomes separated from the original intentions of the agent. Thus the social world is inhabited by actions which have lost their agents. But the *intention* behind these free acts, although it constitutes one of their objective structures, has the singular character of never returning to any consciousness. Intentions without consciousness, actions without subjects, human relationships without men, participating at once in material necessity and finality: such are generally our undertakings when they develop freely in the dimension of objectivity. Admitting that the dispersed reactions of the workers, whose subjective meaning is discouragement, can be seen in their objective results as contributing to make any worker's party impossible, what will they say? This, most assuredly: here is what the workers *have done*. But the objective results of the workers' action refer to a *virtual* intention as to an ideal unity of the moments of the undertaking; they cannot be referred to an actual consciousness—collective or not—nor to a subjective experience. On the contrary, one could say that the objective reality of action, precisely because it is objective, rejects all relation to actual subjectivity. If therefore the result of it should be, later, the negation of all parties, this negation cannot be attributed to the working class, not as a subjective experience—since it has not yet been revealed—nor as an actual intention—since it presents itself precisely as something *other* than what the subject wanted. In short, *you cannot make a class from that*. When you insist on having the proletariat benefit in subjective experience from the objective implications of its conduct, you mystify us, you create a phantom-subject in order to assemble the *virtual intentions* which are, by principle, without subject; you then pretend to uncover this objective subjectivity spread throughout the consciousnesses of individuals and you alienate the individual consciousnesses from this spectre in order to liberate them from the Communist Party. That is what you did for production: it has fatal consequences for capitalism since it unceasingly increases the accumulation of capital. Any productive strategy is subjectively a whole organized of ends and means; objectively, it sustains petrified intentions, among others that of annihilating the present regime. But if you constitute the very basis of proletarian experience as the reinteriorization of these intentions, baptized "revolutionary opposition," you transform the real into unreality, class into ideas of class and experience into the idea of experience. Your working class, Lefort, has never existed; and it is for this reason that it does not have doors or windows. What is it? The objective structure of collective acts, reconstructed according to their results and presented as the subjective and profound content of *all* individual consciousnesses and of each of them, that is to say, as a privileged presence *beyond* actual subjectivities. That is where the ambiguity of this spectre comes from: by its actual objectivity it is, in each, an *object* and you speak of it often as of a cultural "pattern"; but by its unreal subjectivity it becomes only an idea and one suspects in it a sort of ideal activity, or more precisely, the activity of ideas. Your proletariat does not exist: it could not then disapprove of the partics nor experience itself. There is nothing to explain, Lefort, except, perhaps, the obscure roots of your lucubrations: but you have not come quite that far.

Someone said about the English philosophers that their empiricism is optimistic: anyone who denies the power of the mind to prescribe its laws upon Nature and to regulate its course unconsciously believes in the existence of a natural order which imposes itself on the world and on the mind. In other words, the passivity of contemplation demands the activity of the contemplated object. Thus, the harmonious development which you give to the working class has no other purpose than to justify your inaction. You show that it is organized only so that you may may be quit of all duties towards it. You wall it in solitude so as not to be obligated to relate yourself to it. You have taken it out of the sphere of action, and you are out of its reach; passion could not alter your judgments; you share neither its goals nor its style of life. A pure object of knowledge for your pure mind, it develops with the inflexible rigidity of an idea while your only office is to shed light on it. For you the idea of the proletariat is an end in itself. A philosopher I know, after having condemned the folly of the present age, told me once with a proud and bitter smile: "We have only lucidity left . . ." He lost it several months later: today he has nothing left. I fear that you resemble him.

But after all, if your working class does not conceal any passivity and if one cannot act upon it, is it possible that it can act upon others? I assume not. Not dealing with anything but its own activity, the proletariat can only act upon its own action. It organizes itself, in short, and that is all it can do. "The proletariat defines itself only as experience . . . It is not objective . . . That is precisely what makes its character revolutionary, and what points to its extreme vulnerability." This working class never ceases to prepare itself for the great "restructuring" which you predict for it. It readies itself; within itself it slowly transforms the objective conditions of production into human relationships. When the final crisis immobilizes the great mechanism, the proletariat will be ready to welcome its inheritance. But until then, this historical subject will have done nothing at all. You reproach me for seeing in it nothing but the alternatives of hope and despair: and it is true that I do not deny its failures any more than its successes, but at least I know that it acts and struggles and that it forces history to change its course, that it intervened yesterday, that it will intervene tomorrow, that it exercises upon institutions and upon men a pressure which constantly changes. But *according to you* what does it do? In what moment of its long adventure has it acted? Passing from "reformist" exploitation to "Stalinist" exploitation, it has only changed masters. Of course, you show how adversity progressively educates it, but I do not see that it has, in your view, influenced the course of world history. You appear to concede that it made the Russian Revolution, but you add that the Revolution was immediately taken out of its hands. Suppressing its action on the Other and the action of the Other on it, you have transformed the bloody and jagged history of the class struggle into a solipsistic evolutionism. A certain Marxist tradition, I have already said, presents the world revolution as the effect of the progressive derailing of capitalism. But these increasingly serious crises entail the progressive impoverishment and the "brutalizing" of the workers. From that Marx concluded the necessity of a "working class organization" which might compensate for the destructive effects of these crises by a gradual emancipation of the working class. But in your concern to show the uselessness of the leaders, you have transferred their function to the order of production itself. You maintain the strange theory that while slipping towards its destruction, capitalism furnishes the proletariat with ever more numerous occasions to enrich its experience and so to perfect its organization. This is enough in my opinion to put you among your reformist friends: according to whether you reject or admit the presence of the *Other* in every moment of the worker's life and even in the "immediate conditions" of production, you are on one side of the barricade or the other, with the reformist socialist or with the revolutionaries. I would compare your article to those long works which the Germans call *Erziehungsroman,* for, just like Marivaux in *La Vie de Marianne* and Goethe in *Wilhelm Meister,* you recount how adversity makes your hero worthy of the highest tasks.

For the present, will he accomplish these tasks? Will the novel end well? You do not say. "It is one thing to say that the proletariat must of necessity become conscious of its opposition to the bourgeoisie. . . It is another to know if the future will permit it to turn this oppression into something positive in defeating its exploiters. It is enough for us to indicate that the experience of the working class will continue *whatever the outcome. . . ,*" etc. A strange experience which appeared so harmonious is in danger of bursting like a soap bubble. Perhaps the proletariat is only a dream. What then has happened? Insofar as you make of it a pure experience which will not bear fruit until the day of "restructuring," you have left it defenseless in the middle of the real world. You, who are not situated in history, who are lost in your dreaming lucidity, you emerge from it suddenly and you look at your hero from without. All of a sudden how fragile he appears! When you were a Trotskyite, you allowed a fifty-fifty chance that history would deteriorate; at least it was a matter of possibilities and you were ready to struggle against them: the field was still open. One had to see how you found fault with Merleau-Ponty, who was suspect of sympathy towards deterioration: "The difference which separates a revolutionary from Merleau-Ponty is that the latter has placed himself on the side of barbarism while describing it as a fact . . . . while a revolutionary concludes from that the absolute necessity and urgency of militant action." If that is what distinguishes Merleau-Ponty from a revolutionary, I ask you, Lefort, what distinguishes you from Merleau-Ponty? What has happened then to the absolute necessity and urgency of militant action? Yes I know, it was a youthful error. Today the very reasons which prevent you from acting are signs of your youthful maturity. Otherwise, of course, you are still a revolutionary. The day before yesterday the revolutionary acted, today his activity is defined by a militant inaction. Who will be surprised since you are *the* revolutionary. The ruthless experience of the proletariat, however, continues parallel to world history without reflecting it; it resembles those recorded melodies which mount straight towards their apotheosis but which stop forever once the record is broken.

I wonder if all your writing does not, in reality, hide a more secret and cynical idea, namely, that the dialectic was distorted from the start: the bourgeoisie had to produce the proletariat, its own gravedigger; the proletariat had to produce the "Stalinist" machinery as a particular moment of its self-organization, but Stalinism was the gravedigger of the proletariat: and there history stops —the last act of your revolutionary pastoral play represents the end of the World. This quick reversal would be surprising if this apocalypse were not, like your initial optimism, a logical consequence of your quietism. What do you care whether the world is saved or destroyed, as long as it is understood that you are not involved? With only slight changes, one could apply to your case your own definition of the working class: "Lefort never deals with anyone but himself, only with his own activity, only with the problems which his bourgeois position create." Is that not precisely the definition of the solipsist or of the perfect revolutionary?

Glossary

ABBÉ PIERRE: organized a movement to house, clothe, and feed the Paris *clochards* in the 1950's.

ALTMANN, GEORGES: (1901-1960) editor-in-chief of *Franc-Tireur* (1944-1957).

LES ANNALES: famous bi-monthly which last appeared Dec. 10, 1939. Full name *Les annales politiques et littéraires.*

ARON, RAYMOND: b. 1905. Distinguished French sociologist. Editorialist for *Combat* then for *Le Figaro.*

ARTAUD, ANTONIN: (1896-1948) French playwright.

L'AURORE: morning daily founded in 1944. The readers are mainly small businessmen and shopkeepers. Moderate to conservative. Editors: Marcel Boussac, Robert Lazurik.

BAYLOT, JEAN: b. 1897. Parisian *Préfet de Police* (1951-1954).

BIAGGI, JEAN: b. 1918. Founder and President of the *Parti Patriote Populaire* (1957-1958) and co-founder of the *Rassemblement pour l'Algérie française* (1959).

BILLOUX, FRANÇOIS: b. 1903. Member of the Central Committee of the Communist Party and of the Political Bureau. Secretary of the party since 1954. Editor of *France Nouvelle.*

BLANQUI, (LOUIS) AUGUSTE: (1805-1881) socialist and revolutionary who participated in many 19th century revolutionary events.

This glossary was compiled from *The Communists and Peace* by Martha H. Fletcher. Identifications are in most cases as of the time of the events referred to in the text.

BLUM, LÉON: (1872-1950) head of the French Socialist Party (S.F.I.O.). Chief of the Popular Front government of 1936 and of a Socialist government in 1946.

BONY, ROBERT: (real name: Maurice Lazurik) b. 1895. Editor of *l'Aurore* since 1951. Socialist deputy 1936-1940.

BOTHEREAU, ROBERT: b. 1901. Secretary-general of the C.G.T.-F.O., vice-president of the International Federation of Free Trade Unions (1947-1959).

BOULANGER, GEORGES: (1837-1891) French general. Minister of War in 1886. Attempted a coup d'état. Fled to Brussels and committed suicide.

BRIAND, ARISTIDE: (1862-1932) originally a socialist, co-founder with Jean Jaurès of *L'Humanité*. Prime Minister eleven times.

BRISSON, JEAN-FRANÇOIS: b. 1918. Assistant editor-in-chief of *Le Figaro*.

BRISSON, PIERRE: (1896-1964) man of letters, director of newspapers (*Les Annales,* 1934, then *Le Figaro* and *Figaro-Littéraire*).

BUCHARIN (or BUKHARIN), NIKOLAI: (1888-1938) *Pravda* editor until 1928. Head of the Third International (1926-1929). Expelled from the Communist Party (1937). Executed 1938.

CACHIN, MARCEL: (1869-1958) director of *L'Humanité-Dimanche* (1948-1958). Member of the Central Committee of the Communist Party. Deputy.

CAVAIGNAC, LOUIS-EUGÈNE: (1802-1857) Chief Executive (chef du pouvoir exécutif). Suppressed the June insurrection.

CAILLOIS, ROGER: b. 1913. director of *Éditions Gallimard,* author, formerly editor of UNESCO's *Diogène*.

C.F.T.C.: *Confédération Française des Travailleurs Chrétiens.* Founded November 1919. Catholic trade union movement. Now C.F.D.T. *Confédération Française Démocratique du Travail.*

C.G.T.: *Confédération Générale du Travail.* Founded in 1895. After 1902 pact with the *Fédération des Bourses,* it acquired its present structure of two sections: the *Bourses* (local and regional union groups) and the *Fédérations* (national trade unions).

C.G.T.-F.O.: see F.O. (*Force Ouvrière*).

C.G.T.U.: *Confédération Générale du Travail Unitaire.* Organized under Communist auspices in 1921 by seventeen union federations expelled from the C.G.T. Reintegrated into the C.G.T. in 1936.

CHAPUIS, MAJOR: in command of the troops called out at Fourmies, May 1891.

CLARK, COLIN: British economist, author, at Oxford University since 1953.

CLAUDEL, PAUL: (1868-1955) Catholic playwright and poet; diplomat. Member of the *Académie française.*

COLLINET, MICHEL: (b. 1904.) Author of *L'Ouvrier français; Essai sur la condition ouvrière; L'esprit du syndicalisme.* Editor-in-chief of *Volontés* (1945).

COMITÉ DES FORGES: organization of the French steel and armament industry.

CONGRESS OF TOURS: 1920. Congress at which the French Socialist Party split, the majority forming the Communist Party, the minority remaining the S.F.I.O.

C.R.S.: *Compagnies républicaines de sécurité:* police units created in 1945 and responsible for the maintenance of order.

DANTON, GEORGES-JACQUES: (1759-1794) member of the Convention. Promoter of the revolutionary tribunal and the Committee of Public Safety. Beheaded by Robespierre.

DECAZEVILLE STRIKE: January 26, 1886.

DE GASPERI, ALCIDE: (1881-1954) Leader of the Italian Christian Democrats. Prime Minister (1945-1953).

DEPEYRE, OCTAVE-VICTOR: (1825-1891) monarchist. Deputy (1871). Minister of Justice (1873-1874). Senator (1876).

DUCLOS, JACQUES: b. 1896. President of the Communist group in the National Assembly (1946-1958). A secretary and member of the Political Bureau of the Communist Party.

DUVERGER, MAURICE: b. 1917. Professor of political sociology and editorialist for *Le Monde.*

L'ESPRIT: leftwing Catholic review, founded in 1932. Editors: Paul Thibaud, Jean-Marie Domenach.

FAJON, ETIENNE: b. 1906. Deputy (1946-1958). Secretary of the Communist Party (1954-1956). Director of *L'Humanité.*

FÉDÉRÉS: soldiers of the Paris Commune (1871).

FIGARO LITTÉRAIRE: weekly supplement to *Le Figaro*. Started in 1946.

LE FIGARO: conservative morning paper, founded in 1854 (became a daily in 1866). Director: Louis-Gabriel Robinet.

F.O.: *Force Ouvrière* (full title C.G.T.-F.O.) formed in 1948 split from the C.G.T. to break from what the F.O. leaders considered Communist domination of the C.G.T.

FOURMIES MASSACRE: May Day (1891) demonstration in the coal-mining district in the north of France. Nine killed (including four women, three children) and 40 wounded.

FOUR SERGEANTS: accused of a plot against the Restoration, the *quatre sergents de la Rochelle* were executed at Place de Grève, 1822.

FRANC-TIREUR: morning daily (founded in 1941) which emerged from the Resistance. Left-liberal. Became *Paris-Journal* (1957), then *Paris-Jour* (1959).

FRANCE-SOIR: largest afternoon daily newspaper (circulation over one million). Moderate. Director: Pierre Lazareff.

FRIEDMANN, GEORGES: b. 1902. Professor and sociologist. Author of *De la Sainte Russie à l'U.S.S.R.* and numerous works on sociology.

GALLIFFET, GASTON DE: (1830-1909) General. Suppressed the Commune. Minister of War (1899-1901).

GIRONDINS: political party during the Revolution. Occupied the Right at the Convention. Outlawed in May 1793. Most of its members were beheaded in October 1793.

GREFFUELHE, VICTOR: (1874-1923) secretary-general of the C.G.T. (1902-1909). Revolutionary syndicalist.

GURVITCH, GEORGES: (1894-1966) Professor of sociology. Director of *Cahiers Internationaux de Sociologie*.

HALBWACHS, MAURICE: (1877-1945) famous French sociologist.

HERVÉ, GUSTAVE: leader of the pre-World War I C.G.T. left-wing. Superpatriot during the war. Petainist later.

HERVÉ, PIERRE: former editor of *L'Action.* Broke with the Communist Party over the Hungarian insurrection.

JEANNE THE MADWOMAN: (Jeanne la Folle) (1479-1555). Queen of Castille, wife of the Archduke of Austria and mother of Charles Quint.

JOUHAUX, LÉON: (1879-1954) secretary-general of the C.G.T. (1909-1947). Directed the C.G.T.-F.O. after the split.

KIENTHALIANS: A group of European socialists, including Lenin, who met at Kienthal, Switzerland to oppose Socialist Party support of World War I.

KOESTLER, ARTHUR: b. 1905. British (naturalized) author of such books as: *Darkness at Noon, The Yogi and the Commissar,* etc.

LA MORANDIÈRE, TURMEAU DE: author of *Principes politiques sur le rappel des Protestants en France* (1764).

LA ROCHEFOUCAULD: (1613-1680) aristocrat, ardent supporter of *La Fronde,* author of *Maximes* which suggest that self-interest directs all human activity.

LECOEUR, AUGUSTE: b. 1911. Miner. Deputy (1946-1955). Member of the Central Committee of the Communist Party. Left the party in 1954. Joined the S.F.I.O. Director of *La Nation Socialiste.*

LE CHAPELIER LAW: June 1791, prohibited any association of wage earners or employers. Abrogated 1884.

LE LÉAP, ALAIN: co-secretary-general of the C.G.T. since 1948. Former civil service union official.

LEROY-BEAULIEU, PAUL: (1843-1916) economist. Professor at the Collège de France.

LUSSY, CHARLES: b. 1883. Socialist deputy (1945-1958) and former president of the Socialist group of the National Assembly.

MARTIN, HENRI: b. 1927. Young sailor, former resistant. Sentenced to 5 years imprisonment (October 1950) for distributing leaflets against the Indochinese war among other sailors at Toulon.

MARTINET, GILLES: b. 1916. Journalist. Director of *France-Observateur* (since 1950). Assistant National Secretary of the *Parti Socialiste Unifié*.

MAURRAS, CHARLES: (1868-1952) author. Director of *l'Action française*. Condemned in 1945 to life imprisonment for collaboration with the enemy.

MAUSS, MARCEL: (1872-1950) famous French anthropologist.

MERRHEIM, ALPHONSE: secretary of the Metalworkers Federation from 1891. C.G.T. official. Represented the revolutionary syndicalist tendency prior to World War I.

MERLEAU-PONTY, MAURICE: (1906-1961) professor of philosophy. Author. Founder with Jean-Paul Sartre and Simone de Beauvoir of *Les Temps Modernes*. Writer on *l'Express*.

MILLERAND, ALEXANDRE: (1859-1943) first European socialist to sit in a "bourgeois cabinet" (1899) hence *Millerandisme* to indicate class collaboration. Minister of War (1914-1915). President of the Republic (1920-1924).

MONATTE, PIERRE: (1881-1960) C.G.T. militant. At 1907 Amsterdam Congress of Anarchists, he defended revolutionary syndicalism.

LE MONDE: great afternoon daily. France's *New York Times*. Serious, neutral. Publisher: Hubert Beuve-Méry.

MONNEROT, JULES: b. 1908. Broke with the Communists in 1936. Active in the Resistance. Author of several books, including *Sociologie du communisme* (1949). Gaullist.

MONMOUSSEAU, GASTON: Syndicalist turned Communist. Secretary of the Railroad Workers in 1920. Condemned to death during the Occupation. Secretary of the C.G.T. in 1945.

M.R.P.: *Mouvement Républicain Populaire*. Post-World War II Catholic welfare party which accepted state economic intervention and nationalization of industries.

NENNI, PIETRO: b. 1891. Secretary-general of the Italian Socialist Party (1926-1958).

NIEL, LOUIS: Syndicalist-reformist, elected secretary-general of the C.G.T. in February 1909 but replaced by Jouhaux in July 1909.

LA NOUVELLE CRITIQUE: founded in 1948. Cultural monthly of Communist intellectuals.

L'OBSERVATEUR: (*France-Observateur* since 1954, *Nouvel-Observateur* since 1964) founded 1950 by Claude Bourdet, Roger Stéphan and Gilles Martinet. Noncommunist left weekly.

PARIS-PRESSE: large conservative afternoon paper.

PAUL, MARCEL: b. 1900. Head of the national gas and electric workers' union and former Minister of Industrial Production (1945).

P.C.F.: *Parti Communiste Français,* formed in 1920.

PELLOUTIER, FERNAND: (1867-1901) anarcho-syndicalist. In 1895 became secretary-general of the *Fédération des bourses du travail.*

PETSCHE, MAURICE: (1895-1951) Minister of Finances in 1949.

PINAY, ANTOINE: b. 1891. Industrialist. Former deputy and senator. Prime Minister (July 1950-February 1951; August 1951-January 1952).

PLEVEN, RENÉ: b. 1901. President of *Union Démocratique et Socialiste de la Résistance,* (U.D.S.R.). Prime Minister (July 1950-February 1951); (August 1951-January 1952).

POUGET, EMILE: (1860-1932) anarcho-syndicalist, C.G.T. militant, editor of *Le Père Peinard,* leading anarchist journal of the 1890's.

PREUVES: monthly review supported by the Congress for Cultural Freedom. François Bondy, editor-in-chief.

PRAVDA: morning daily, official organ of the Communist Party of the Soviet Union.

P.S.U.: *Parti Socialiste Unifié,* small left-wing socialist party founded in 1958 whose membership includes Pierre Mendès-

France, several former Socialist deputies and some left-wing Catholics, ex-Communists and Radicals.

RAVACHOL, FRANÇOIS (CLAUDIUS KOENIGSTEIN): (1859-1892) French anarchist. Responsible for many assassination attempts. Guillotined.

RENAN, ERNEST: (1823-1892) 19th-century rationalist with great faith in science; author concerned with the history of languages and religions.

REVUE DES DEUX MONDES: French large circulation literary review. Founded in 1829. Superseded by *Revue* (1944).

R.G.R.: *Rassemblement des Gauches Républicains,* electoral alliance of the *Parti Républicain Radical et Radical-Socialiste* (usually simply called the Radicals) and similar groups. Moderates; anticlerical but defenders of private property and opposed to socialism.

R.P.F.: *Rassemblement du Peuple Français,* founded by de Gaulle (1947) and dissolved by him (1953). Strongest party in the 1951 elections. Former members helped form the U.N.R. (*Union pour la Nouvelle République*) for the 1958 election.

ROBINET, LOUIS-GABRIEL: b. 1909. Journalist for *Revue des Deux Mondes,* then editor-in-chief of *Le Figaro.*

SALLE GAVEAU: A concert hall in Paris.

SAUVY, ALFRED: b. 1898. Statistician, economist, sociologist. Professor of social demography at the Collège de France. Author of many works on population problems.

SCHNEIDER, EUGÈNE: (1805-1875) with his brother Adolphe, founder of Creusot. President of the Legislative Body under the Second Empire.

SÉMARD, PIERRE: leader of the railroad workers union. General secretary of the Communist Party. Shot as a hostage in 1942.

SOREL, GEORGES: (1847-1922) gave revolutionary syndicalism an autonomous doctrine independent of anarchism.

SOROKIN, PITIRIM: b. 1889. Distinguished Harvard sociologist.

STALIN'S NOSE. . . STALIN'S HEART. . . : references to Pascal's *Pensées* [94] "If Cleopatra's nose had been shorter, the whole face of the earth would have been changed."

STIL, ANDRÉ: b. 1921. Editor-in-chief of *Ce Soir* (1949): of *l'Humanité* (1950-1959). Stalin Prize (1951).

TAINE, HIPPOLYTE: (1828-1893) philosopher, historian and critic. Tried to explain artistic and literary works by the triple influence of race, milieu and period.

LE TEMPS: famous daily; predecessor of *Le Monde*. Confiscated after the Liberation for alleged collaboration.

LES TEMPS MODERNES: review founded in 1945 by Jean-Paul Sartre, Maurice Merleau-Ponty and Simone de Beauvoir.

THIBAULT, PIERRE: political editor of *France-Soir*.

THIERS, ADOLPHE: (1797-1877) historian, statesman. President of the Republic in 1871. Suppressed the insurrection of the Commune.

THOREZ, MAURICE: (1900-1964) miner, general secretary of the Communist Party (1930-1964). Deputy Prime Minister in several cabinets (1945-1947).

TOGLIATTI, PALMIRO: (1893-1964) a founder (1921) and the leader (from 1944) of the Italian Communist Party.

TURGOT, ANNE-ROBERT: (1727-1781) controller general of finance under Louis XVI.

VAILLANT, EDOUARD: (1840-1916) a Communard in 1871, headed the Blanquists at the C.G.T. Congress at le Havre (1880).

VALLON, LOUIS: b. 1901. Left-wing Gaullist. Deputy (1951-1955). Administrator in de Gaulle's governments. Political author.

VÉRITÉ: (*La Vérité des travailleurs*), Trotskyist review.